Concepts of
Transportation
Economics

Concepts of
Transportation
Economics

Barry E Prentice
Transport Institute, University of Manitoba, Canada

Darren Prokop
College of Business and Public Policy, University of Alaska Anchorage, USA

EW JERSEY · LONDON · SINGAPORE · BEIJING · SHANGHAI · HONG KONG · TAIPEI · CHENNAI · TOKYO

Published by

World Scientific Publishing Co. Pte. Ltd.
5 Toh Tuck Link, Singapore 596224
USA office: 27 Warren Street, Suite 401-402, Hackensack, NJ 07601
UK office: 57 Shelton Street, Covent Garden, London WC2H 9HE

Library of Congress Cataloging-in-Publication Data
Prentice, Barry E.
    Concepts of transportation economics / Barry E Prentice (Transport Institute, Canada &
University of Manitoba, Canada) & Darren Prokop (University of Alaska Anchorage, USA).
    pages cm
    ISBN 978-9814656160 (alk. paper)
    1. Transportation. 2. Transportation and state. I. Prokop, Darren. II. Title.
    HE151.P73 2015
    388'.049--dc23
                                            2015020409

British Library Cataloguing-in-Publication Data
A catalogue record for this book is available from the British Library.

In-house Editors: Rajni Gamage/Dipasri Sardar

Typeset by Stallion Press
Email: enquiries@stallionpress.com

Printed in Singapore

Contents

About the Authors

Barry E Prentice is a Professor of Supply Chain Management at the I H Asper School of Business, University of Manitoba; and an Associate of the Transport Institute and was the Institute's third Director (1996–2005). His major research and teaching interests include logistics, transportation economics, urban transport and trade policy. Barry E Prentice holds degrees in economics from the University of Western Ontario (1973) and agricultural economics from the University of Guelph (1979) and the University of Manitoba (1986).

Barry E Prentice has authored or co-authored more than 250 research reports, journal articles and contributions to books. His scholarly work has been recognized for excellence in national paper competitions and awards. In 1999, National Transportation Week named him Manitoba Transportation Person of the Year. Through the Transport Institute, Barry E Prentice has organized national and international conferences on sustainable transportation (*Railways and the Environment*), supply chain logistics (*Planes, Trains and Ships*), agribusiness logistics (*Fields on Wheels*), the potential use of airships for northern transportation (*Airships to the Arctic*) and food trade between Canada and Mexico (*La Cadena de Frio*). In 1999 and 2003, he received University of Manitoba Outreach Awards. In 2009, Barry E Prentice was made an Honorary Life Member of the Canadian Transportation Research Forum.

Barry E Prentice was instrumental in founding a major in transportation and logistics within the B. Comm. (Hons.) program at the I H Asper School of Business (Fall 2003). Since that time, a new Department of Supply Chain Management has been formed, and in 2006, a MSc program in supply chain management was initiated. Barry E Prentice has served on the Boards of Directors of several transportation organizations: National Transportation Week (President, 2001 and 2003), Canadian Institute for Traffic and Transportation (Honorary President, 2001–3) and the Canadian Transportation Research Forum (President, 1997). In 2005, he co-founded ISO Polar, a not-for-profit research institute, to promote the use of airships as sustainable transport for the northern latitudes. He is Associate Editor of the *Journal of Transportation Research Forum*. In addition, Barry E Prentice has served on the Board of Winnipeg Airports Authority, Inc. (1998–2003), Winnipeg TransPlan 2010, the Mid-Continent International Trade Corridor Task Force, the Rapid Transit Task Force, Council of Canadian Academies (2012–14), Statistics Canada Industry Advisory Committee (2010–present), expert committees, and is frequently asked to speak on the topics of trade and transportation.

Darren Prokop is a Professor of Logistics in the College of Business and Public Policy at the University of Alaska Anchorage. He is also the director of the Master of Science in Global Supply Chain Management Program. He received his PhD in economics from the University of Manitoba in 1999. Prior to his academic career, Darren Prokop worked in the government as an economist and in the private sector in inventory planning. Darren Prokop specializes in transportation economics and its effects on international trade and transportation security. He has published seminal research in leading academic journals with topics ranging from the microfoundations of logistics to air cargo logistics to supply chain security modelling. He has contributed chapters to many books in his field and edited a collection of readings for the two-volume, *The Business of Transportation* (Praeger).

Darren Prokop is an active consultant to both governments and businesses. Prominent transport carriers, shippers and policy-makers have relied on his modelling of complex problems in order to develop workable solutions to meet their needs. An expert on cabotage regulations, Darren Prokop's opinions in this area are actively sought by international shippers and carriers. A popular speaker and writer, he has contributed to numerous business conferences around the world and has written for many national trade publications, on issues ranging from trade liberalization and weathering economic cycles to sensible environmental planning for businesses.

Being based in Alaska for many years, Darren Prokop has enjoyed the rich opportunities for research and consultation afforded in the US's largest state — and one leading the nation with innovations in air cargo liberalization, maritime shipping and the opening of the Arctic. Darren Prokop has written and spoken extensively on each of these issues and has received multiple awards for his scholarship, teaching and speaking.

Structure of the Text

This text covers concepts in transportation economics that are global in perspective. By this we mean that an individualistic treatment of transport modes is not our purpose. While a mode-specific treatment is sometimes necessary, our purpose is to introduce applications of modern economic theory in order to understand the provision of transportation services. Economic theory is used specifically to define, analyze, and solve problems that arise when such concepts are fitted to the specific characteristics of the individual modal markets.

Economic models of transportation are abstractions of the real world drawn from the various theories found in modern economics. The models developed in this text are applied, as appropriate, to the rail, air, truck, bus, car, and ocean vessel markets.

The text is written in a detailed manner befitting the way an economist is expected to formulate models. Diagrams are used to clarify the arguments where possible. The student should carefully study the structure of these diagrams for their value lies in their compactness. At the same time, these diagrams are not the final word; rather, these figures come about from underlying economic theories that employ various assumptions. It is through an appraisal of these assumptions that one may assess the validity of any theory and allow one, by contrast, to propose alternative assumptions as necessary. The models in this text lend themselves to policy-making and, in that regard, any policy maker in the transport sector must have confidence in the theoretical basis from which his policies are derived. We encourage healthy skepticism; it is the engine of improved theory.

The text is structured into two distinct parts. The first part consists of Chapters 1–10, which introduce the unique problem of transportation to modern economic analysis. These chapters also build a comprehensive tool kit for use by the transportation analyst. These chapters should be examined in sequence. The second part consists of the remaining chapters (11–14), which may be seen as stand-alone examinations of specific applications of transportation economics. These chapters may be examined in any order.

The material found in the text is more than sufficient for a university half-course. The instructor may wish to cover the first six chapters and then proceed to two or three of the remaining application chapters based upon his own interest.

The keywords listed at the end of each chapter serve as signposts to aid in the understanding of the material. Each of these terms is fully defined in the glossary to aid in cross-referencing through the other chapters. The keywords are listed column-by-column as they appear in the particular chapter, and are printed in italics at the first instance in the text. A new feature of this edition is the addition of exercises that permit the application of the theory in the chapter.

A student with some background involving introductory microeconomics and who possesses a good reference text in microeconomic theory written within the last 10 years will find this text challenging but comprehensible. The level of mathematical understanding required is no more than that found at the high school algebra level. But be forewarned, if you master this text, you will never again look at a passing freight/passenger vehicle without wondering at the miracle of its journey.

Transportation and Economic Theory

A Prologue to the Text

The purpose of this prologue is to outline how economic theory can aid in the understanding of transportation activity. Issues will be raised that should motivate the reader to examine the material in the chapters themselves. The reader should be in a position to understand these issues and answer any questions arising out of them after having read through the text and devoting some thought to the material.

What is Transportation?

Transportation is an activity that takes place all around us. Every physical good that may be purchased at a retail outlet required transportation in order to get there. Even if the good were purchased where it was produced, it is likely that transportation was required in order to get the inputs necessary to produce the good. Production and trade in the economy is dependent upon transportation. In other words, economic performance from the smallest town to the largest country is a function of transportation activity. So too is the other aspect of one's quality of life — leisure activity. From well-defined travel and tourism to simple things such as a Sunday drive or a stroll down a sidewalk; these ways to spend free time are a form of transportation.

Anyone or anything that has to move from one well-defined place to another is dependent upon transportation. This presents a challenge to the economist. Transportation is a physical activity that an economist must analyze using theory; that is, the "real" is to be explained by way of the "conceptual". Economic theory has been refined for hundreds of years now and many of its first breakthroughs concerned international trade and the pricing of agricultural produce, both of which are dependent upon transportation. So where is the challenge? It comes from the fact that transportation, as an activity, is easy to see but not easy to define.

Transportation could be undertaken at zero monetary cost and for its sheer enjoyment; for example, a walk in the neighborhood, browsing past store front windows, a bike ride through the park, etc. Of course, such enjoyment could be purchased; for example, a bus tour of city attractions, a train ride through the country-side, an ocean cruise, etc. Thus, transportation could be a final good. But, alternatively, it could be an input or factor of production. The drive to work can occur on roads and bridges that are used free of charge (unless, of course, a toll is charged). Business travelers may fly directly from one city to another or they may be laid-over at another city in-between. Shipments might be moved to store-shelves in bulk, or on an as-needed basis. Long-distance freight may move relatively slowly by rail or relatively fast by air cargo shipping. The challenge to economic theory is to properly define and analyze particular forms of transportation activity; that is, transportation as a consumption activity and as a production activity.

Transportation is time, space, and form dependent. Most economic models concern transactions that take place without concern for time; that is, the disposition of people or freight in-transit is often ignored. But it is what happens, or perhaps what is desired to happen, during this in-transit stage that may determine whether or not the transaction will take place. In terms of space, it must be remembered that the surface of the earth is not topographically constant; mountains and rivers, for example, interfere with the ability to connect to places with a straight-line roadway. Air currents affect flight paths and ice built-up affects the use of seaways and canals. Thus, out of time and space concerns, the problem of location occurs. Should a firm locate its production near its customers, near the source of its inputs (e.g., a mine, a forest, a farm, etc.), or somewhere in-between? Product form will influence this decision. Transport may be too slow or rough for some products to be shipped. Processing or disassembly of perishable products may be necessary to allow transport. Alternatively, the transport vehicle may need modification, e.g., refrigeration, to extend the product's life and enable saleable merchandise to reach their market. The challenge to economic theory is to help identify the parameters by which it is possible to answer these questions; that is, to understand the geographic and demographic lay-out of marketplaces.

Transportation is a service that facilitates trade. If an exchange of goods between two places is agreed to, the goods have to be moved. Exports and imports cannot exist without transportation services. Focusing on one good for a moment, if it is worth more in another place then an incentive exists to move it there. Of course, if the cost of transportation is more than the extra value assessed to the good in that other place, then it will not be moved. Conversely then, transportation services may be looked upon as an impediment to trade in that it is a transaction cost that has to be borne in order for trade to take place. Now consider one firm for a moment, if its customers would prefer that the good it produces be delivered to their homes it has a need for local transportation services. A fleet of trucks could be purchased and used exclusively by the firm or it could set up a contract with a for-hire trucking firm to move the goods. The challenge to economic theory is to note that transportation, while part of the production process is a service that can be undertaken by the firm itself or can be contracted-out to another firm. Whether that is in-house or contracted to a third party, transportation services can have important consequences for the cost of production and the prices of goods.

Finally, transportation activity is dependent upon both the private sector and the public sector. City streets and sidewalks are provided by the government and financed through taxes. Governments can provide highways in the same way so that all taxpayers finance it. Conversely, the government could charge a toll so that only the actual users finance the highway. Certainly, a private provider of a highway would wish to charge a toll.

Some airlines remain government owned, but most are run by private organizations. In the reverse, most urban transit systems are government-operated monopolies. The structure of transportation industries depends on government policy as much as the inherent economics of transportation. All modes of transport face some level of government regulation; though it is the case over the last 20 years or so that the economics of transport activity have been less regulated. In other words, while safety and insurance regulations exist, and in some cases have been made more comprehensive, regulations affecting foreign ownership, geographic operation and types of goods carried have, in general, been relaxed. The challenge to economic theory is to explain why a balance between the private and public sectors has been struck and why it is that the sectoral mix within that balance changes from time to time.

What is Transportation Economics?

Transportation economics is a specialized area within the overall discipline of economics. It is, by and large, applied microeconomics. However, as was pointed out in the previous section, transportation applies to such diverse areas as manufactured and agricultural production, trade, consumption, location and government activity. In this regard, transportation economics makes use of other areas of applied economics such as: production and competition theory, international trade theory, consumer behavioral economics, spatial economics, cost–benefit analysis, public finance theory, taxation theory, and the economics of regulation. In short, transportation economics employs a rich body of knowledge.

Transportation economics involves basically what all economists are well versed in doing: (1) gathering facts; (2) developing theories of human behavior; and (3) proposing and evaluating policies designed to achieve a particular goal. Each of these points will be considered in turn.

Facts

Facts are information and they come in a variety of forms. They may be numerical such as a raw data set listing, for example, the freight rates (in, say, dollars per 100 pounds) for several types of goods to be transported from Chicago to Dallas. They may be statistical meaning that the raw data has been converted into statistics such as, for example, an average freight rate that applies to a typical bundle of goods traveling from Chicago to Dallas in a boxcar. In that case the statistic is known as a weighted-average freight rate.

Facts may be historical in that they are based on observations of the recorded past such as, for example, the year when air travel between Chicago and Dallas became more widely used than rail. Finally, facts may be anecdotal in that an observation is made concerning the behavior of one or a few elements often with the hope that generalizations to all of the elements within the set may be made. An example of this would be noting that when a certain airline on the Chicago to Dallas run has a seat sale it tends to take away passengers from other airlines operating along the same route. A generalization might be that all seat sales have this effect but, again, the fact was anecdotal and there may be other elements at work here that might not apply to other airlines offering seat sales.

Theory

What is an economic theory? It is a generalized statement or model of behavior involving human activity. All theories, economic or otherwise, are dependent upon facts in order to establish their validity; that is, a theory ought to be testable and falsifiable. By falsifiable we mean that the theory is drawn up in such a way that existing facts can be used to either verify or falsify the theory. This does not mean that the theory has to appear "realistic"; rather it must, in the end, be able to explain the facts. For example, the text offers a theory as to why airlines often charge their passengers more if they book their flights close to the travel date. In other words, we wish to explain this pricing "fact" by way of a "theory of last minute travelers". The theory, by the title applied, may sound unrealistic when it comes to understanding how an airline sets its fares; but if it stands up to the facts then the theory is valid and useful.

Of course, a theory is an abstraction from reality, which is why the term "model" is often used synonymously. As a model of reality and not reality itself, facts deemed relevant are given a lot of weight and those deemed to be irrelevant facts are ignored. In other words the model has to be tractable so that its workings can be understood. In the real world, everything may be dependent upon everything else; however, to model something requires ignoring some of these possible dependencies.

Consider two different ways to theorize about economic behavior. One way is to carefully examine raw data and conduct field experiments. Another way is simply to postulate a pattern of behavior, call it a theory, and test it against observable facts. Which method is superior? One might be tempted to say the first because it appears to be more "scientific" in that the economist lets the facts speak for themselves and the relationships he finds will suggest the theory. The second method has the economist dreaming up a theory and then hoping that the facts will bear it out. Given that the facts play a role in both methods and are instrumental in validating the theory, they are both reasonable ways to theorize. The method of using the facts to come up with a theory is known as induction while the method of taking a theory and testing it against the facts is known as deduction. Because economists rarely are able to test the behavior of human beings in controlled environments, they more often use deductive methods in their theorizing. The models to be examined in this text tend to assume a particular way for consumers, producers, and government to act. Again, the validity of the model is not in the assumptions but in the way it holds up to the facts.

If facts are gathered that do indeed falsify the model, it is time to reassess the model's assumptions. The model itself is a logical system that is derived out of the particular facts chosen and assumptions made. A model cannot be illogical; therefore, if it is faulty it is because of certain assumptions being invalid. Suppose two transportation economists are appearing on a television program and are being questioned on the issue of increased taxes on gasoline and their effect on pollution emissions. Economist A says that an increase in such a tax would make driving more expensive and thus increase carpooling and decrease leisurely Sunday drives. Emissions and thus pollution would decline. Economist B says that while the tax would make driving more expensive, government would take that tax revenue and, among other things, improve the quality of existing roads and even build new ones. More and better roads mean more driving and so the effect on emissions and pollution could go either way. Which economist is correct? Whoever it is will be determined based on the facts: how drivers, in fact, react to the tax increase and whether government does invest in roads. Both economists are postulating perfectly logical theories, and may differ only on their assumptions. The value of their prognostications will depend mainly on how accurately they assess the reactions of drivers and the government.

Policy

Continuing with the case of the two economists above, suppose they are asked what they would have the government do to achieve lower pollution levels. Economist A recommends an increase in the gasoline tax. Economist B, noting his theory that gasoline taxes and pollution are not inversely related, actually recommends decreasing the gasoline tax. He believes that more cars on the road will end up increasing traffic congestion and creating more potholes that will, by themselves, eventually deter enough people from driving that pollution levels will fall. Without the same level of gasoline tax revenue the government cannot fix the potholes and, therefore, no new drivers will be tempted to use the road. The two different theories suggest two different ways to achieve the goal. How a theory is used to achieve a particular goal is known as a policy. In other words, one cannot suggest a policy for achieving any goal unless he has a theory that he feels explains the environment in which the goal is to be achieved.

Policy is not something confined to government; it is applicable to all decisions made in the economy ranging from consumers and single firms to entire industries. In a transportation context consider the following types of policies and the theories they presuppose:

⇒ A rush-hour commuter continues to use his car to drive to work even though a new light rail transit (LRT) system is now available for free use during that time. The use of the car comes with a monetary cost while the LRT does not. Obviously, the commuter has a theory of rush-hour travel that compares the car and the LRT such that a low-weight is assigned to the monetary cost. The commuter's theory of rush hour travel likely assigns a high-weight to such things as travel time, comfort, directness, etc.

⇒ A shipper decides to maintain his own private fleet of trucks, as opposed to contracting a for-hire trucking firm, in order to ensure better customer service. This shipper must, therefore, have a theory about how his customers' demands operate and, in this regard, has determined that full control of his transportation activity is necessary to increase the satisfaction of these consumers.

⇒ An airline wishes to create an alliance with another airline in a different country so that it can reap the benefits of being a larger airline but without the need for actually merging the two. This airline has a "bigger is better" theory and has determined that governments will maintain foreign ownership restrictions on domestic airlines. Nonetheless, some of the benefits of merger can be achieved by such tactics as flight code-sharing and flight-time coordination. The airline's theory holds that such coordination would provide a more seamless service that is likely to attract more passengers and increase profits.

In summary, the decision (or policy) that is to be made concerning how to provide and use transportation services is conditioned by a theory that is, in turn, dependent upon the facts that have been used to validate that theory. This is expressed in the following figure:

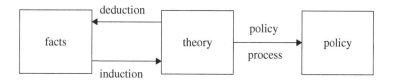

The richness of economic reasoning may be seen in the context of how to proceed from theory to policy. Keeping this in mind allows one to sharply scrutinize the economic decisions that people make as well as to offer ways to improve those decisions.

Chapter 1

Transportation, Logistics and Technology

The linkage between economic development and the growth of international trade is well established. Increased trade leads to an expansion of global wealth. What is less appreciated is the role of transport in this complex phenomenon. Efficient transportation is a key to competitiveness in foreign trade. A backward transportation network is incompatible with the needs of an industrially advanced economy. The quality and sophistication of a country's transportation *infrastructure* is one of the strongest indicators of its *economic development.*

The importance of transportation and logistics is widely recognized, but the factors that determine these costs are only superficially understood. Anyone who owns a car may feel that they can comprehend the essential costs of transport. For most people, however, the determination of a simple airline ticket's price or a railway freight rate may seem to be a complete mystery. The purpose of this text is to explore the economics of the transportation market, and remove the enigma that surrounds this industry.

Communications and Technical Change

Negotiation of transactions always involves questions of transportation and logistics. Bids and offers of sale are quoted with respect to the location of exchange, e.g., *free-on-board* (FOB)[1] which could be the production plant, the receiver's door, or any point in between. Sales contracts set out the seller's and buyer's transport and storage obligations. The share of transport costs in final product prices varies with the characteristics of

---

[1]FOB is a sale's term that indicates the point where the buyer takes possession of the good and arranges for transportation beyond that point.

the merchandise, distance shipped, and a myriad of other influences. For some products, transportation costs can be the largest single impediment to international exchange.[2]

Transportation is a necessary condition for trade but, except for direct barter exchanges, transport is seldom sufficient to conclude trade. Traders must communicate to identify potentially profitable exchanges of goods and services. Improvements in communications create a virtuous circle between trade and transportation. Better communications permits more sophisticated supply chains to emerge that lower cost through the specialization of production. This generates wealth and the impetus for technological improvements that leads again to a demand for more transport, better communication, and new rounds of the virtuous circle.

The invention of the telegraph marked a turning point in transportation and trade. Before the telegraph, information was "glued" to the freight. Knowledge could not be transported in advance of the physical product. Consequently, ownership often remained in the hands of the original producer until the goods were sold at a terminal market. All risks of unfavorable price changes and physical damage were borne by the shipper. The telegraph was the initial technological innovation that overcame the barrier of distance. With electronic communications, transactions could be undertaken prior to physical delivery. Supply chains became more efficient and the pace of the world economy increased markedly.

The correspondence between the economics of communications and transport is striking. Data transmission networks and freight transportation networks are conceptually the same. One system conveys bits of information over its "right of way", often in electronic form, while the other carries tangible goods. Transportation and communications industries have high capital costs associated with the provision of network infrastructure.[3] The fixed investments in these networks enjoy increasing "economies" until they approach full utilization. If demand contracts or technology

---

[2]The cost of transporting bulk commodities like grain can be equal to half the value of the delivered shipment.

[3]Odlyzko provides an interesting comparison of the similarities of the pricing systems employed in transportation and communications. Odlyzko, Andrew. "The Evolution of Price Discrimination in Transportation and its Implications for the Internet." *Review of Network Economics*, Vol. 3, No. 3 (September 2004), 323–346.

changes however, railway tracks, pipelines and transmission cables have no alternative economic use. Finally, both systems are prone to elements of non-competitive behavior and are strategically important to security and sovereignty. As a result, governments exercise extensive regulation and oversight of transportation and communications industries, and often this has led to public ownership and provision of these services.

Complementarities between transportation and communications reinforce the adoption of new technologies. Advances in one field promote quicker implementation in the other. For example, the railways were limited to slow speeds and small-scale operations until the development of a telegraph code that could signal the approach of an on-coming train. At the same time, the railway provided the telegraph with a right-of-way through the placement of the over-head wires along-side the track, and created an immediate demand for its services.

Technology change

Often, a technological advance in transportation could not have occurred without the corresponding advance in communications. Table 1.1 contains a partial record of technological advances in transportation and communications. Note the timing of developments. Trans-oceanic air transport could not have developed without radio communications. Similarly, the trucking industry owes much of its flexibility and dependability advantages to the telephone and, more recently, to satellite communications. Perhaps the technological advance that we are most familiar with is booking airline tickets over the Internet (Table 1.1). The components of the computer reservation system that are hidden from our view are the coordination of crews and scheduling of equipment for use or maintenance. No modern airline, railway or trucking company could function without the advances in computer assisted communications and data retrieval.

Since the Industrial Revolution, world trade has accelerated because of new developments in transportation and communications. About every 35 to 50 years a new transportation development has emerged that propelled further economic growth. Observation would reveal however, that the lag time between invention and wide spread adoption is often measured in decades. Like any other technology, transportation and communication follow a life cycle process similar to the conceptual model presented in

Table 1.1.   Technological advances in transportation and communications.

Time period	Advance in transportation	Advance in communication
About 3000 B.C.	Horses tamed; Egyptians sailing ships; wheeled carts; first aqueduct Nineveh 691 B.C.	First systems of writing emerge, first mail service in 550 B.C. in Assyria
300 B.C. to A.D. 500	Liang wheelbarrow; Romans construct roads; iron horseshoes and stirrups are invented; Chinese canals	Paper invented in China
Between 500 and 1000	Horse collar is invented; Viking ships cross the Atlantic; Chinese compass	Chinese produce movable type to produce books
Between 1000 and 1500	First modern rudder; Vreeswijk pound lock (1373); three-mast ship (1450)	Paper currency in China; Gutenberg printing method in Europe (1456)
Between 1500 and 1800	Newcomen steam engine (1712); Cugnot steamcar (1769); Montgolfier balloon flight (1783)	Printed newspapers regularly published
Between 1800 and 1850	Fulton steamboat (1807); the bicycle (1816); McAdam surfaced roads (1816); Stockton and Darlington steam railroad (1825); Davenport electric streetcar (1834); Brunel iron ship (1843)	Daguerre photograph (1830); Morse telegraph code (1844)
Between 1850 and 1875	Gifford Airship (1852); compound steam engine (1854); London subway (1863); Van Syckel oil pipeline (1864); Otto internal combustion gasoline engine (1866); transcontinental railway (1869); de Smedt asphalt paved road (1872)	Trans-oceanic telegraph cable service (1858); Sholes typewriter (1867)
Between 1875 and 1900	Parsons steam turbine engine (1884); Benz gasoline powered car (1885); Dunlop pneumatic tire (1888); Diesel engine (1895); Daimler truck (1896); Reno escalator (1891)	Bell telephone (1876); Berliner microphone (1877); Marconi wireless radio (1895); loudspeaker (1898)
Between 1900 and 1925	Wright brothers airplane (1903); first helicopter flight (1907); Ford Model T (1908); Zeppelin scheduled passenger flights (1910); diesel-electric locomotives (1917); passenger airplane flights (1919); Cierva Autogiro (1922)	Trans-Atlantic radio signal (1900); KDKH-AM commercial radio station (1920); facsimile transmission (1925); Armstrong FM radio (1933)

(*Continued*)

Table 1.1. (*Continued*)

Time period	Advance in transportation	Advance in communication
Between 1925 and 1950	Goddard liquid propelled rocket (1926); Autobahn (1933); Sikorsky helicopter (1939); Whittle jet engine (1941); tractor-trailers; Comet passenger jet (1949)	Radar systems (1940); WNBT commercial television service (1940); ENIAC electronic computer (1946); Bell labs transistor (1947)
Between 1950 and 1975	Hovercraft (1956); intermodal container service (1957); Sputnik 1 (1957); Boeing 747 (1966); Concord SST (1969); maglev train (1969)	Berkley Personal computer (1950); integrated circuits (1958); Xerox copier (1959); Gould laser (1959); Telstar 1 comm. satellite (1962); Internet (1970); Cooper cell phone (1973); RFID tags (1973)
Between 1975 and 2000	Satellite dispatched trucks, Space Shuttle (1981); double-stacked container train service (1984); unmanned aerial vehicles (1991); Toyota fuel cell forklift (1996); Prius hybrid electric car (1997)	Xerox laser printer (1977); Fiber optic cable (1978); global positioning system (1978); Archie search engine (1990); Blackberry wireless (1998)
Between 2000 and 2025	Jet taxi (?); cargo airships (?); space elevator (?)	Holographic television (?), universal translators (?)

Figure 1.1. During the initial years, market sales growth is very slow and the new enterprise may fail. Often this is because the new technology has to displace an established system that has already depreciated a large share of its fixed costs. It may also be a materials problem holding back the new technology, like the lack of metal to make reliable rails for trains, or batteries to give electric cars sufficient endurance, or the limits of vacuum tubes in the development of computers. Once these technical issues are resolved, and if the new forms of transport and communication do lower costs, increase speed or provide some unique advantage, they can experience a tipping

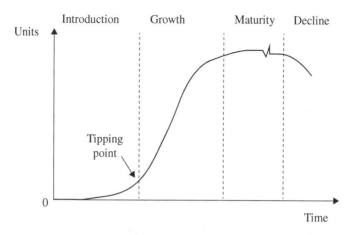

Figure 1.1. Product life-cycle stages.

point when an extended period of rapid growth stage begins. In the growth stage, new competitors enter the market and a dominant product design emerges.[4]

At some point the market becomes mature and sales growth slows to the pace of the underlying general economy. The length of the mature stage in the product life cycle is indeterminate, and during this period technological improvements and refinements continue to be made. If a better alternative is introduced however, a transportation technology can ultimately enter into a declining phase. An example of this phenomenon is transcontinental passenger rail service. It began slowly in the early 1800s, but did not hit the tipping point until after the telegraph was perfected in the mid-1800s. Subsequently, passenger rail services in North America grew rapidly until reaching maturity near the beginning of the 20th century.[5] Afterwards, growth slowed as automobiles and airplanes were introduced. By 1950, passenger rail services were in decline, and by the 21st century, passenger

---

[4]The Boeing 247 (1933) is considered to be the first airline with all-metal, semi-monocoque construction, fully cantilevered wing and retractable landing gear. This approach was joined quickly by the DC-1 (1933). Every airliner since that time has followed the same basic design.

[5]In the United States, the total railway network reached its maximum in 1916, at 266,381 miles of track. As of 2012, the network had declined to 136,623 miles of track. Available at http://www.railserve.com/stats_records/highest_steepest_railroads.html.

rail services were all but abandoned except for a few high density urban corridors.

The adaptation of cost-reducing technological innovations in transport and communications is spurred by the double stimulus that the falling costs of logistics have on international trade. A reduction of transportation costs can increase the profits for sellers in the export trade, while it lowers prices for buyers in the importing country. The pull of trade generates a push in both markets to invest in the newest transportation developments.[6] The rapid growth of the railway freight industry in the 19th century is an example of the double stimulus of trade. As railway lines were extended into undeveloped locations, farming opportunities emerged that were previously uneconomic. This encouraged trade and settlement that made demand for the railways self-perpetuating.

A similar experience has been occurring over the past four decades in ocean transport. Advances in ocean container ships, double-stack trains and faster port handling equipment have lowered the unit costs of international supply chains. The productivity improvement in container transportation has occurred simultaneously with the economic growth of the "Asian Tigers", Chinese and Indian economies. The economic stimulus of cost-reducing innovations in container shipping cannot be ignored in the rapid growth of trade among the countries of East Asia, North America, and Western Europe.[7]

Location

The economics of location can be altered by technological innovations that affect the costs of transport and communications. Until the mid-1800s, the commercial regions of the economy were limited to the major seaports and navigable rivers. The combination of telegraph communications (1844) and advances in railway engineering during the 1850s permitted an extension of international trade to the centers of the continents. Subsequently, the

---

[6]Kindleberger, Charles P. *Foreign Trade and the National Economy.* New Haven, Conn: Yale University Press, 1962.

[7]For a concise history of the development of containerization, see Levinson, Marc. *The Box: How the Shipping Container Made the World Smaller and the World Economy Bigger.* Princeton, NJ: Princeton University Press, 2006.

industrial core areas grew to encompass an area in which deliveries could be made within one to two days. By 1950, the development of tractor trailers, divided highways and telephone communications expanded the industrial core of the North American economy to encompass an east/west area from New York to Chicago and north/south from Montreal to Pittsburgh.

In the next decade, links between industrial core areas became more international as the reliability of airplanes enabled scheduled trans-oceanic flights.[8] By the late 1960s, wide-body aircraft like the Boeing 747 were bringing the cost of air travel into the reach of the masses, while the Concord SST pushed air travel to supersonic speeds.

Location decisions continue to be affected by technological changes in transportation and communication. In the last quarter of the 20th century, per unit cost of communication has declined at a stunning pace. From telegrams that charged by the word, to the Internet that charges by the month, no costs have fallen as dramatically as those for communications. It is less expensive now to e-mail a book from North America to Australia, than to mail an invoice across the city. As the economy becomes more service oriented, the transmission of information may replace the transport of products or people. Video-conferencing is an example of direct displacement of passenger transportation by communications. Although it has yet to rise up to its early expectations, communicating face to face over a computer screen is becoming more prevalent with services, like Skype, available on the Internet.

Communications can replace transportation indirectly by making less transportation necessary. For example, better communications have helped the retail distribution system reduce transportation costs. Previously, chain stores used a "push" system to ensure customer service. They would dispatch all inventories to retail outlets in anticipation of consumer demand. Subsequently, unsold merchandise would be *transshipped* between stores or returned to a central warehouse for redistribution or disposal. With low-cost

---

[8] Historically, the Zeppelin Company began trans-oceanic air passenger service in the 1932. The ticket prices on the Zeppelin were the equivalent in real terms of a first class flight on the Concord 50 years later. Of course in terms of opportunity costs, the time savings on the Concord were small relative to the days saved on a Zeppelin of the 1935.

communications, chain stores now ship only small volumes of inventories to each store and re-supply from the central warehouse based on sales reported nightly through computer connections. This "pull" system has reduced their need for transportation capacity and has cut the costs of inventory as well.

The change in communication costs has had a profound impact on the advantages of location. As communication costs fall, the geographic core of the economy expands. While some advantages of location in the industrial heartland still exist, the penalty of location at the fringe has diminished greatly. In no sector of the economy is this more evident than in information technology (IT).

IT workers can choose to live in communities based on esthetics (Vancouver, Denver) rather than proximity to the economic core (Toronto, Chicago). Even more extreme, IT workers in India compete directly with their North American counterparts. Falling transportation and communications costs have created a global village in the work sense, as well as Marshall McLuhan's media sense.

Communications between peoples affect the routes of trade and thus the routing of transportation. New trade routes are usually preceded by diplomatic and political links. In colonial times trading areas were generally a reflection of military power; in the modern era, trading blocks are now more likely to reflect financial stability and the level of industrial development among members. "Trade follows the flag" is still true today except that, to some extent, the "flag" can now be a metaphor for a multinational corporation as much as a country. The integration of markets internationally means that risks of "exposure" to foreign political uncertainties are diminishing. Transportation firms are becoming part of this multilateral network through direct ownership, and "alliances", which are formed where foreign ownership restrictions continue to exist, such as in the airlines.

Logistics and Supply Chain Management

Before international trade can occur, firms must be able to acquire the *factors of production* (land, labor, capital, and entrepreneurial ability) necessary to produce trade goods and services. Of course, both inbound transport of resources from suppliers to the firm and outbound transport of goods away from the firm to the marketplace must occur. This is where the concept of *logistics* comes into play. Logistics involves the management of inventories through the functions of acquisition, handling, storage, and transportation. Each logistics manager in the supply chain from primary producers to retail outlets may use the services of specialized intermediaries: transport carriers, public warehouses and terminal operators, freight forwarders, customs brokers, banks, and cargo insurance firms. The supply chain encompasses the entire structure of raw material suppliers, processors, distributors and consumers linked by transportation and communications.

For the logistician, the complication of the supply chain is not simply its many components but the proper balancing of functions and costs. The customer service goal of business is to get the right goods to the right place, at the right time, in the proper quality, at the lowest total cost. Increased customer service could expand sales, but if the firm wishes to maximize its profits, the expenses of increased customer service must be considered.

For example, the firm could offer more reliable delivery by increasing the number of warehouses it operates, or by using a faster transportation service. Lower inventory costs would be traded off against an increase in information management and transportation costs. Of course, once this "proper" balance has been struck, it is only a matter of time before it will have to be re-balanced. Changes in technology, competition, customer tastes and incomes can alter the optimal combination of the warehousing, inventory, transportation, order processing and other logistical functions.

Transportation is the largest cost component of the logistics process and can differ widely among tradable goods. Similar goods from several different continents may compete for the consumer's dollar. At the same time, some products such as sand, gravel and concrete are available only on a very local basis. The characteristics of a good such as its weight, configuration and perishability determine choice among the available modes of transport and sources of supply.

General freight is usually carried in a standardized intermodal container, boxcar or trailer. If the freight is perishable, it may need a heated vehicle, or one that is refrigerated. The value of the freight is also very important. Low value freight must often seek transport in bulk, while high value freight is carefully packaged.

Characteristics of a trip such as distance, terrain, and speed further affect the choice of transport. Ocean barriers, mountains and other geographical features limit the choice of transportation mode. Deficiencies in transport infrastructure or service can further impede the efficacy of any particular mode of transport within an area. For example, freight shipments that would normally move by truck are made by air when the destination is the Arctic because no all-weather roads or rail lines exist.

Route choice often entails transfer between different modes of transport. This is usually the case for any transoceanic shipments. A complete trip involves a land-based pick-up, marine travel, and a land-based drop-off of the good at the final destination. Trans-shipments add to the cost of transport, and increase the risk of damage to the cargo in-transit.

The military originated logistics management because the efficient movement of armies proved to be a significant advantage in fighting wars.[9] Logistics theory was pioneered by agricultural economists who recognized that farm incomes are very sensitive to the costs of marketing food products. Agricultural commodities have low value to weight ratios and often must be transported long distances. Moreover, perishability makes storage and handling costs of food products a high proportion of the supply chain cost.

Agricultural economists developed the concept of marketing utilities to represent the *value added* by logistics of the supply chain. *Place utility* is the value added to the product by transportation and handling. As the goods are moved closer to the point of consumption, they are of more value to the final consumer. *Time utility* is the value added in the supply chain by inventory holding and storage services. The maximum value of the product occurs when the final consumer wants it to be available. *Form utility* is the value added in the conversion of a raw material into a finished good. Form changes may also include packaging, preparation (e.g., pre-cooking) and other customer service elements. *Possession utility* is the value added as ownership changes throughout the supply chain. Data management, document preparation and financial transfers are some physical functions associated with ownership changes.

A simplified supply chain that depicts the transportation, storage and conversion of wheat into bread is presented in Figure 1.2. The supply chain

---

[9]Baluch describes fascinating accounts of historic military success and failure based on logistics. Hannibal's crossing the Alps with elephants to attack Rome is one success. Hitler's failed airlift at Stalingrad is compared to the success Berlin airlift after WW2. Baluch, Issa. *Transport Logistics*: *Past, Present and Predictions*. Dubai, UAE: Winning Books, 2005.

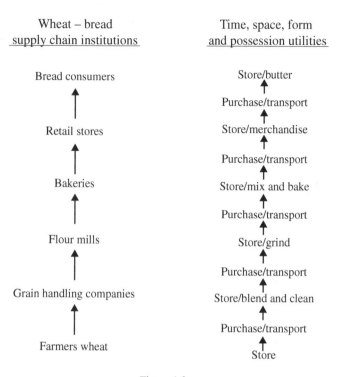

Figure 1.2.

comprises institutions that pass the product along like a relay race from raw material origin to final consumer. It is possible to combine one or more of these institutions, but amalgamating middlemen, does not eliminate the logistical functions. The provision of logistics services can only be shifted from one business to another.

The institutions of the supply chain can be expressed in the economist's price/quantity space as a family of demand curves. In Figure 1.3, each demand curve is dependent on, or derived from, the demand for its products in the supply chain. A shift in demand for bread at the consumer level creates a ripple effect through the *derived demands* (DD) for inputs. The demand for wheat creates the DD for flour. In turn, the DD for flour creates more DDs for other factors of production. Within each of these individual DDs lies another level of DDs (not illustrated) for transportation, storage and other logistical functions.

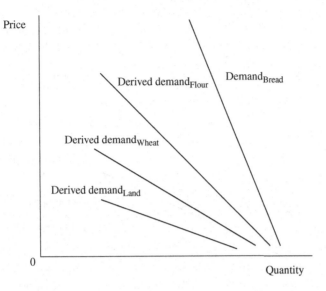

Figure 1.3.

Factors of production do not in and of themselves directly satisfy the demands of consumers. Rather, they indirectly satisfy consumer demand as part of the value added through the supply chain. The demand for a factor of production (i.e., a transportation or logistical service) is a DD. The demand that one or more firms have for that factor is based upon the demand for the final goods and services that factor is used to produce.

Every supply chain provides examples of DD. The demand for automobiles generates a DD for its factors of production, such as steel and assembly-line workers. The demand for savings accounts generates a demand for bank tellers. Demand for the movement of freight and passengers generates a demand for transportation equipment and operators. The concept of DD highlights the value-adding processes between the market for outputs (final goods and services) and the market for inputs (factors of production).

Value-adding logistic services can be depicted in terms of supply and demand. The diagram in Figure 1.4 illustrates two levels of the market, or the beginning and end of what is commonly called the supply chain. The quantity Q^* represents the units of final product, and the equivalent amount of raw material used in its production. For the sake of this example, imagine

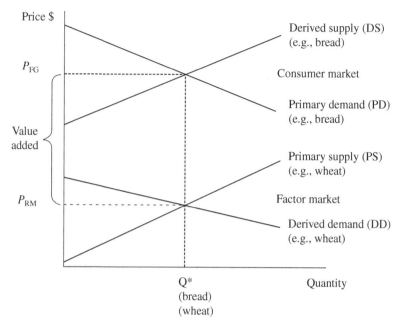

Figure 1.4. Economics of the supply chain.

Q^* as the quantity of bread consumed at the retail level, and the quantity of wheat required at the wholesale level to make this much bread.

The quantity of finished product (bread) available is represented by the derived supply (DS) curve. The DS is based on the raw material supply and the sum of value-added services provided by all the supply chain intermediaries. This includes logistics providers that modify, store, move, and make the finished good available where and when the consumer chooses to purchase. The retail price (P_{FG}) and quantity of finished goods (bread) purchased is determined by the intersection of the *primary demand* (PD) of the consumer the DS curve of the product.

The DD for raw material reflects the prices that intermediaries are willing to pay, subject to the prices received for the equivalent quantities of finished goods needed to satisfy the primary consumer demand for the product. The primary supply (PS) is determined by the costs of production of the raw material (wheat). The wholesale price (P_{RM}) and quantity of raw materials supplied is determined by the intersection of the PS and DD curves.

The vertical difference between the retail price for the finished product (P_{FG}) and the wholesale price of the raw material used to make this product (P_{RM}) equals the value of the supply chain services, or the value-added. The value-added represents the compensation to all the marketing and processing activities of the supply chain including transportation.

Economics of Technological Change in the Supply Chain

The supply chain model can be used to illustrate the double stimulus to trade created by a cost reducing innovation in transportation and communications. First, it is necessary to review the difference between a shift in a supply or demand curve, and a movement along a supply or demand curve. Figure 1.5 illustrates a shift in supply and the resulting impact on product prices.

The supply shifters are changes in the factors of production and technology. The main factors of production are labor and capital, in which capital represents all purchased inputs. An increase in the cost of labor or capital causes a supply curve to shift up, or to the left. At every price, a lower quantity is produced than before the cost increase. A decrease in the cost of inputs causes the supply curve to shift down, or to the right. Now, at every price more is produced. Changes in technology have similar effects. If technology improves production efficiency, the supply curve shifts right, while a loss of technology, say a ban on a previously used

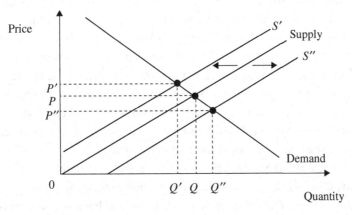

Figure 1.5. Supply shifts and price movements along demand.

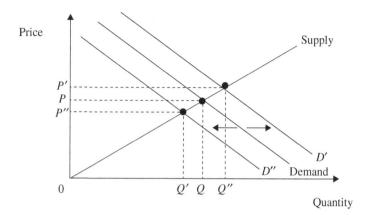

Figure 1.6. Demand shifts and price movements along supply.

chemical or process, could cause the supply curve to shift left. Note, that these supply shifts cause a movement of the product price along the demand curve.

Figure 1.6 illustrates a shift in the demand curve and a corresponding price movement along the supply curve. The arguments underlying the demand curve are more complicated than the supply curve. Demand shifters can be changes in the prices of complementary goods or the prices of substitutes.

A complementary good is one that is used in conjunction with the product in question. An example is airplane trips and airports. If the price of a complement rises (e.g., higher airport user fees), consumers may shift their purchases to an alternative product (e.g., private cars) that results in less demand for the product in question. Consequently, the demand for the product (i.e., airplane trips) shifts down or to the left. The converse is also true, if the complementary product drops in price, the demand shifts right.

A change in the price of a substitute causes the demand for the product to shift in the opposite direction. If a substitute product becomes more expensive, consumers will shift purchases to this product which causes demand to shift up, or to the right, and vice versa.

The other demand shifters are income and population. For normal products, demand shifts out if people have more money to spend, or if the population grows. The assumption is that tastes and habits remain constant. Of course, some goods are considered to be inferior and when consumers have more income they will switch to a good that they like better. An example is public transit, which for most people is a second choice, if they can afford to drive a car. As young people enter the job market and increase their incomes, many buy a car and stop riding the bus. However, demand shifts also depend on demographics and the location of population. If the young population migrates to live downtown, they may decide to put off buying cars, even if they can now afford to own them.

Changes in tastes and habits can also affect demand. If consumers in the suburbs come to believe that riding the bus reduces carbon emissions and helps to slow climate change, they might park their car and take the bus to work instead.

Changes in tastes and habits can shift demand, but in some cases they also have the power to alter the shape of the demand curve such that consumers react differently to price changes. Sales of electric cars continue to increase even though they remain more expensive (total costs to own and operate) than traditional gasoline-powered automobiles.

Note that product price changes resulting from shifts in the demand curve trace out movements along the supply curve.

The review of demand and supply shifts can now be applied to a case in which a cost component of the supply chain changes. A reduction in logistics costs because of a technical improvement in transportation is illustrated in Figure 1.7. In this case, only the final product (bread) supply and demand curves are presented and the one raw material (wheat) supply and demand curves. The intermediate DS and demand curves for transport, storage, processing, etc. are not illustrated, and only the cumulative effect is shown in the raw material and final good prices.

Consider the following scenario in which the grain industry abandons bulk handling in favor of containerization grain shipments. Container shipments of wheat permit foreign flour millers to employ a Just-in-time system that lowers their inventory holding costs and improves customer service to the bakeries. These benefits are passed on to consumers through competition causing the DS of bread (DS_0) to shift to down, or to the right (DS_1). At every price, more of the product is now available for purchase because the total cost of the supply chain has been reduced.

PD at the consumer level stays fixed, but the falling price from PR_0 to PR_1 leads to an increase in the quantity (of bread) demanded from

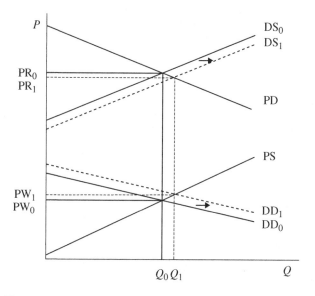

Figure 1.7. Impact of productivity improving logistics innovation.

Q_0 to Q_1. A price movement along the PD (for bread) at the consumer level is accommodated by a shift in the DD (for wheat) at the wholesale level. This is represented as a shift to the right in the DD curve from DD_0 to DD_1. At every price, more raw material (wheat) is now desired. The PS curve is unaffected by the change in logistics costs and stays fixed.[10] The greater quantity (of wheat) demanded raises the wholesale price from PW_0 to PW_1, which calls forth more resources or a movement along the PS curve from Q_0 to Q_1.

In summary, a reduction in logistics costs causes a shift to the right of the DS for the finished good and the DD for raw materials. The double stimulus to trade occurs because the benefits of innovation are shared between consumers and producers. As consumers increase their consumption of lower priced bread, the DD for farmer's wheat shifts to the right. Farmers receive high prices for wheat that encourages more

---

[10]The assumption behind the upward sloping supply curve is that some resources are limited in quantity or quality and prices are bid up from PW_0 to PW_1. The PS of wheat does not shift because nothing has affected the cost of producing wheat. The technological change only affects costs beyond the farm gate.

production. The transportation example of technological change is easy to visualize, but any improvement in the efficiency of value adding service could create a double stimulus for growth because both consumers and producers are made better off.[11]

The method used in this economic model is called comparative statics. The diagram depicts the market before some economic stimulus and an end state of the market when complete adjustment has occurred. The model assumes that the market is at equilibrium before and after a sufficient time has passed for adjustment. In reality, prices and quantities could easily overshoot the end state, and then contract beyond the end state before settling on the new equilibrium. Comparative statics is incapable of predicting the precise magnitude or speed of any adjustment, but sets out the logical direction of change.

The complexity of the logistics process accentuates the possibility that the "optimal" balance may not be struck due to the informational or time limitations involved in physical movement. The economics of logistics is not the focus of this textbook. Our purpose is merely to highlight the role of efficient transportation services in the consumption process of a modern economy.

Traditional microeconomic theory stresses optimal solutions, but real world applications require merely finding "satisfactory" solutions. Quite often, as long as transport costs are below some threshold, they are considered acceptable. An understanding of transportation economics helps to identify the logistical possibilities.

Keywords

derived demand	infrastructure	time utility
economic development	logistics	transshipped
factors of production	place utility	value added
form utility	possession utility	
free-on-board (FOB)	primary demand	

---

[11]WalMart is a modern example of the phenomenon. WalMart expanded its sales by passing the gains in logistics efficiency to consumers in the form of lower prices.

Exercises

1. Imagine that a bacterial problem occurs at a beef slaughter plant that kills hundreds of people. The government reacts by imposing stricter regulations that increase the cost of the cattle/beef supply chain.

   Draw an appropriate economic model and explain the impact of these new safety regulations on the prices paid by consumers for beef, and on the prices paid to farmers for cattle.

   Explain how the prior economic model would change if consumers began to substitute pork and chicken for beef because of health concerns.

2. A recent pig disease, Porcine Epidemic Diarrhea (PED), has caused the death of millions of piglets. The effected farms are losing their total pig production for that cycle, and problem can be prolonged for several cycles because the disease is easily spread and there is no vaccine.

   With the use of an appropriate diagram, explain how this pig disease would affect the prices, supply and demand of pigs on farms and of pork products (like bacon) at the retail level.

   Since the PED disease became widespread, the farm price of pigs has increased over 50%, but the price of pork products (like bacon) has only increased about 15% at the retail level. Explain why the percentage change in prices paid in the retail market is so much less that the percentage change in prices received by pig farmers.

3. Carbon taxes on fossil fuels would increase the cost of supply chain services like transportation and processing in the bakery industry. Wheat producers would be exempt from the carbon tax because their crops provide a carbon offset.

   Draw and explain an appropriate economic model(s) that illustrate(s) the impact of a new carbon tax on retail and wholesale prices in the bread supply chain.

   Explain the net economic impact on the bread supply chain, if the government cut income taxes to reduce the impact of carbon taxes on bread consumers.

4. The government proposes to increase the sales taxes by 1%. Each business in the supply chain would charge the tax and add it to the cost of their services (value added). Consumers, who have to pay more taxes, would have less disposable income to spend on new houses. The forestry companies are also going to incur more expense because this

sales tax is not rebated back to producers when they buy inputs to harvest and process trees into lumber.

Use an appropriate model to illustrate and explain the impact of this sales tax increase on the price of new houses and the prices received by lumber producers.

5. Over the past 15 years, pulp and paper plants that produce newsprint have closed across North America. The companies have experienced unanticipated events. The Internet attracted advertising dollars away from newspapers. As a result, the newspapers downsized or ceased operations. Forestry harvesting and paper manufacturing are energy intensive. The rising price of petroleum made pulp and paper plants more expensive to operate.

Use an appropriate model to illustrate and explain the impact of these unanticipated events on prices received by pulp and paper plants and quantities produced.

Adding to the woes of the pulp and paper industry, the technology to recycle waste paper improved to the point that it can now compete directly with newly manufactured newsprint processed from trees. Illustrate how this change would affect prices and quantities.

Chapter 2

The Demand for Transportation

The demand for transportation has unique attributes that make it an interesting topic. Transportation is a service that can be enjoyed by the individual consumer, but it is also a factor in the production process of most goods. As a factor of production, the demand for transportation is a service generated by the trade within markets for goods. It is easier to obtain a directional balance in passenger transport because short of migration, people make return trips. Freight transport demand is more difficult in this respect because few markets have a balanced volume of trade. The imbalance of trade between markets creates a surplus of transportation vehicles in at least one direction. In a variation of *Say's Law of the Markets*, the "*backhaul*" demand for transport could be said to be created by virtue of its own supply. The other complications of transport demand are perishability, externalities, opportunity costs and joint consumption. Sharing the road in a private automobile is a case of joint consumption. Deciding whether to drive this car for 12 hours or to take an airplane is an example of weighing opportunity costs. Missing the airplane because of road congestion on the way to the airport illustrates both negative externalities and the perishability of transportation services. Despite these idiosyncrasies, the theory of demand can be applied to transportation just as it can for other goods and services.

Elements of Transportation Demand

A demand curve for transport can be thought of as a locus of the willingness to pay on the part of a passenger/shipper for various quantities of a (constant-quality) transportation service provided by a carrier. For the demand curve to be captured: (1) the passenger/shipper has to be able to value those service quantities; and (2) these values must come from a well-defined set of preferences that are correctly revealed in the marketplace.

In valuing a transport service that is used to move a person or good from point A to point B over a given period of time with a specific degree of comfort or reliability in transit, a passenger's/shipper's valuation is dependent upon whether or not transportation serves a primary demand or a derived demand. Most forms of leisure or recreational travel are serving the primary demand for transport where the experience itself is the purpose of the trip. For example, a pleasure cruise through the Caribbean would be a case of primary demand. After two weeks of travel, the passengers end up exactly where they started. Passenger travel for sight-seeing or joy-riding is a primary demand.

A derived demand serves functional passenger travel in which the principal reason for the trip is to get from one location to another. Taking a leisurely bicycle ride through the park is clearly a primary demand for transport. Riding this same bicycle to work is more likely to serve a derived demand. Even though some pleasure might be obtained in riding the bicycle, the purpose of the trip is just to get back and forth from work. In this sense, the bicycle could easily be substituted for another means of transport such as a bus or a car.

The distinction between primary and derived demand is important. Most transportation services are purchased on the basis of a derived demand. Passenger travel may involve elements of both primary and derived demand, but no one transports freight so that it can enjoy the trip. All freight transportation is serving the derived demand created by final (primary) demand for the trade of final goods and services. This is demonstrated in Figure 2.1.

In a primary demand, the value of the user sets is based on a personal measure of satisfaction or pleasure that the user gains from the journey. The monetary value of the service to the consumer may be compared with the price of the service. Thus, for a particular quantity of the service, such as the duration of a pleasure cruise, the passenger reveals a willingness to pay for it equal to the monetary value of the satisfaction received in taking it.

Of course, this narrow view of demand ignores the issue of affordability. For example, one may assign a high dollar value to the satisfaction received in traveling through a planetary orbit on a NASA Space Shuttle but few

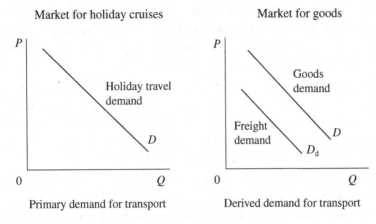

Figure 2.1.

would be able to pay their share of the cost involved in doing so. This is the difference between effective demand and latent demand. Some people are able and willing to pay (effective demand) while others would like the product or service, but are unable to pay (latent demand).

An alternative way of looking at the demand is in terms of the willingness to acquire a specific quantity of a good under a given price. This serves to create a subset known as feasible demand on the part of the consumer.

The locus of willingness to pay, when drawn in a price–quantity space, depends on a variety of things such as: one's current income or wealth level, the prices of substitute and complementary goods, individual tastes and preferences, and opportunity costs. Expectations about the future can also affect demand, but only to a limited extent. One can decide to take a trip earlier to avoid a price increase, but it is impossible to "stockpile" trips in anticipation of future consumption. Nonetheless, all of these variables serve to shift the demand curve when they change.

The relative prices of different modes of transport can be the most important determinants of consumer demand for a particular mode.[1] A key

---

[1] The absolute price of any good or service is often less important than the difference between its price and the price of a close substitute. Think of truck versus rail transport or perhaps even car pools versus a bus ride. The freight rate for truck transport is more likely to be compared by a shipper to that for rail rather than just considered in isolation. Likewise, a

problem in urban transportation is the difficulty of making realistic price comparisons between the different forms of transport. The cost of a transit bus ticket may be known with certainty but most people have only a vague idea of the equivalent taxi fare, or the cost of using a private automobile. From society's perspective, the decisions of such consumers are likely to be economically inefficient. This is made worse if direct and indirect subsidies distort the prices paid by individuals. If prices are not visible, or do not reflect true economic costs, individuals will consume too much of what is actually scarce, and too little of what is abundant.

The demand for travel is further complicated by the joint consumption of some transportation infrastructure (e.g., road ways). Joint consumption of the street network is supported by a pooled contribution of revenues from fuel taxes and other levies. Through the purchase of fuel, car owners gain unlimited access to the entire network of a public infrastructure. The direct cost of using any street is the same, regardless of whether it is a main arterial road or quiet residential street. As a result, the higher demand for strategic routes tends to be rationed through *congestion costs*. As the users increase in number, the congestion of traffic increases travel time. This represents an indirect "price" that influences consumer decisions on route choice and means of transport.

So far it has been taken for granted that the preferences or willingness to pay on the part of the demanders would be correctly revealed in the marketplace. This need not always hold. When it does not hold, the market is said to fail in that truthful information on the part of demanders is not reaching suppliers so that the latter may decide not to provide the good.

Goods for which the market alone will not cause correct preference revelation are known as *public goods*. By definition, public goods are non-rival and non-excludable. Non-rival means that one person's use of the good does not in any way affect another person's use of that same good. Non-excludability means that once the good is provided, it is provided to everyone and it makes no sense to try to prevent anyone else from using the good.

---

rider in a car pool will no doubt compare his cost of participating in the car pool with the cost of a bus ride to and from the same points. In terms of derived demand, there are many close substitutes that a shipper/passenger may choose.

An example of a public good in the context of transportation is a street improvement plan in a city or town. The market will fail to provide improved streets because it is rational for no one to reveal a preference for better streets even when every member of the community wants it. Thus, true preferences will not be revealed in this private transaction. Why? Assume that a block of houses faces a common unpaved street and that each homeowner desires to have the entire through-road paved to allow ease of access to other adjoining roadways. A private contractor might get many residents to agree to pay their proportional share of the costs in paving the street but an incentive exists for one or more owners to refuse to join. These residents realize that if enough of the others pay, the street will be paved and free use will be provided to those who chose not to pay. Appropriately, these individuals are referred to as "*free-riders*". The problem is that the homeowners who agreed to pay would not stand by and have the road paved knowing that some will use it for free. If everyone decides to become a free-rider (a *market failure*), the street stays unpaved. Where roads do allow members of society to be excluded (e.g., divided highways), private toll roads can be organized to collect revenue. In this way, drivers are required to reveal their true preferences. Where excludability is impossible, such as urban streets, the government constructs the roadway and forces everyone on the block to pay tax levies.

Freight versus Passenger Demand for Transportation

When the business passenger or shipper is confronting a derived demand, his willingness to pay is calculated to equal the value of the increase in productivity with respect to the final benefit that accrues to the business passenger or shipper from using an extra unit of the transportation service. The term that economists use for this definition is the value of the marginal productivity (VMP) of the factor of production.

In the sense of transportation as a factor of production, the VMP of an extra unit of a certain transport mode is simply the extra quantity of freight or worker output that can be brought to market during a specific period of time multiplied by the price at which this quantity is sold. Thus if a shipper, by hiring one more truck, is able to bring, say, 100 more units of a good to market where they could be sold with a $4 price markup then the value of that truck to the shipper would be $400. This would represent his maximum willingness to pay for that truck at the margin, or the VMP.

Differences exist in the demand for transportation of passengers and freight shippers. Freight transport always occurs under a derived demand while passenger travel can occur for business and/or leisure reasons. From the point of view of the carrier, however, passengers can be, in a somewhat demeaning sense, considered "freight that complains". Of course, such a term does put the quality of service into context. While a shipper may complain about the quality of the goods after shipment, a passenger is likely to complain every second of the journey if the comfort and convenience fails to meet *a priori* expectations.[2]

Income and *opportunity costs* create more differences between passenger travel and freight transport demand. *Income elasticity* of demand measures the sensitivity of the quantity demanded of a good or service with respect to a change in the level of income of the consumer. More specifically, it is the ratio of the percentage change in the quantity demanded to the percentage change in income. For a shipper, the income elasticity of demand for all modes of transport is positive in value meaning that, *ceteris paribus*, as the shipper obtains more revenue from the sale of goods, the more that shipper will avail himself of any particular means of transporting his goods.

Passenger demand does not behave so simply because of competition between the transport modes. As income rises, individuals are willing to trade off monetary costs for improvements in other attributes of travel like convenience and their opportunity costs.

Comfort and security are attributes of travel whose demand generally rises with income levels. Ostensibly, the higher the cost of transport, the greater the comfort and security provided to and expected by the passenger. Higher income consumers are likely to choose more expensive means of

---

[2]In travel demand the passenger is always the decision-maker. Consequently, bad service has a more direct effect on repeat business. Carriers are responsible for damage to freight in-transit, and pay claims to shippers. However, the shipper is not present to observe damage that goes undetected.

transport, because of comfort and security attributes, even if time is not a constraint. Compare the demand for an airline service to that of an intercity bus between two distant cities.

Growth of income can lead to substitution. For example, the income-elasticity of demand for urban bus travel is negative because, as the user obtains more income, the more likely it is that the user will travel by automobile instead. Low-income consumers have little choice but to accept the comfort/security that is available with the more time-consuming means of transport. Any good with a negative income-elasticity of demand economists call an *inferior good.*

Opportunity cost is defined as the value of the next best alternative foregone to undertake the present activity chosen. For example, the opportunity cost of working is the value of one's favorite leisure activity foregone by working. In transport, the fare to purchase a faster means of transport is generally higher than the fare of a slower mode. The passenger using the slower mode still arrives at the same location, but gives up time (opportunity cost) that could be used for doing something else, in place of the higher monetary expense.

Of course, a rational decision is to choose the activity that provides the greatest possible satisfaction or economic profit out of all possible activities. In terms of freight transport, opportunity cost is the profit that might have been earned by producing a good that did not require as much transport time or cost to reach its market. For example, the capital used to finance larger safety stocks inventory during transit could have been used for other purposes. The firm has to bear for the opportunity cost of longer transit times for the goods it produces. Some or all of those costs are passed on to consumers in the form of a higher sale price. So long as the profits earned using the current transport mode exceed those of the alternatives, the present decision is rational for the shipper.

The need exists to build the opportunity cost of transport time into the total cost of goods production because manufacturing areas and retail areas are separated. Speed of delivery may be considered by a shipper to be a valuable attribute for which its customers would pay. The derived demand aspect of freight transport means that any premium paid for speed or reliability of transport may be passed on to consumers in the form of higher output prices.

The same opportunity cost does not hold true for passenger travel except, perhaps, for business travel. The opportunity cost of passenger travel is the value of the time foregone by traveling. The attractiveness of the premium necessary for shorter travel time varies with the income of the traveler and their corresponding opportunity cost. A passenger traveling as a sightseer or to a vacation spot may not value speed all that much. A shipper derives no extra satisfaction while his goods are in transit whereas some passengers might obtain extra satisfaction while in transit based on the sights and/or amenities offered by the carrier. A business traveler may only want to return home in time to be with family on the weekend.

A journey's total cost is the sum of the money cost and the time cost (which encompasses the opportunity cost). For both freight demand and passenger demand one may wish to know, in general, their price-elasticity of demand. To begin to answer this, one needs to determine the sensitivity of the quantity of transport services demanded to a change in the price of transport. Following a price-elastic demand relationship, if the money price of transport falls by a certain percentage the quantity demanded is expected to increase by a greater percentage. If time is a major cost however, the demand may be much more price-inelastic.

Current and potential users may be insensitive to a drop in the money cost of transport if the time cost, which has not changed of course, is a large proportion of total cost. Such a point would help to explain why even drastic cuts in urban transit fares would not be enough to induce some people to give up their cars and travel by bus; the opportunity cost of travel time for them is very high.

The parallel in the freight market would be a fall in the price of a slower mode relative to a faster one. Because of the derived demand aspect of freight travel, the money savings in using the slower mode would have to exceed the money-denominated extra travel time cost as far as the shipper is concerned so that a lower net price could be passed on to his consumers.[3]

---

[3]Interestingly, most shippers are less concerned with the total time of transit than the reliability of carrier in achieving the delivery target on time. The rationale is obvious. The shipper can control lead times and set safety stocks to deal with customer demands if the carrier is dependable. If the carrier is unreliable, the seller can experience customer service failures that result in buyers switching suppliers. Not all buyers return after such experiences.

A priori, it is impossible to say whether a passenger has greater time sensitivity than does a shipper.

Urban transportation services can be presented as a function of price (fares or private costs), and a bundle of quality attributes that represent speed of travel, comfort, convenience, and security. The bundles of quality attributes generally decline as the travel time increases. Rather than a "smooth" supply curve of transportation options, individuals have to choose between discrete alternatives. The general trade-off is between the monetary cost of the trip and the time involved in making the trip. If money is scarce, consumers are willing to take a more time-consuming, but less expensive mode of transportation. If time is limited, the consumer is more likely to opt for the more expensive, faster means of automobile transport.

Figure 2.2 presents the inherent opportunity cost trade-off between travel time versus monetary cost available to the consumer of urban transportation. At one extreme is the alternative of fast and convenient, but expensive, automobile travel. If consumers are willing to spend more time traveling, they can obtain lower cost means of transport, such as buses, or an essentially "free" bicycle or walking.

Any conceptual model suffers when confronted with the reality of application. In the case of travel times the generalization depicted in the model will depend on the three factors: length of trip, route, and time of day. For very short trips city buses and bicycles can experience the travel times of private automobiles (if one includes the time required for

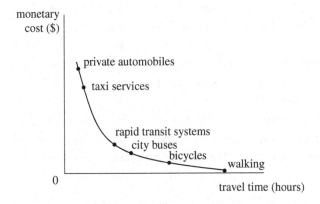

Figure 2.2.

locating a parking spot). On main corridor routes, the travel time of city buses is likely to be closer to the private automobile. As the length of the trip increases, the general model above is more likely to apply. Time of day exaggerates these relationships because of congestion. During peak travel periods, rapid transit systems with exclusive right-of-ways are likely to perform better than the private automobile or city buses. Off the main corridors, the general model is more likely to be accurate.

Most transportation services are provided by a combination of public and private investment. The public sector provides the long-lived infrastructure (e.g., streets), while private individuals or firms provide the vehicles.[4] But governments can also use subsidies and regulations to influence the demand for passenger transportation. In part this can be explained by the tendency of transportation toward *monopoly* control and the desire to use transportation as an instrument of social policy. Governments try to influence demand through subsidies that lower the price, by investments in transportation infrastructure and through regulatory controls.

In many jurisdictions, governments regulate taxi and transit services. Taxi licensing arrangements are used to limit the number of cars and set maximum fares. This helps to maintain the incomes of taxi owners and, in theory, improves the quality of the cars and guarantees service.

Transit bus services are an example of direct government intervention. Most transit services were converted to public monopolies after they were driven into bankruptcy during the first half of the 20th century. Government regulations that required operators to provide service on routes at uneconomic fares were the source of the private transit companies' problems. Where the governments could not achieve their social goals of income distribution through regulation, they have used subsidies to provide uneconomic services. Today, very few urban transit services generate enough revenue from the passenger fare box to pay for half their costs; the balance is provided by subsidies.

Overall, transportation regulation restricts demand by narrowing the range of choices available to consumers, while subsidies provide levels of service that would not otherwise be provided, or in some cases wanted.

---

[4]The freight railways in North America are a notable exception to the rule. Private companies own and maintain the right-of-way (track) and rolling stock.

The longer government regulations and subsidies are sustained, the more insensitive the transportation service becomes to the evolving consumer demand. The quality and quantity of services provided may no longer match the demand. Evidence of this phenomenon in most cities are suburban bus routes served by 45-seat buses with only a few people on board, and the emergence of Uber as a lower-cost alternative.

Elasticity of Derived Demand for Transport

Movement of freight or passengers to and from a marketplace creates place utility. In other words, transportation adds value to what is being transported because it is worth more in one place than in another. Coal found in the mine is worth more at the dock of a power plant. Society gains when the coal reaches the power plant in order for electricity to be generated. This creates the derived demand for the railway to haul coal to the plant.

The derived demand for transportation is very much dependent upon the scope and stability of consumer demand. The various modes of transportation face a demand for their services that is cyclical in nature. The transportation industry expands and contracts with the cycle of the general economy. The demand for transportation is the first to be ill-affected by an economy-wide recession, and the first to react positively to a general economic expansion.

The transportation industry can exhibit a procyclical economic nature. A procyclical industry expands and contracts more so than the general economy. This is because many industries served by transport face a cyclical demand, such as housing, forestry, and retail distribution. Those industries that are less cyclical, such as education, medicine and government services, use little commercial transportation services. The transportation industry sizes itself to the demand because it is a service that cannot be hoarded or stockpiled. When the general economy begins to recover from years of slow growth, consolidation and reduced inventories, the demand for transport quickly outpaces the available supply. The changes in prices that result lead to changes in quality demanded. This depends on the price elasticity of the derived demand for transport services.

The *price elasticity of demand* expresses an important relationship between changes in prices and total revenues. The formula for the elasticity of demand is given in Figure 2.3, and is illustrated in Figure 2.4. If the

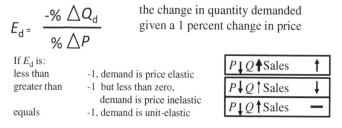

$$E_d = \frac{-\%\,\triangle Q_d}{\%\,\triangle P}$$ the change in quantity demanded
given a 1 percent change in price

If E_d is:
less than   -1, demand is price elastic
greater than   -1 but less than zero,
                 demand is price inelastic
equals   -1, demand is unit-elastic

Figure 2.3. Price elasticity of demand E_d.

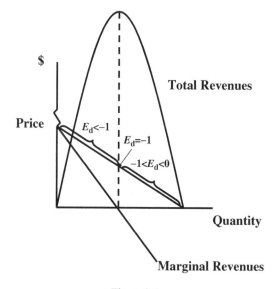

Figure 2.4.

demand is elastic and prices go down, then total sales or revenues go up because the percentage increase in the quantity demanded is greater than the percentage drop in prices. If the demand is inelastic and prices go down the quantity demanded will still increase, but not enough to compensate for the lower prices and consequently, total sales or revenues go down. These relationships are symmetrical if prices go up.

The only point on the demand curve that revenues are constant is at the point of unit-elasticity. In this case the change in prices is exactly offset by an opposite change in the quantity demanded, so that total revenues stay constant. The implications of the price elasticity for the derived demand are more complicated. Transportation faces the elasticity its own derived demand, but is also affected by the elasticity of the final demand that transport serves.

An analysis of the dependency of the market for factors to the market for final goods and services is worthwhile before moving into the specific nature of the derived demand for transportation. Two relationships of note are:

(1) The larger (smaller) the proportion of total costs accounted for by the factor, the more (less) price-elastic is the demand for it.
(2) The more (less) price-elastic the demand for the final good or service, the more (less) price-elastic is the demand for the factor.

Point (1) means, for example, that if the price of the factor fell and the factor's cost accounts for a small proportion of the total costs of production then overall costs to the firm fall by a small amount as well. The output from the firm only expands by a small amount as a result. The quantity of the factor demanded will only increase by a small amount. This is demonstrated in Figure 2.5.

The first panel shows demand and supply for the firms' final output while the second shows the derived demand for a factor used in the production of that output. When the price of the factor falls from P_0 to P_1 as seen in the second panel, firms are inclined to purchase more of it, *ceteris paribus*, and in so doing produce more output. Production of more output

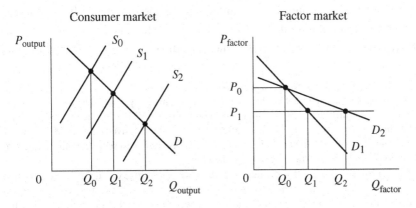

Figure 2.5.

for the consumer market is reflected in the rightward shift of the supply curve away from S_0. If the factor's cost accounts for a small proportion of overall cost, the firm buys only a relatively small amount of the factor. This is shown by the increase in the quantity demanded by the firm from Q_0 to Q_1 along demand curve D_1 in the second panel. It translates into an increase in supply of output from S_0 to S_1.[5]

If the factor's cost had been a larger proportion of total cost then the fall in the factor's price would have triggered a larger increase in the quantity of the factor demanded. This is shown by the increase from Q_0 to Q_2 along demand curve D_2 and would translate into a greater increase in supply as shown by the increase in supply from S_0 to S_2. It should be noticed at this point that D_2 is more price-elastic than is D_1.[6]

In terms of transport costs, a shipper of manufactured goods has a relatively price-inelastic demand for transportation services because these costs are a small proportion of the overall cost — most of the value-added comes in the manufacturing process itself. The derived demand for transport is more price-elastic for bulk goods such as coal, grain, and iron ore. These bulk goods have a low value to weight ratio, compared with manufactured goods. Consequently, transportation costs are a large source of value-added in bulk goods, and the derived demand is very sensitive to changes in freight rates (price elastic).

The explanation for point (2) focuses on the price-elasticity of the final demand. When the output demand is price-elastic (price-inelastic), a small change in price translates into a larger (smaller) change in the opposite direction for the quantity demanded of the factor. In the first panel of Figure 2.6, the final demand D_1 is price-inelastic and D_2 is price-elastic. If the price of a factor falls, the increase in output supply brought about

---

[5]An astute observer may notice that there is more to this story. Once the supply curve for the final good shifts and the price of the final good falls, the VMP (i.e., the derived demand) will shift leftward. While this does not affect the slope of the derived demand (drawn under the assumption of a constant output price) this "output effect" will serve to diminish the size of the Q_0 to Q_1 differential in panel 2 somewhat.

[6]The student should note that the relationship between the slope of a demand curve and its price elasticity is by no means simple. It is only for convenience that we have shown two intersecting linear demand curves because it is indeed the case that the flatter curve is the more price-elastic.

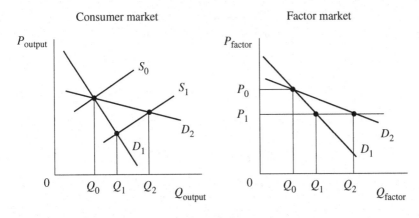

Figure 2.6.

by demanding more of the factor will lead to an increase in output from S_0 to S_1.

The fall in the price of the factor from P_0 to P_1 shown in the second panel leads to an increase in the quantity of the factor demanded that is dependent upon the elasticity of the demand for the output. Given D_1 in the first panel, the increase in supply from S_0 to S_1[7] leads to an output increase from Q_0 to Q_1 that translates into an increase in the quantity of the factor demanded from Q_0 to Q_1 in the second panel. Notice that if the output demand curve were more elastic as given by D_2 both output and thus the quantity of the factor demanded would increase from Q_0 to Q_2 instead.

As an intuitive test for point (2), which factor demand is likely more price-elastic: business class seats or regular cabin seats on an airline? The answer is cabin seats, for a variety of reasons. Paraphrased in terms of our two points above: (a) personal travel is usually a larger proportion of one's own income because this is not a business trip that a firm subsidizes in whole or in part; (b) the set of "activities" that are possible under a personal trip, which comprises the trip's "output", is more varied than that for a business trip which is also of a more compulsory nature.[8] One final point in this

---

[7] The same caveat as discussed in Footnote 2 applies here.

[8] The rapid growth of air travel after the introduction of discount airlines illustrates the impact of demand price-elasticity. The majority of the new passengers used the discount airlines for leisure travel. In fact, some discount airlines completely eliminated the business class seats in favor of the cabin class.

Derived demand for fransport

	Inelastic	Elastic
Inelastic	Q_{1a} Oil & pipelines	Q_{1b} Gravel & dump trucks
Elastic	Q_{2a} Grain & rail cars	Q_{2b} Tourists & charter airlines

Primary product demand

Figure 2.7.

regard is adjustment time as a determinant of price elasticity. A personal trip is easier to cancel or postpone because it is usually planned further ahead of time than is the business trip.

The sensitivity of the quantity of the factor demanded to a given change in its price is based upon both the proportion of this factor's cost to total cost of the final output and to the price elasticity of demand for the final output itself. The derived demand is very much dependent upon the nature of the market for the final output. It is not impossible that a product with an inelastic demand could have a factor market with an elastic demand, and vice versa. Figure 2.7 presents a matrix of possible examples. The impacts of the factor price changes are illustrated in Figure 2.8.

Finally, the price-elasticity of demand applicable to a specific mode of transport is dependent upon the substitutability of the various modes with respect to the shipment type. The more substitutes there are, or the increased similarity of any two particular substitutes, the more price-elastic will be the demand for any particular mode and thus the more sensitive shippers are to freight rate changes within that mode. This can be seen in Figure 2.9.

Quantity (Q) in this diagram can be taken to mean either quantity of freight or passengers per trip or the frequency of trips over a fixed amount of freight or passengers. For a given increase in supply of transport services,[9]

---

[9]Technically, this is a shift in the supply of transportation services that would require a change in input costs. For example, a large drop in the price of petroleum could enable more transportation services to be offered at every freight rate level.

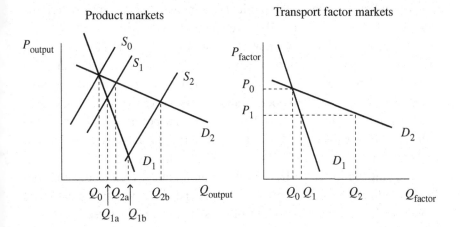

Figure 2.8.

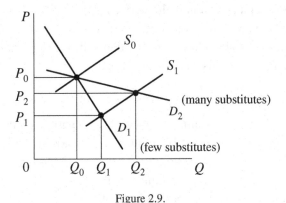

Figure 2.9.

from S_0 to S_1, the freight rate or ticket price falls by a lesser amount along the more price-elastic demand (D_2) than along D_1 and yet the increase in the quantity demanded is greater with respect to the former. The number and/or closeness of existing substitutes make for a more competitive market while a more price-inelastic demand suggests a market that is less competitive. Intermodal competition (to be discussed in Chapters 6 and 11) and other technological changes have increased the substitutability between trucking and rail. Each mode is finding an increased price-elasticity of demand with respect to certain shipments.

The relationship between product weight and distance may determine whether shipping will actually take place. Goods with a low value to weight ratios are sensitive to transport cost. A high freight rate may prevent such goods from being transported over large distances and limit trade to localized markets. For example, crushed rock is a freight sensitive good that is restricted to local trade by its very low value to weight ratio. Even over short distances the value of transportation can exceed the value of the crushed rock at the quarry. The freight sensitive group would include primary goods, such as crude oil, coal, iron ore, and feed grain that are shipped in bulk. Higher value commodities, such as dimensional lumber, refined metal, and coffee can withstand containerized freight rates. Goods with high value to weight ratios such as manufactured goods can overcome transport costs more easily, but the costs of distribution cannot be ignored. Even for high value-added goods, transportation costs for imports still offer a degree of protection to local manufacturers.

The next chapter examines the derived demand for transportation in a trade context. The foundations of trade theory are put forward that lead to the demand for trade. Based on this demand, the derived demand for transportation to serve this trade is developed.

Keywords

backhaul	inferior good	public goods
ceteris paribus	market failure	Say's Law of the
congestion costs	monopoly	Markets
free-rider	opportunity cost	
income elasticity of	price elasticity of	
demand	demand	

Exercises

1. The demand for urban transport is complex, but the two most important considerations, usually, are time and money. The speed of transport and the cost of providing transport are closely related.

   Draw and explain an appropriate economic model(s) that illustrate(s) the trade-off between time and money in urban transportation and why it is so difficult to generalize the transportation options.

Explain the considerations that can modify an individual's demand for urban transportation.

2. Some products have elastic demands, while other goods have inelastic demands. Typically, the derived demand for transport follows a similar pattern to the elasticity of the final good, but not always. The share of transportation costs in the final price of the goods may be large or small, regardless of the product's own demand elasticity, and this can affect the elasticity of the derived demand for transport.

   With the aid of an appropriate economic model(s) explain the conditions in which the derived demand for transport would be elastic or inelastic.

   Explain why an increase in the number of transportation substitutes would affect the elasticities of the derived demands for transport, regardless of the product carried.

3. Feed barley used to fatten cattle is a large share of the cost of finishing a steer. In contrast, the value of the malt barley used in the production of beer is worth less than the cost of the cardboard package. Whether the barley is used for malting or feed the transport cost is the same. Assume that the cost of transporting barley falls by half; both beef and beer can now be produced at lower prices.

   Draw and explain an appropriate economic model(s) that illustrate(s) the impact of falling factor prices (transport cost) on beer and beef prices.

   Explain the economics of the derived demand model and why the output of the two finished products is affected differently.

4. Air passengers can be divided into two groups: leisure travelers and business travelers. We know that leisure travelers are more sensitive to price changes because they are paying for the fares personally. Business travelers do not really care that much about the price of an air ticket because the company is paying. Leisure travelers take longer trips than business-people who only go or a day or two, at most. Consequently, leisure travelers are more likely to have bags to check with their extra clothes.

   The airlines are starting to charge passengers $25 to check a bag. Using an appropriate model or models, illustrate how this increase in the cost of air travel is likely to affect the demand for tourism versus the demand for business meeting travel.

The $25 per bag price is the same whether a passenger is travelling on a short-haul flight (under 500 kilometers) or a long-haul flight (over 500 kilometers). Explain how the economies of distance would affect the derived demand for leisure and business travelers.

Chapter 3

Trade and Transportation Costs

Transport costs have been declining over time relative to total production costs because of technological changes. As a result, the critical weight-to-value ratio of trade has been rising and more goods are moving between international markets. The importance to trade of transportation is obvious, but the role of these costs in determining the composition and volume of trade needs to be more firmly established. The case for efficient trade of goods and services is based on the *gains from trade argument*. The development of the argument begins with the assumption that transportation and communications costs are "free". Subsequently, the impact on trade of introducing transportation costs is made clearer later in the chapter.

Role of Transport in Trade: The Zero Transportation Cost Case

Trade can lead to a gain in wealth that would not otherwise exist so long as the following assumptions are satisfied: (1) gains from the *division of labor* exist; (2) all regions and countries operate according to their comparative trade advantages; and (3) trade is free from government intervention in the form of customs duties (tariffs) and quotas. Each of these points is explained in turn.

An assumption of gains from the division of labor should strike one as basic. Each person is endowed with a unique set of skills, talents, and interests. The division of labor allows each of us to specialize in that part of the production process to which we are best suited. Without a division of labor, everyone would be forced to be self-sufficient such that we would be responsible for finding and making all of the goods that we wish to consume.

Our modern society enjoys an abundance of complex, assembly line produced items that range from ballpoint pens to jet planes. Producing our own personalized versions of these items is impossible. The high standard of living in the industrial age is dependent on specialization and division of labor in the production of goods and services. Rather than attempt to acquire all of the specialized knowledge necessary to produce a series of items, each worker needs only the skill necessary to produce a component within one stage of the production process. In the process, salaries are earned such that the worker can buy a whole range of goods produced elsewhere.

All workers sell their labor skills to an organization that can best employ them. In the production of an automobile, an assembly line process is employed that is sandwiched between the design and financing processes on the one hand, and the marketing and sales processes on the other. Within the assembly process in particular, one can envision skilled workers specializing in processes such as: steel welding, glass fitting, electrical wiring, and engine assembly to name just a few. A more sophisticated automobile results because its production involved state-of-the-art techniques for the production and fitting of all components. It should be obvious, however, that if the division of labor is to work to the advantage of everyone, a system of trade in goods and services must necessarily develop.

The theory of *comparative advantage* shows that gains from trade exist once a region or country specializes in the production of those goods and services that it is better able to produce relative to other regions or countries. This specialization allows for more to be produced in the world than would be the case if each region or country remained self-sufficient. To see this, consider the example in Figure 3.1.

country \ product	A	B	
x	4	6	– each number indicates the amount of labor required for the production of 1 unit of each good.
y	2	12	

Figure 3.1.

Assume that the world consists of just two countries each with the possibility of producing only two goods. Each cell in the table shows the amount of a constant quality of labor necessary to produce either of the two goods within each country. It can be seen that Country A has an *absolute advantage* over Country B in the production of both *x* and *y* in that it takes less labor to produce these goods. Though A is more efficient in the production of both goods it should not produce everything unless we, unrealistically, require that all labor in B is willing and able to emigrate to A.

Assuming immobility of labor across countries, specialization by each country will increase world output. To see this, one must identify each country's comparative advantage. Country A requires 2/12 or 17% the amount of labor B requires to produce a unit of *y*, while for *x* it requires 4/6 or 67%. Thus, A's absolute advantage is greater in *y* and that is also where it has its comparative advantage. B's absolute disadvantage is least in *x* and thus its comparative advantage will lie there.

Assume further that Country B is more populous with 18 units of labor, while Country A has 6 units of labor. Figure 3.2 illustrates the production

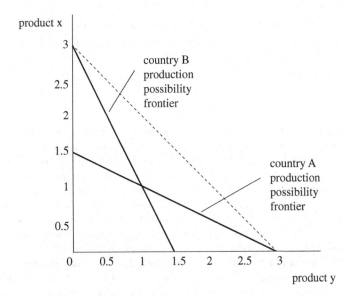

Figure 3.2.

possibility frontiers (PPF) for the two countries based on the information in Figure 3.1 and their labor resources. Country A could produce 1.5 units of *x*, or 3 units of *y*, or any combination along the PPF. Similarly, Country B could produce any linear combination of *x* and *y* on its PPF between 3*x* and 1.5*y*. If the countries specialized and traded, they could jointly produce and consume as if they operated along the dashed line between 3*x* and 3*y*.

Based on their endowments, A will specialize in *y*, and B will specialize in *x*, with the prospect of each trading with the other for the product that they do not produce. With A giving up one unit of *x*, it frees up four units of labor that will, according to the table, produce a further two units of *y*. Before specialization, A could produce a unit of both *x* and *y* and use up six units of labor; but after specialization it can produce three units of *y* using the same six units of labor. B can produce three units of x using its 18 units of labor. So world output can grow from four units (i.e., two of *x* and two of *y*) before specialization, to six units (three of *x* and three of *y*) after specialization.[1]

Specialization was possible because trade enables both goods to be consumed: A can trade some of its good y for B's good *x*. Assuming zero transportation costs, Country A will export *y* and Country B will export *x*, as determined above. The world price ratio is known as the *terms of trade* and can be written as p_x/p_y. It is irrational for either party to accept a rate of exchange that leaves them worse off than they would have been without trade.

---

[1]One may ask what determines comparative advantage. The Heckscher–Ohlin Theorem serves, given its specific assumptions, to answer this question. Countries and regions possess different factor endowments and there is a limit to the substitutability of factors of production across the different goods that might be produced. Basically, the theorem says that a country will export only the good whose production is most intensive in the factor that the country has in the most abundance. Figure 3.1 shows only one factor's productivity and not total abundance of *all* factors in each country. In this way, the *Heckscher–Ohlin Theorem* is more realistic than is the simple theory of comparative advantage because, while the latter assumes *constant costs* of production, the former is not so restricted. In other words, Country A needs only half the amount of labor for a unit of *y* than it did for a unit of *x* independent of the amount of *y* to be produced. It is more realistic to have this labor productivity advantage of *y* over *x* diminish as more *y* is produced. Trade is beneficial so long as factors of production are unevenly distributed among trade partners.

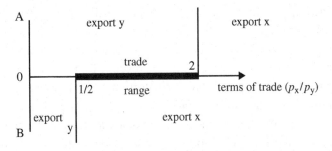

Figure 3.3.

In Figure 3.3, it can be seen that the only viable terms of trade ratio in this two-country case is between $p_x/p_y = 1/2$ and $p_x/p_y = 2$. The ratio of the world price of x to the world price of y in both countries is between 1/2 and 2. Economists refer to this trading range as the core. Exactly where the terms of trade will be struck within the core cannot be predicted. Better negotiating skills, coercion, timing and desire are but a few of the influences affecting trade bargaining.

The indeterminate points when the ratio is precisely 1/2 or 2 imply, respectively, that Country B or Country A is indifferent to trade. In the real world, which is made up of many countries, this ratio can fluctuate greatly across goods and has great implications for trade patterns. Appendix presents an example that helps explain the importance of the terms of trade ratio and the rationale for upper and lower bounds.

One of the ways that economists have looked at transportation costs is as if some part of the traded goods are consumed during transport. If we assume that countries A and B settled on the terms of trade that gave each country $1.5x$ and $1.5y$, by the time the traded portion arrived, each would get less (say $1.2x$ for Country A and $1.2y$ for Country B). As an aside, this theoretical construct actually has a parallel in the trade of electricity. Some portion of the electricity that is exported is consumed during transmission (because of resistance). In essence, the line losses are the costs of electricity transportation.

The existence of gains from trade has driven international trade agreements in which government agrees to forego the use tariffs or quotas to protect local domestic producers. A detailed review of tariffs and quotas will not be given here, suffice it to say that a tariff is a tax imposed on the price of the import upon entry into the country, while a quota creates a strict volume limit on imports.

A tariff on imports makes it easier for domestic producers to raise their prices while, at the same time, earning tax revenue for the government. This sounds positive at first glance, but the distortion of domestic prices reduces consumption and leads to less trade which shrinks the global economy. Transportation costs act in the same manner as tariffs. Transportation costs increase the price of imports relative to domestic goods and offer local producers a "natural" protection. However, this natural protection leaves everyone worse off because there are fewer opportunities for specialization. Consequently, global output drops. This is illustrated in Figure 3.4. If transportation costs were zero, then everything would be traded and complete specialization would occur in both countries. The higher the transportation costs, internally and externally, the lower the combined production possibilities obtained through trade. In this sense, it is the opportunity for specialization that creates the derived demand for transportation.

Trade with Real Costs for Transportation

Opportunities for specialization are realized by the arbitrage activities of traders. Arbitrage refers to buying goods in one market and selling them in another. If a trader can buy in one market, and sell in another for more than the transfer costs they can earn a profit. As the traders continue buying and selling, they raise the prices in the low-cost market and depress the

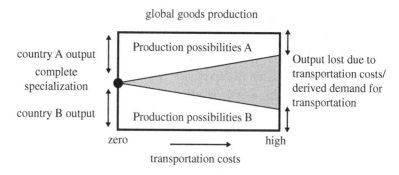

Figure 3.4.

prices in the high-cost market. Once the price difference in the two markets is equal to the transfer costs (which are mainly transportation), no more profits are available through arbitrage and a new equilibrium is reached. In this manner, the prices in all markets are connected through transportation costs, or what is known the *Law of One Price* (LOOP). An interregional trade model that is based on LOOP is presented in this section.

The interregional trade model presents transportation as a facilitator of trade rather than as a factor in the production process. Assume a world of two regions where price differences for a product exist in the absence of trade because of differences in factor endowments. Region A is a low cost producer, while Region B is a high cost producer of this product. If transportation between the two regions were possible, and the cost of transport did not exceed the difference in prices in the two regions, then Region A could be an exporter, and Region B could be an importer.

The export supply potential for Region A is called the excess supply (ES) curve and the import demand potential for Region B is called the excess demand (ED) curve. The ED and ES curves depend on all properties and parameters that lie behind the domestic demand and supply schedules in the respective regions. Figure 3.5 presents the ES of the good in the exporting region A. In the absence of trade, the equilibrium price in Region A is determined where supply and demand are equal. If the prices in Region A were higher, consumers would cut back consumption while producers would have an incentive to produce more. The ES curve is plotted out by the horizontal difference between the supply and demand curves at every price above the equilibrium price.

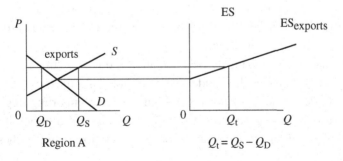

Figure 3.5.

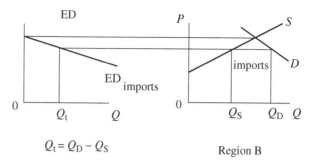

$$Q_t = Q_D - Q_S$$

Region B

Figure 3.6.

One horizontal difference between the Region A's supply and demand curves is illustrated. At higher prices consumers would want to cut back purchases. Simultaneously, producers would want to increase production to take advantage of the higher price available in the export market. At this specific price level, the quantity Q_D would be consumed domestically and the quantity Q_S would be produced. This would leave the quantity $Q_t = (Q_S - Q_D)$ available for export.

Figure 3.6 presents the ED for this same good in Region B.

In the absence of trade, the equilibrium price in Region B is determined where supply and demand are equal. If additional supply could only be obtained from imports, prices in Region B would be lower. Consumers would increase consumption, while producers would cut back production. The horizontal difference between the supply and demand curves at every price below the equilibrium price plots out the ED curve. One horizontal difference between the Region B's supply and demand curves is illustrated. At this price level, the quantity Q_D would be consumed and the quantity Q_S would be produced domestically. This would leave the quantity $Q_t = (Q_D - Q_S)$ made up by imports.

Let us now develop the derived demand for transportation between the two regions for this product under the conditions of a fixed exchange rate and free trade. In the upper portion of Figure 3.7, the importing Region B's ED curve is superimposed over exporting Region A's ES curve. In lower portion of the figure is the market for transportation between these two regions.

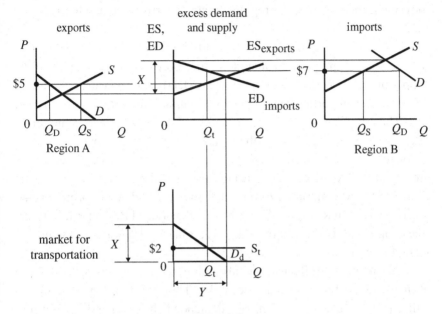

Figure 3.7.

Where the ES and ED curves intersect is the maximum quantity of goods that would be traded at zero transportation costs. This is the distance Y in the market for transportation services (as shown in the lower portion of Figure 3.7). An exchange between Region A and Region B will occur only if the costs of transport and handling do not exceed the price differences that exist without trade.[2] The very most that would be paid for transportation between these two markets is represented by X, which is the difference between the equilibrium price in Region A and equilibrium price in Region B. The derived demand (D_d) for transportation can be obtained by vertically subtracting the ES curve from the ED curve. The potential for product

---

[2]One may recall the famous *Factor Price Equalization* Theorem, which states, under several restrictive assumptions that free trade will serve to equalize factor prices across trade areas. In this way, free trade is a substitute for factor mobility. But for the Theorem to hold, transport costs must be zero. The Theorem does not require that regions be completely specialized in the production of a good. Our purpose here is to show how trade-dependent prices will adjust when transport costs are positive. For a complete analysis see: Samuelson, P. "International Factor-Price Equalisation Once Again." *Economic Journal* (1949), 181–197.

movements between the two regions creates a derived demand for transport services.

The derived demand for transportation captures the relationship between the freight rate and quantity of transport services demanded. If the supply of transport (S) is assumed to be perfectly price-elastic, commodity prices in the importing and exporting regions will differ by the freight rate. Thus in this diagram the freight rate is $2 per unit. Given this freight rate, traders arbitrate between the markets, buying in the low cost market and selling in the high cost market. This process continues until the prices are separated by the cost of transportation and there are no more profits available to the arbitrators. In this case, the new trade equilibrium occurs when the price in Region A rises to $5 and the price in Region B falls to $7. The quantity Q_t is shipped from the export market Region A to the import market Region B.

This model is, in effect, a general equilibrium framework in that we have an interaction within more than one market. The quantity of exports supplied will equal the quantity of imports demanded. In a general equilibrium model ES, when it exists in one market, must always equal ED in another.[3]

The derived demand curve is nothing more than the locus of a shipper's willingness to pay to move goods from A to B. The marginal willingness to pay for transport is equal to the price differential in the good across the regions. With the derived demand curve now obtained one can work backwards to determine just how much would be shipped at given transport prices. If the transport price were set higher than $2 by either the government or the carriers themselves, the higher transportation cost would force down the price in the export market, and increase the price in the import market, thus implying less trade. An important point is that the transportation supply curve, to the extent that it is technologically determined, governs the volume of feasible trade across regions. This is the heart of the concept of transportation as a facilitator of trade.

---

[3]This is known as *Walras' Law*. In other words, the world is a general equilibrium system made up of many sub-markets. It is not possible for the world to experience either ED or ES alone. If there are m markets for goods and services in the world, when $m - 1$ of them are in equilibrium the other one remaining must be as well.

As with the case of zero transportation costs, the two regions are better off with trade than without trade because more of the product is produced and consumed. Note that the exporters and importers share the costs of transportation, but the division is not necessarily equal. The relative elasticities of the ES and ED determine the share of transportation costs borne by the exporter and the importer. The party with the more inelastic curve will bear the greater share of the transportation costs.

Specialization resulting from trade leads to a growth of income within the import and export markets. Producers in the exporting region are happy to receive higher prices; while consumers in the importing region see the prices they pay drop. The double stimulus for trade creates the derived demand for transportation. This has been shown in Figure 3.7.

The implicit assumption of the interregional trade model is that the supply of transportation S_t is perfectly elastic. Any amount can be transported at a fixed price of $2 per unit. This assumption may be correct for the marginal change in trade, say a few truckloads, but eventually freight rates would begin to rise. The nature of transportation supply depends on the cost structure of the industry, intermodal competition, management and idiosyncrasies of the mode. The next three chapters consider the characteristics and costs that determine the supply of transportation services. The available freight rates will also depend on the balance of trade between the two regions. This is addressed in Chapter 9.

A question that often creates confusion is whether the importer or the exporter bears the cost of transportation. Usually this arises when transportation costs change. The answer, as in many cases of economics, is it depends on the elasticity of supply and demand. In Figure 3.8, the trade section and derived demand for transportation have been extracted to illustrate the point. In this case, the cost of transportation is assumed to increase from P to P'. This reduces the demand for transport and the trade volume from Q_T to Q'_T. As a result, the exporter's price falls, and the importer's price rises, but as is obvious, the importer's price has increased the most. The reason is that the ED is more inelastic than the ES. Whichever party to the bilateral trade has the most inelastic relationship pays the greatest share of a transportation cost increase. Conversely, they also benefit most from a transportation cost decrease.

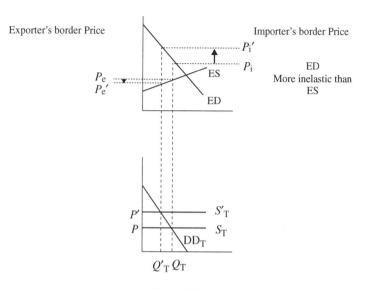

Figure 3.8.

Appendix

To understand the terms of trade concept more clearly, we can use the same situation as presented in Figure A3.1 for each country but impose a terms of trade price ratio of, say, $p_x/p_y = 10$ meaning that x happens to be 10 times more expensive in the world market than is y.

Taking the case for Country A, direct production of x costs it four units of labor. Alternatively, it could import a unit of x that, according to the terms of trade, requires 10 units of y in trade thus requiring 20 units of labor as seen in the table. Direct production of y costs two units of labor but it could, alternatively, be imported through trade with x thus requiring 1/10 units of x, which costs 2/5 units of labor. The acquisition of y through trade costs A less labor as compared to x meaning that x should be the good specialized in. Of course, this figure shows in the panel for B that it should specialize in x as well — a result that is not viable.

Keywords

absolute advantage	factor price equalization	Law of One Price
comparative advantage	gains from trade argument	terms of trade
division of labor	Heckscher–Ohlin Theorem	Walras' Law

A

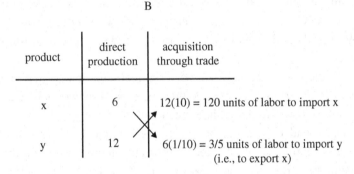

product	direct production	acquisition through trade
x	4	2(10) = 20 units of labor to import x
y	2	4(1/10) = 2/5 units of labor to import y (i.e., to export x)

B

product	direct production	acquisition through trade
x	6	12(10) = 120 units of labor to import x
y	12	6(1/10) = 3/5 units of labor to import y (i.e., to export x)

Figure A3.1.

Exercises

1. When the cost of international transportation falls (assume a technical change) both exporters and importers benefit.

   Draw and explain an appropriate economic model(s) that illustrate(s) the impact of falling transportation costs on importers and exporters.

   Clarify in your answer, why the benefits of lower transportation costs may not be divided equally between the importer and exporter. Explain the conditions under which importers could gain more of the benefits of lower transportation costs than exporters.

2. LOOP holds that all prices are connected geographically by differences in logistics costs. The prices of commodities like wheat and corn across North America is an example of spatial price distribution. These prices

are kept in line by the actions of buyers and sellers that arbitrate the market.

Use an appropriate model or models to explain how the actions of arbitrators can influence prices and trade flows within or between regions, and the impact when the cost of transportation rises or falls.

3. Country A and Country B, use ocean transport to ship bulk materials. Both countries can produce grain, but Country A exports to Country B which has a much larger population.

   Draw and explain an appropriate economic model(s) that illustrate(s) the impact on prices, production, consumption and trade if rising oil prices that raises cost of ocean transport.

   Imagine that following the oil price rise, a serious recession occurs that lowers price for ocean transport below where it was before. How would this impact the trade, prices, production, and consumption of grain.

4. The development of a new soil bacteria treatment doubles the yields of grain in Country A. Assume that this treatment only works here and not in Country B where the grain is exported.

   Draw and explain an appropriate economic model(s) that illustrate(s) the impact of this technological change on the production, consumption, prices in each country, and the volume of grain traded.

   Imagine that this technological change increased total income in Country A. Explain how this would affect trade volumes.

5. Increased potassium fertilizer prices raise the cost of wheat production in Country B, which is an importer, but not in Country A because the soils are naturally rich in this element.

   Draw and explain an appropriate economic model(s) that illustrate(s) the impact of rising potassium fertilizer prices on the prices, production, consumption and trade of wheat in Country A and Country B.

   Explain how imports of wheat from Country A would be affected, if the people in Country B reduce their intake of wheat in favor of corn that is available at a lower price.

6. Region A is the lowest cost producer of beef in the country. Large volumes of beef are trucked to Region B where the cost of beef production is much higher. An *E. coli* outbreak disrupts this trade pattern because frightened consumers in Region B buy less beef.

Draw an appropriate model and explain the economic impact on the derived demand for transportation between Region A and Region B caused by the change in consumer demand for beef and the impact on prices and production in each region. Assume that Region A consumers ignore the problem.

Assume now that the consumers in Region A are frightened by the *E. coli* outbreak, too. Explain how consumption, production and prices would be affected in each market and the change in the quantity of beef shipped from Region A to Region B.

7. China is the world's largest pork producer, but they also import pork from North America. The Chinese economy is doubling every 8 years. Meat has a positive income elasticity, as incomes grow, people buy more.

Draw and explain an appropriate economic model to illustrate the impact of increased incomes in China on pork imports, production and consumption and the demand for transport between North America and China.

Imagine that a serious drought in the U.S. corn producing states doubles the price of grain to feed pigs in North America. How this will impact your previous model. (Draw a new version, if you wish).

8. Economists universally agree that countries are better off importing from their neighbors than trying to be self-sufficient in everything they consume.

Use an appropriate diagram to explain the gains from trade theory, and how even countries with an absolute advantage in producing everything, can still be better off by trading with their neighbors.

Canada has a well-educated workforce and a well-developed industrial economy, but we concentrate on the export of raw materials (like lumber, wheat, oil, and copper) and import mass produced manufactured goods (like clothing) and specialized medical equipment like MRIs. Some politicians would like to turn Canada into an exporter of manufactured goods instead of raw materials. Explain why the Heckscher–Ohlin Theorem predicts that our current pattern of trade is unlikely to change.

Chapter 4

Laws of Variable Proportions and Scale

The demand function for transport services, as discussed in Chapter 2, is a set of quantity preferences given particular prices. It is also described as a set of willingnesses to pay for various quantities of a transport service. Technically, the quantity demanded is a function of, among other things, the given price and this relationship allows one to trace out a demand curve, *ceteris paribus*. Such a view abstracts from the profile of the set of preferences that consumers have, but is a necessary simplification at this stage. For the actual setting of prices, it is necessary to derive supply curves, and the material in this chapter forms the foundation for that task.

In its simplest sense, supply decisions of firms are based on the selling price of its good or service, and the costs of producing these goods and services. Selling prices are determined by the interaction of supply and demand, while the firm, to some extent, can control the costs of production. Thus, the costs of production that are components of the supply decision is the focus of our attention in this chapter.

Direct Costs

Most costs of production are borne directly by the firm. Transport carriers face *direct costs* for the factors of production they use: wages for labor; payments to capital, called interest; compensation to the use of land, called rent; and remuneration to the organizer of the production process, called the normal profit accruable to the entrepreneur. Specific costs for items such as fuel, electricity, telephone, etc. can be simply combined into the capital component. The indirect or external costs of production are covered in Chapter 8.

At this point we can state the relationship between the factors used and output produced that is called the *production function*. Specifically,

$$Q = f(K, L, N, E),$$

where:

$$Q = \text{output}, \quad K = \text{capital}, \quad L = \text{labor}, \quad N = \text{land},$$
$$\text{and} \quad E = \text{entrepreneurial ability}.$$

It should be stressed that this production function of a transport service is firm-specific, it abstracts from, in the truest sense of the transportation process, the other direct logistics costs that exist but are not borne by the carrier. For example, freight requires packaging by the shipper before pickup as well as the transaction costs of arranging terms with the carrier and the receiver at the drop-off. Passengers as well, face similar time and transaction costs when undertaking long distance travel in terms of the opportunity cost of in-flight time and the purchase of luggage. These examples of direct costs applicable to the shipper and passenger, but not to the carrier, are nonetheless direct costs of the transport process. Thus, output (Q) in the production function above is exclusive of shipper- and passenger-specific direct costs. It is the output of the carrier above and not the production function for freight carriage or trip-making.

A final point about Q concerns its unit of measure. There are two choices: (1) the number of trips over a specific period of time; or (2) the total payload over a specific period of time. Obviously point (1) does not highlight the different weights or configurations over each trip that are occurring while point (2) does not indicate over how many trips the total payload was moved. In the short run, it is not important whichever measure is used except that consistency should be maintained when comparing different production functions. In the long-term technology and relative price movements may cause some divergence in these two measures.

The output is the quantity that the firm supplies to the market if we assume that no inventories are allowed to accumulate. The costs are functionally related to this output produced as illustrated in Figure 4.1. Panel 1 is the graph of the production function drawn when various units of a factor, say labor, are hired and added to a fixed amount of every other

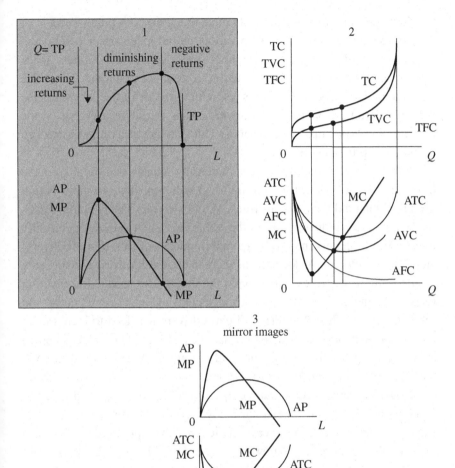

Figure 4.1.

factor. Another name for the output (Q) of the firm is the total product (TP). To make things simple, assume that output comes from only two factors of production, capital and labor. Furthermore, assume that all factors have a constant quality, meaning that the 1st worker hired is just as intelligent and skillful as, say, the 150th. With these assumptions, the shape of the production function in panel 1 can be understood.

Consider the following story. Assume that a firm has purchased a less-than-truckload business. In this operation, partial loads are picked up and taken to a terminal where the freight is sorted with other shippers' loads that are going to a common destination (a terminal in another city). The terminal is staffed, but the firm has yet to hire drivers for the fleet of trucks. Adding one unit of labor (i.e., a driver) means a truck can go out on the road and make pickups and deliveries. This increment in output is tracked as marginal product (MP).

For a time, the truck firm faces increasing returns as more drivers are hired in that each extra truck on the road will contribute to more output produced than did the previous truck. Why? Two reasons: (1) more trucks on the road mean more options for the whole fleet, such as more opportunity to *interline* shipments and to offer greater frequency of pick-up and delivery; and (2) even after all trucks in the fleet are in use the extra drivers will serve to allow the trucks to operate around the clock. The production function rises at an increasing rate. Of course, increasing returns will not go on forever. After a while, the hiring of extra drivers will lead to increases in output but each increase will be less than the previous. This range is known as diminishing returns. In this range of output, the average product (AP) reaches a maximum and starts to decline.

Now that enough drivers are employed to keep the fleet on the road 24 hours per day, hiring an extra driver will crowd the others meaning that each extra driver will add increasingly less to the output process. Think of the extra drivers being hired now as relief drivers sitting on the trucks with the other drivers. Each relief driver is sitting and ready to take over and can even help with the load/unload process. The relief driver is productive, but because he is not driving the truck, he is less productive than the driver. One might say that the relief driver should be used to take over when the first driver gets fatigued but we have assumed this away by specifying that all factors (i.e., drivers) are of constant quality.

The production function curve (TP) rises at a decreasing rate over the range of diminishing returns. Finally, as ever more drivers are added, not only is each extra driver less productive than the previous, he is so much so that the output of the entire fleet begins to drop. Think of there being so many relief drivers on board each truck that the driver is not able to drive properly or that the truck cannot move as fast due to vision problems arising from extreme crowding. That situation is known as negative returns and is shown by the production function decreasing at an increasing rate.

This outlines the hypothetical production response of a truck firm operating first with zero drivers, and thus zero output, up to the point where so many drivers are employed that they impede each other's movement, and output falls back to zero again. It is from this story in panel 1 (Figure 4.1) that all costs functions of a firm can be derived in panel 2 of Figure 4.2.

From panel 1 we can analyze the cost functions of panel 2 using the same story as above. First, it should be noticed that direct costs are divided into variable and fixed costs. Because the capital factor (the truck fleet) is fixed in quantity its cost is fixed giving a total fixed cost (TFC) function that is a horizontal line in the panel. The labor factor (the drivers) can be any amount that the firm desires so that its cost is variable giving a total variable cost (TVC) function as shown. The shape of the TVC function follows the same reasoning as does the production function (TP) except that the story is in terms of cost for the former. As diminishing returns set in, the variable costs increase at an increasing rate.

Consider the inverse relationship between variable cost and productivity in panel 3. In the range of increasing returns, the first driver produces two units of output, say deliveries, while the second is more productive by producing three. Marginal productivity has increased from $2Q/L$ to $3Q/L$. Another way to write these ratios is as $Q/(1/2)L$ and $Q/(1/3)L$, respectively, meaning that the first unit of output required only 1/2 of a driver's productivity while the second unit required even less at 1/3 of a driver. Because these drivers are paid equally for a unit of productivity, 1/3 of a driver's productivity costs less than 1/2. So as TP is rising at an increasing rate, the TVC of labor is rising, of course, but at a decreasing rate because each extra driver is more productive and thus costs less for every unit of output produced.

After the peak of technical efficiency (maximum MP/minimum MC), a range of diminishing returns begins. Each driver adds less and less productivity meaning that each extra unit of output produced costs more. Thus, as TP rises at a decreasing rate, TVC rises at an increasing rate.

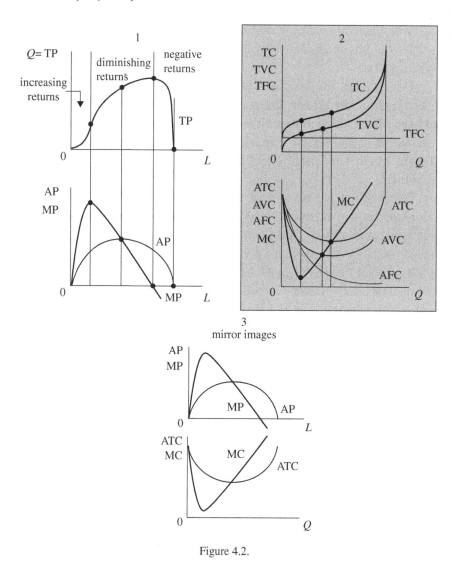

Figure 4.2.

In the range of negative returns, the TVC function would bend backward (not shown) indicating rising cost with falling output but that portion of the line will be irrelevant for our purposes. With the TVC function understood, the total cost (TC) function is simply the vertical sum of the TVC and TFC functions as shown in panel 2.

One might wonder at this point what the optimal level of labor to hire is and thus what is the optimal amount of output. The diagram is not equipped to answer that question because the firm's goal is assumed to be maximization of total profits. Total profits are simply total revenue from sales minus the TC of production. Because we have not specified total revenue yet, it is impossible at this point to determine the profit maximizing level of output. However, it will always be the case that the optimal level of production will occur somewhere along the range of diminishing returns.

The average cost curves are derived by simply dividing the total cost curves by the quantity (Q) produced. In the lower half of panel 2, the average fixed cost (AFC), average variable cost (AVC), average total cost (ATC) are derived in this manner. The marginal cost (MC) function represents the incremental costs associated with each additional unit of output.

Panel 3 highlights further the inverse relationship between variable cost and productivity by showing the "mirror image" result of AP and MP as compared with MC and ATC. Note that the lowest (highest) average cost (product) occurs where the marginal cost (product) function crosses. This is the point of maximum economic efficiency, but not necessarily maximum profit in the *short run*. As stated above, this depends on the price received for output as well as the costs of production. In the *long run*, the firm can adjust to the point where maximum economic efficiency and maximum profit do coincide.

Scale Economies

The analysis of productivity and cost has used a variable factor along with a fixed factor. If one or more factors are fixed, the firm is operating in what is known as the short run of the production process. If all factors are variable then the production span is known as the long run. In the example used above, a trucking firm had fixed capital in fleet size while additional labor (drivers) could be hired. The story has elements of truth, and is realistic in the short run. The carrier will maintain capital (terminals, vehicles, office space, etc.) that is less variable at a given moment than is labor. Also, in specific modes of transport, infrastructure (roads, rail networks, canals, etc.) is fixed for different durations of time across modes.

In the rail mode, locomotives can remain viable over about 20 years with the track remaining so for about 50 years. For water vessel transport, the canals can last indefinitely. No specific real-time is given to the short run versus the long run. In reality, firms face a great deal of fixed costs — from building mortgages to insurance coverage — so it is reasonable to look at the firm's operations within a short run time frame. The task for the carrier in the short run is to determine the optimal amount of the variable factor to use given the amount of the fixed factor in place. The long run analysis is employed at times to highlight how firms and industries (collections of firms) respond to changes in the marketplace when enough time exists to adjust their capital structure.

Some idea of long run analysis is given in Figure 4.3. Here, a carrier can now alter the amount of capital along with labor used. In this sense, the firm does not face a capacity constraint such as when the truck firm discussed above operated with only a fixed number of trucks in its fleet. The cost functions derived in panel 2 of Figure 4.2 have a capacity constraint based on the fixed fleet size. But when everything is variable, a variety of possible short run cost functions are applicable to different amounts of capital and labor used.

The long run average total cost (LRATC) function is the lower "envelope" of all of the possible short run average total cost (SRATC) functions. We see that the set of SRATC curves fall at first as the output or scale of operations increase and later on begin to rise. This fact gives rise to the U-shaped LRATC. The falling portion of the LRATC indicates a phenomenon known as economies of scale while the rising portion indicates

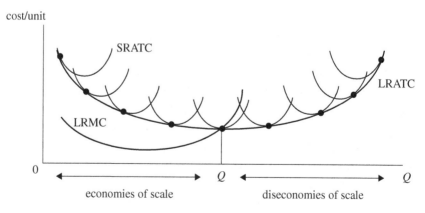

Figure 4.3.

diseconomies of scale. Economies of scale indicate that as the size of the firm's operation expands, its average costs fall. Recall that SRATC falls under the range of increasing returns because the increase in marginal productivity of variable factor makes the cost of the fixed factor easier to carry. Having the extra variable factor validates having the current amount of the fixed factor. In the long run, economies of scale cause the LRATC to fall due to internal and external causes.

Internal causes would be: indivisibilities, division of labor, and overhead costs. Each will be considered in turn. Indivisibilities of capital may be present whereby, for example, the efficient use of a new supertanker would, because of its fixed size, require the scale of oil transport to increase greatly. But as the scale increases the average cost of the tanker falls because it is being put to better use. The division of labor, first mentioned in Chapter 1, leads to a lowering of average costs because as the firm expands capacity it is natural for the production process to be broken up into more specialized departments. The productivity gains from the division of labor make the average cost of the labor force drop. Finally, as capacity expands, the average cost of overhead such as advertising drops because, while the cost of a newspaper advertisement is constant, it is easier for the firm to validate having it if the firm is larger and produces more.

External economies would be due to the fall in average cost of one firm leading to a fall in average costs of all other firms in the industry. For example, the presence of an extra firm in an industrial park might prompt the government to put in a paved road system that will serve to lower the transport costs of all of the firms in the area. TC of production would be easier to carry meaning that average costs would fall. Another example might be that the presence of more firms leads to a greater incentive for all firms to engage in research and development. To the extent that this greater time and effort on the part of the industry leads to more technological advances, all firms will gain and this validates the extra expenditure.

Of course, when the LRATC rises, diseconomies are occurring and these are due to both internal and external causes. An internal cause would be that the firm is now so big that its many departments are burdened by bureaucratic "red tape" in the form of coordination difficulties. The average cost of production would increase. An external cause may be that the number of firms in the industry is so large that the transport infrastructure becomes

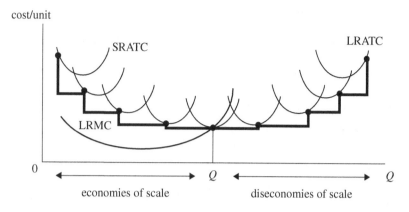

Figure 4.4.

congested which thus raises the costs facing all firms. It should be noted that the external causes of economies and diseconomies are obviously not part of the direct costs of the firm. They have merely been included to facilitate a complete view of the phenomenon.

In transportation economics, especially, it is likely the case that LRATC will not be a smooth curve as drawn; rather it might trace each SRATC between the dots shown in Figure 4.4. The resulting LRATC would be one indicative of "*lumpy costs*". Basically, transport facilities may only be expandable in discrete amounts. In other words, cost minimization is only approximated by the technologically determined increments of capital expansion. For example, an airline that wishes to expand the size of its fleet is constrained by the size of aircraft that is available. The more a mode faces discrete factor costs of operation the more prevalent is the problem of lumpiness.

A railway's operational expansion involves more fixed cost outlays than do, for example, a trucking firm's. While a railway's expansion may involve the laying of new track or the expansion of its yard, a trucking firm can more easily lease a vehicle (to be used on publicly provided roads) and may set up "drop-lots" instead of building a new terminal. In this way, a trucking firm can, in smaller increments, expand its operations more easily than a railway. The difficult policy question that arises from lumpiness is: given the discrete choice of over- or under-provision of an infrastructure or service, which should be chosen? The investment decision will be discussed more

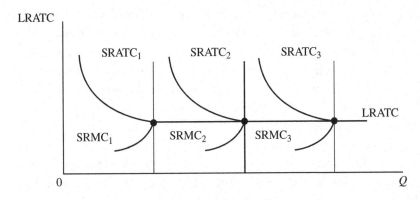

Figure 4.5.

fully in Chapter 11 while an example of indivisibilities will be discussed when peak load pricing is introduced in Chapter 9.

In some cases neither economies nor diseconomies of scale exist over the long run cost functions, meaning that the expansion of the firm's size neither adds to, nor subtracts from, the burden of carrying existing costs. If such is the case, production exhibits what is known as constant returns to scale. LRATC would be constant as shown in Figure 4.5. In certain modes of transport constant returns to scale are to be expected. For example, each vehicle in a fleet has a capacity constraint meaning that the addition of another vehicle will simply raise the cost of the fleet as seen by SRATC2 which is higher than SRATC1 when past the latter curve's capacity constraint.

Efficient utilization of each vehicle will achieve a minimization of cost along the LRATC function where all vehicles in the fleet are at capacity. Constant returns to scale will apply if and only if the addition of an extra vehicle does not allow for a more efficient use of the existing vehicles. The best examples are truckload trucking and ocean shipping. Another vehicle will only be brought into service if all others in the fleet are at capacity and the firm expects sufficient demand for the extra service.

Incentives exist for bulk cargo ship owners to utilize as much capacity as possible before an extra vessel is brought on line because vessels operate on independent routes and the expense of the vessel is so great,. Thus, in Figure 4.5, once the minimum SRATC for the fleet is achieved, the fleet is at capacity, and when a new vessel is brought into the fleet, a new SRATC is applicable. The assumption of constant returns to scale for an ocean liner firm is reasonable because the cost structure of the existing vessels does not change when another is brought on line. Notice the contrast this has with other modes such as aviation which allows for the possibility of interlining. When another vehicle is brought on line additional traffic can be spread across the entire network.

A tendency towards constant returns to scale can also affect the structure of competition in the transportation industry. If a mode of transport reaches constant returns to scale at relatively few vehicles, then the structure of the industry can be more heterogeneous, such that very large firms and very small firms compete simultaneously. For example, in truckload (TL) trucking the vehicles are dispatched on point-to-point moves with minimum scope for interacting with other vehicles in the fleet. As a result, firms with as few as 10 trucks can survive in a market that has competitors that operate 1,000 trucks. Chartered buses exhibit the same characteristics, as do taxis in a deregulated market.

It is worth bearing in mind that increasing, diminishing and negative returns are short run concepts signifying productivity and cost changes when at least one factor of production is fixed. Recall that our discussion of the short run concept that increasing returns depended on each driver creating such efficiency gains in fleet usage before the capacity constraint of the fleet was reached. Economies of scale, diseconomies of scale, and constant returns to scale are long run concepts applicable when no factors of production are fixed and the firm can adjust the overall size of its operation.

Keywords

constant returns to scale	long run	production function
direct costs	lumpy costs	short run
interline		

Exercises

1. Small truckload carriers that have less than 20 or 30 trucks are able to compete with truckload carriers that have much larger fleets (more than 500 trucks).

Draw and explain an appropriate economic model(s) that illustrate(s) the cost structure of the truckload market that permits carriers with small fleets to compete with large fleet owners.

In your discussion of the economic model(s), explain why the less-than-truckload market does not exhibit the same degree of competition.

2. The number of competitors in unregulated transportation markets differs widely between rail, air, marine, truckload and less-than-truckload (LTL) trucking.

Draw and explain an appropriate economic model (or models) that illustrate(s) why in some modes of transport, like airlines and LTL trucking, firms are few in number and in others, like truckload trucking, companies are so many in number.

Describe in your explanation how internal and external economies might affect the structure and location of the industry.

3. Capital inputs, like airplanes, come in unique sizes. This is said to make the LRATC curve "lumpy".

Draw and explain an appropriate economic model (or models) that illustrate(s) what is meant by this and why these inputs may be considered to be lumpy.

Describe why lumpy inputs would not be the cause of diminishing returns?

Chapter 5

Cost Economies and Traceability

The direct costs of transportation are fairly straight-forward. Theoretically, direct costs can be classified as either fixed or variable components. In practice, some costs become very hard to trace because the linkage is more indirect. For example, when a process yields multiple outputs it can be difficult to identify the appropriate share to attribute to each input.

Management of production functions can also have cost implications. Managers make choices regarding equipment size, organization of networks and activities to pursue. These choices can have important cost implications because they involve questions of efficiency. With respect to transportation, economies of scale is a misleading and incomplete term in that "scale" of operation can be achieved in a variety of ways. The benefits of scale may derive from the economies of vehicle size, fleet size and scope; distance and weight relationships; and, infrastructure and traffic density. Each will be explained in turn.

Cost Economies

Vehicle size

Economies of vehicle size occur because as the size of the vehicle used increases, its volume (capacity) increases by a greater magnitude than does its surface area. This is known as the Square–Cube Law (SCL). In the simplest exposition, consider an empty cube of $3 \times 3 \times 3$ units. If all sides doubled to $6 \times 6 \times 6$ units the surface area increases from 9 square units to 36 square units while the volume increases from 27 cubic units to 216 cubic units. Thus, a doubling of all side-lengths increases surface area four-fold and increases volume eight-fold.

73

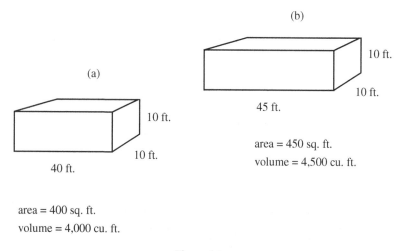

Figure 5.1.

The physical limits of infrastructure and materials limit the benefits of the SCL for transportation. Nevertheless, all modes of transport can gain if the vehicle's footprint increases by the square, while the volume increases by the cube. This is illustrated in Figure 5.1 by the two blocks (a) and (b). While both area and volume share the same percentage increase (12.5%), area increases by 50 square feet and volume increases by 500 cubic feet in using (b) over (a).

For most transport vehicles, construction costs per unit of capacity falls as the vehicle size increases; that is, their average total costs (ATCs) fall with respect to capacity. Doubling the material used to make a transport device (e.g., a container, pipeline, dirigible or ship's hull) will more than double its carrying capacity. Meanwhile the costs of engines and control systems are likely to increase by less than double.

Labor cost savings are another source for vehicle economies of size. The amount of operators or crew need not increase by the same magnitude as capacity. Figure 5.2 presents four truck configurations that are common in North America. Regardless of the number of trailers, the truck only requires one driver. Based on a recent report on the operating costs of trucks in Canada[1] a twin trailer unit is only 25% more expensive to operate than a

---

[1] Transport Canada. *Operating Costs of Trucks in Canada.* (by Bulk Plus Logistics) 2003.

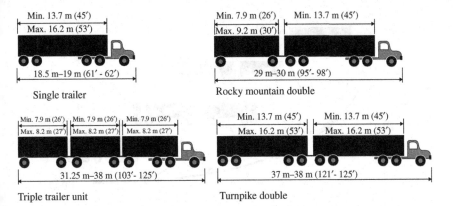

Figure 5.2.

single semi-trailer unit. With double the payload, the potential savings per ton/km could be as much as 35% to 40% for the larger vehicles.

Economies of vehicle size do have limits in that eventually "bigness" can drive up costs faster than the gains from increased volume. For instance: technology may not be equipped to provide ever-bigger, yet fuel-efficient, engines; seaports, airports and highways face maneuverability limits; sea traffic lanes may have draft restrictions that require more circuitous routes[2]; and, terminal costs of shipment consolidation may become large given that the vehicle can transport so much at once. For example, the loading and unloading of ever-larger ocean container vessels requires more and larger cranes. Such ships also require bigger hinterlands to serve which can affect the land-based side of the total shipping costs. Specifically, large ships generally have to draw freight from a greater radius.

The other limit to bigness is regulations. The economies of vehicle size are very significant in trucking so that in every jurisdiction constant pressure

---

[2]Oil tankers of more than 200,000 deadweight tons (dwt) are classed as VLCC (Very Large Crude Carrier), while oil tankers of more than 300,000 dwt are ULCC (Ultra Large Crude Carriers). The Jahre Viking, which is the largest ULCC ever built at 564,763 dwt, was constructed in 1979 at Oppama Shipyard, Sumitomo, Japan. With a draft greater than 21 meters, the ULCCs cannot pass the Malacca Straits or the Suez Canal, and must sail much further than the VLCC ships. In 2005, China commissioned a ULCC at 300,000 dwt, but this is the first new ship of this size in recent years.

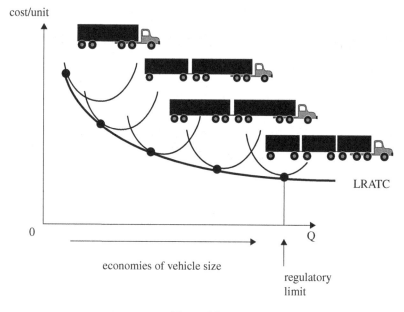

Figure 5.3.

is applied by the industry to relax the length and weight limits.[3] The long run ATCs associated with truck size is truncated before it reaches the point of minimum costs as illustrated in Figure 5.3 Although the size limit looks inefficient, the LRATC only considers the narrow costs of the trucking firm, and not the full social costs of their operations. If the additional social costs of road damage and negative effects on other road users associated with size are included, the socially efficient vehicle limit is less than what would be optimal according to the private costs of the truck operator.

Fleet size

Economies of fleet size have been alluded to above and exist when the provision of another vehicle makes for a more efficient use of the existing vehicles in the fleet. Again, some modes are more likely to allow for this than others. The contrast can best be seen in modes that allow for interlining of shipments among vehicles in comparison to those modes that do not.

---

[3]Trucks cannot expand in width without widening the roads and streets. Similarly, they cannot be made taller than the existing bridge and tunnel infrastructure will permit.

The trucking industry provides a useful contrast of fleet economies. The truckload (TL) trucking sector involves door-to-door freight shipping in which the truck usually handles only one shipper's goods per haul. In contrast, less than truckload (LTL) trucking involves the hauling of goods from many shippers at once. These loads are picked up at, and delivered to, freight terminals located in every major population center that handle the consolidation and de-consolidation processes. The TL sector is characterized by constant returns to scale and does not enjoy significant fleet economies, while the LTL sector has the increasing network economies as more vehicles are added.

The TL carriers do experience some gains from size. For example, savings can accrue in bulk purchasing of tires and fuel, and the overhead costs of the headquarters are spread out over more vehicles, but there are also disadvantages. A small carrier with 10 trucks only has to find loads for the tenth truck to exceed 90% utilization. A carrier with 1,000 trucks would have to find loads for the last 100 trucks to achieve the same efficiency. Adding one more truck to this operation does not generate many benefits for the existing vehicles in the fleet.

The LTL carriers have long haul trucks that operate between their cargo hubs, and city trucks that move freight to and from these consolidation warehouses. Adding another city truck to pick up and deliver freight would be like connecting another spoke that feeds traffic to and from the entire network. LTL carriers have high fixed costs. As long as the consolidation warehouses are free of serious bottlenecks, adding another vehicle will increase efficiency of the fleet and help spread the fixed costs over more units.

Scope

Economies of scope occur when efficiency gains exist from multi-product production. Examples include: an airplane being pressed into charter service when the demand for commercial flights declines; an LTL carrier taking on TL activity from time to time when the LTL market declines; and an inter-city bus providing intra-city service when passenger space allows for it while on the way to the city terminal.

Economies of scope highlight a corollary to the division of labor concept. A firm may be more efficient, or have some cost economies if it is not too specialized. Care must be taken however to not be mesmerized by scale effects. It is possible for economies of scope to exist at some level of operations and not at others. The major scheduled passenger airlines have cargo operations as a function of their available belly space, but have a spotty record with dedicated air cargo operations. In this case the economies of scope for utilizing maintenance bases, airport presence and existing cargo handling equipment has been insufficient for the scheduled carriers to dominate the air freight market, or in some cases sustain their dedicated cargo aircraft.

Distance and weight

The *taper effect* in freight rates, which arises because of economies in distance traveled, is best seen in terms of a linear total cost function: $TC = a + bD$ where (a) is the fixed cost per unit shipped and (b) is the variable cost that is, itself, a linear function of travel distance (D). In for-hire trucking, (a) can be considered the terminal (load and unload) costs which are independent of travel distance while (b) is the marginal cost of transporting a unit of fixed-weight freight an extra unit of distance. These variable costs involve fuel, driver costs, vehicle maintenance and depreciation, which, in the transportation industry, are referred to as *line-haul* costs.

Figure 5.4 presents the model of freight costs with respect to distance. Spreading the terminal costs (a) over a longer distance serves to make the ATC decline as the trip lengthens. The benefits of distance are passed on to shippers through competition between carriers. This is known as the taper effect in transportation pricing.

Air travel benefits significantly from the taper effect. Terminal costs, the extra fuel used in take-offs and landings, as well as landing fees charged to the airline are all costs that get spread out with distance traveled. In the short-haul markets the taper effect is mitigated and average seat-mile or cargo-mile costs are higher than in long-haul markets. However, demand in short-haul markets is relatively price-elastic because cars, buses and trucks are viable substitutes. Alternative means of transport provide a counter-pressure to keep air rates low in short-haul markets. This is one reason why regional and short distance airlines are subject to more volatile performance than airlines that serve trans-oceanic markets.

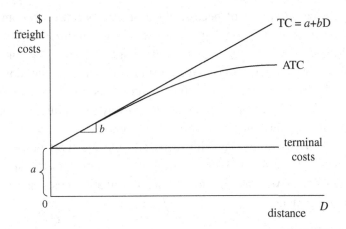

Figure 5.4.

Now consider the effect of increasing shipment weight over a constant distance traveled. Doubling the shipment's weight, for example, will not double fuel cost (though it would still increase). As well, driver costs, to the extent they would increase, do so in a less than proportional manner. Only terminal costs would be expected to increase greatly. As long as total cost rises proportionally (or less) with respect to shipment weight, ATC will decline with respect to weight. Of course, once the weight impedes the hauling capability of the vehicle, or strains the ability of the terminal to handle the shipment, this "economy" disappears. Moreover, the transportation costs for oversized, indivisible freight accelerates rapidly because special equipment must be used, movements require escorts and in some cases bridges may need strengthening.

Infrastructure and traffic density

Economies of infrastructure occur when traffic over a particular route is heavy enough to benefit from more options along the transport network. Consider that along a busy rail line a twinning of the track will more than double rail capacity because the conflicts between directions that existed will have been eliminated; that is, no train will be delayed due to a right of way conflict. Similarly, adding two extra lanes to a one-lane, two-way road will likely more than double capacity because the new median lane on each side may now be used as a faster through-lane. Economies of infrastructure are directly linked to the costs of congestion.

Zero congestion is not necessarily desirable because economies of density occur as part of making better use of a given infrastructure. One example occurs with respect to railway usage. The rail line increases scale by way of increasing usage of the track and, when doing so, the ATC inclusive of the track infrastructure falls. Of course, as traffic density increases it becomes easier for the railway to establish specialized trains (coal or grain transport, for example) and allow for more frequent scheduling that is important with respect to the transport of perishable goods. Again, the limits to these economies are maintenance costs due to higher density as well as the increase in coordination costs due to extra traffic management.

Network efficiencies

The hub-and-spoke formation of a transport network, as shown in Figure 5.5, links together economies of scope, size economies and economies of density. The three hubs labeled A, B and C each has a variety of spokes intersecting them. A common spoke connecting to each hub links them. The figure shows that transport from x to y will not occur directly; rather, passengers or goods on the x spoke will lead to hub A and from there proceed along the common spoke to hub B from where the trip to y will be completed.

The economies of scope allow one operator to serve this range of destinations more economically than several operators each providing

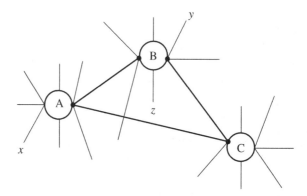

Figure 5.5.

point-to-point service. The operator serving this network can employ a larger fleet of aircraft, achieve better utilization, manage better, deal with weather incidents easier, etc. The hub-and-spoke pattern focuses the traffic (or density) to the hubs and serves to increase the load factor on the x to A run because passengers or goods may depart from A in a variety of directions which takes advantage of any existing economies of vehicle size. As well, the x to y run can draw in freight or passengers wanting the A to B run and, for example, the A to z run. Of course, larger vehicles are used on the hub-to-hub run while smaller ones may be used on the spokes providing economies of vehicle size. Although passengers and cargo face longer travel times because of connections at the hubs, residents in smaller communities have access to more destinations at lower cost than would be the case if only point-to-point service were available.

Examples of hub-and-spoke transportation networks can be found in the airlines, LTL trucking and courier services. The hubs of LTL trucking firms can be consolidation warehouses or "cross dock" terminals. The cross docks are long narrow structures where trucks backup on both sides at assigned slots. Shipments are sorted and loaded to the appropriate destinations as the cargo crosses the terminal.

The U.S. airlines embraced hub-and-spoke systems immediately following deregulation in the late 1970s. The individual airlines chose airports where they could acquire the majority of the loading gates and eliminate competition. Discount airlines have challenged these "fortress" hubs with faster point-to-point services. One advantage they have is shorter dwell periods. If we assume that the banks of airplanes converge and depart from a hub over a three hour period, the average time on the ground is 1 to 1.5 hours. This time is necessary to exchange bags and for passengers to walk through the terminal to their connecting flights. In contrast, Southwest Airlines that operates only point-to-point services averages 20 minute turn-around times.[4] These faster turn-around times allows the discounter to complete one extra flight per day for each airplane. Given the capital value of airplanes and wages to crews that remain unchanged, the extra revenues obtained from greater utilization permits

---

[4]Freiberg, Kevin and Freiberg, Jackie. *Nuts! Southwest Airlines' Crazy Recipe for Business and Personal Success.* New York, NY: Broadway Books, 1997.

the discounter to offer lower fares than the hub operators on these point-to-point routes.

The legacy airlines are struggling to compete with discount airlines, but hub-and-spoke systems are unlikely to disappear. Instead, large network hubs are becoming specialized for international services where long haul flights favor the economies of wide-body aircraft manufactured by Boeing and Airbus. Global air passenger hubs like Heathrow (London), Chek Lap Kok (Hong Kong) and O'Hare (Chicago) are vibrant and dominate their region.

A new hub-and-spoke network is beginning to take shape in the marine industry. As intermodal container ships keep growing larger they are reaching the limits of port size in terms of water draft and market demand. Container ships greater than 8,000 TEUs have reduced the line haul costs, but this means that more containers need to be unloaded and distributed from individual ports. Only a few locations, e.g., Ports of Los Angeles/Long Beach, have sufficient space or economic hinterlands to be able to absorb the volumes now carried by these post panamax container liners.[5] On the east coast, a container hub has already developed at Freeport, Bahamas where large ships are served by feeder routes to U.S. east coast and gulf ports. More developments like this seem inevitable.

Cost Relationships: Joint, Common, and Constant Costs

The discussion so far has been concerned with the specific direct costs of carrier operations. The distinction between fixed and variable cost is relevant for model building and where periods of adjustment differ across factors. Some costs, however, may be related to each other in functional ways. Non-specific forms of direct costs are known as *joint costs*, common costs and *constant costs*. For these costs categories, there is some difficulty in allocating them among the total costs of production. This is known as the *traceability or separability problem*.

Joint costs represent the costs of two or more factors in the production process that have a constant, and well-defined functional relationship.

---

[5] "Yesterday's terminals with 1,200 feet of berth, 50 acres of backland and five gantry cranes cannot accommodate today's mega-ships. Terminals now have 3,000 feet of berthing place, 300 acres or more of backland and at least eight cranes." Mongelluzzo, Bill. "Winning combination." *Journal of Commerce*, (May 23, 2005), 14.

A joint cost would occur in the fuel costs on the *fronthaul* and backhaul movement of freight or passengers. A one-to-one relationship exists between these two movements. But even if the total cost of the round trip were known, it is difficult to separate out the cost of the fronthaul and backhaul. Simply dividing the total cost in half for each leg is incorrect because for the backhaul, to take place, requires the fronthaul to have taken place; indeed for another fronthaul to occur, a backhaul was a necessary cost preceding it. It is not easy to attribute the proper proportion of fuel on the loaded fronthaul that is necessary for the backhaul. Presumably the fuel consumption on a fronthaul is what is needed for the calculation but such a figure requires knowledge of the weight of the fronthaul shipment and its effect on the vehicle's fuel economy. While it is impossible to allocate the costs between the two legs of the trip, it is possible to accurately assign different prices for the service. This will be shown in Chapter 9.

Figure 5.6 presents an example of joint costs in the airline industry. Two products are derived from air transport (passengers and freight) that have distinct markets. As far as the consumer is concerned his desire for travel is not in the least affected by the demand for cargo and vice versa. The figure shows that the demand for travel happens to be greater than that for the air cargo. We can go so far as to assume that the *cross-price elasticity of demand* for the two goods is zero.

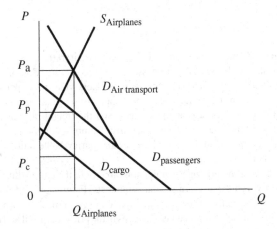

Figure 5.6.

The problem for the airline managers is that passenger seats and cargo space are derived in fixed proportions from the same source: the wide-body airplane. Thus, overseas flights leads to a production of passenger and cargo services, and the costs for each are joint in nature because of the clear functional relationship i.e., passengers will not ride in the belly.[6] The airline supplies both passenger seats and cargo space by flying, meaning that the airline managers must consider two markets at once. The combined demand curve that the airline faces ($D_{\text{Air transport}}$) is the vertical sum of the separate demands for passengers ($D_{\text{passengers}}$) and air freight (D_{cargo}).

The intersection of the combined demand for passengers and cargo and the supply of airplanes determines the equilibrium quantity of aircraft. Assuming that P_a covers the total cost, the price of the passenger tickets (P_p) and the price of air cargo (P_c) is demand-determined. Ticket prices and freight rates are set independently of the allocation of total costs toward the flight.

If the demand for passengers increased, its demand curve would shift to the right ($D_{\text{passengers}}^1$) and the combined demand curve would do likewise. This is shown in Figure 5.7. The price of airfares increases because of demand from P_p to P_p^1 but the freight rates declines from P_c to P_c^1. Why? Because, the greater demand for passenger seats increases the total demand for airplanes to fly across the ocean to satisfy the higher demand for passengers. The price of air cargo must fall in order to induce those whose demand for air cargo have not changed to purchase the extra belly space that is in joint supply with the passenger seats.[7]

---

[6]Of course, cargo will ride on the upper deck and some aircraft have been converted to carry freight in what would normally be passenger space. These "Combi" aircrafts have not become prevalent in most markets because passengers yield more per kilogram than freight. An exception is in the Arctic where the population is small, no other alternatives exist for freight movements on a year round basis, and the freight rates are much higher. However, once the airplane has been converted to a Combi configuration, the passenger space is not easily recaptured so that for all intents and purposes the ratio of passengers to freight becomes fixed.

[7]The reader can observe the pricing phenomenon directly in the commodity market prices for oilseeds, like soybeans, that share similar joint costs. Futures prices for soybeans, soy oil and soy meal are published in the daily newspaper. Oil and meal are produced in fixed proportions from the crushing on soybeans. Changes in the prices of the oil and meal products influence the price of the raw material.

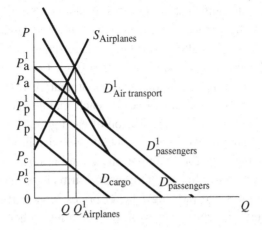

Figure 5.7.

Common costs occur when the costs coexist with no functional relationship, but with joint consumption occurring. A common cost would occur with respect to the maintenance cost of a railway that provides both passenger and freight service. It is not clear how the total cost of track maintenance should be allocated between the two services. Proportion of trips made? Proportion of weight on the track? A weighted average of trips and weight? Proportion to total revenue generated? Absence of a clear answer to cost allocation is the essence of non-traceability.

Consider a train made up of several boxcars. If they are to be dropped off at different yards it is not possible to allocate the total costs of haulage to each separate boxcar. Haulage is a common cost to each boxcar. An airplane carrying both passengers and cargo will face common costs. Ticket processing costs may be allocated directly to passengers and terminal-handling costs may be allocated directly to cargo; but how would the wages of the ground crew that fuels the airplane be allocated? Because they are non-separable with respect to the transport of passengers and cargo they represent a common cost to these two types of transport. Under joint costs, the production of one good or service leads inevitably to the production of another and the breakdown of costs for each is not traceable. For common costs, the production of one good or service need not lead to the production of another.

The model of joint costs (Figure 5.6) shows that the traceability problem is not really a problem in practice. The separate demand curves are instrumental in setting the allocation of prices even if they do not correspond to the cost proportions seen at the production stage. Common costs do not lend themselves as easily to diagrammatic treatment. A model of common costs would need two diagrams, one for each market incorporating the identical costs common to the production of each good. The examples of common costs stated above highlight the subjectivity in allocating these costs to transport users. For example, the common costs in rail and air usage are still somehow allocated to transport firms in terms of the setting of actual cargo rates and passenger ticket prices for a particular train or airplane. A simple practice is known as "cost-plus" whereby each user faces a rate equal to the sum of his specific costs plus a contribution toward common costs. The latter part of the sum is obviously subjective.[8]

Constant costs refer to general overhead expenses that are incurred as part of business operations, but not necessarily in the provision of the transportation service. From memo pads to the bar stocks in the president's office, supplies are acquired that have no direct transportation service relationship. In this way they act like a common cost when more than one service is provided and the allocation of these costs among the services is not straightforward.

Constant costs are simply part of the fixed costs of the firm and are modeled as described at the beginning of this chapter. They are part of the total costs of operation but, as will be seen in the next chapter, it is sometimes the case that competitive transport firms may not fully allocate these costs to their users. This is known as short run loss minimization.

Keywords

common costs	fronthaul	taper effect
constant costs	infrastructure	traceability or
constant returns to scale	joint costs	separability problem
cross-price elasticity of demand	line-haul	

---

[8]An appraisal of various "rules" for the allocation of common costs is provided in Talley, W. *Transport Carrier Costing*. New York: Gordon and Breach Science Publishers, 1988.

Exercises

1. Between October and December, the short run demand for belly cargo space on passenger air flights from Asia to North America increases because retail distributors want to bring in popular toys for the Christmas market that will not arrive in time, if shipped by sea.

   Draw and explain an appropriate economic model or models that illustrate(s) the impact that increased Christmas cargo demand has on freight rates and passenger ticket prices.

   Explain why airline management would resist shipper pressure to increase passenger service to serve this short run demand.

2. When Prairie farmers delivered their grain in 5 ton trucks they were captive to the price offered at the local buyer. Now they can hire tractor-trailers (26 ton loads). If the grain price is $1 per ton better, farmers are just as happy to sell to a buyer 100 kilometers away as they are to a local one only 10 kilometers away.

   Draw and explain an appropriate economic model that illustrates how tapering freight rates could affect a farmer's decision to ship farther using larger for-hire trucks.

   Why would be willing to ship their grain even farther, if they could hire truckers with double-trailers that carry 52 ton. Explain the relevant economic model.

3. Cost traceability is a problem in many industries including transportation because some costs are constant, some are common and others may be a joint.

   Assume you are analyzing an inter-city bus company's costs. The bus carries passengers and freight and operates out of bus terminals in each city. Provide examples of constant, common and joint costs for the bus lines and explain why these examples fit.

   The cargo business of the bus line has exceeded the capacity in the lower deck, and the company recently acquired 20-foot long cargo trailers to tow behind the bus. Present an argument for whether the trailer should be treated as a common, constant or joint cost.

4. Transportation carriers and logisticians try to consolidate loads so they can ship as much as they can, in as big a vehicle as they can, as far as they can.

Draw and explain an appropriate economic model(s) that illustrate(s) the economics of consolidating loads.

Most efforts to minimize costs involves operational trade-offs in which some costs may rise, while other costs fall. Explain the economic and customer service trade-offs inherent in shipment consolidation.

5. A discount domestic airline operates a point-to-point domestic air passenger network, while the competing full-service airline offers a network of domestic and international passenger flights mainly through its hubs airports.

Draw and use appropriate economic model(s) to explain the competitive advantages of these two airlines.

Outline the customer service advantages and disadvantages of these networks designs in your discussion of the economic model(s).

6. Airplanes come in many different sizes as illustrated in the table:

Airplane model	Seat #	Range (km)
Bombardier CRJ 100	50	1,574
Embraer 190	93	3,540
Airbus 320–200	146	4,442
Boeing 767–300	301	10,549
Boeing 777–300	349	14,594
Boeing 767–300	467	14,816
Airbus 380	525	15,372

Draw and use appropriate economic models to explain the economies of size, distance, and traffic density associated with the use of aircraft.

(Note, you do not have to refer to any specific airplane, these are provided for illustrative purposes.)

No formal model exists for the economies of scope or fleet size. Explain these concepts with respect to the airline industry.

Chapter 6

Modal Supply Characteristics

The supply function may be determined by way of specifying production or cost functions and developing a curve on the basis of competition among firms in the industry. In this section we may abstract from such things and discuss firm and/or industry supply as the relation of the quantity supplied to the given prices for transport services. The underlying ratio of fixed to variable costs has a bearing on competition within various modes of transport, while the unique nature of the technology creates differences between the modes. One would not assume that technologies as different as river barges and airplanes would share the same supply characteristics, and indeed they do not.

Elasticity of Supply

The *price elasticity of supply* refers to the change in output, or quantity supplied, given a percentage change in price. Because an increase in the quantity supplied is normally associated with a rise in price, the elasticity of supply is positive. It is convenient to speak about "the" price elasticity of supply, but the reality is that the change in supply has a time dimension. Figure 6.1 illustrates the role of time in the response of supply to a permanent change in price.

In the very short run, when no time exists to alter supply, the elasticity is zero and the supply curve is infinitely inelastic. No matter what price consumers are ready to pay, it is not physically possible to increase supply. Under these conditions the price will simply be bid up by demand until all the supply is exhausted.

In the medium run, given two or three production periods, it is possible to purchase new equipment, hire more labor and generally expand

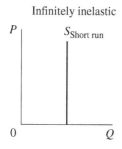

Infinitely inelastic

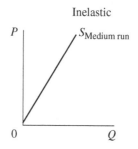

Inelastic

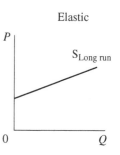

Elastic

(A) Short run — within a
    given production period;
    no time to increase
    variable or capital inputs

(B) Medium run — extending
    over 2 or 3 production
    periods; time to invest in
    new equipment

(C) Long run — extending over
    many production periods;
    time to invest in new land
    and plant expansion

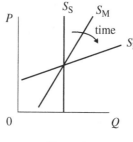

The elasticity of supply
is a function of time

Figure 6.1.

production within the constraints of the physical infrastructure. The supply
could still be inelastic, which means that the percentage change in price is
greater than the percentage change in quantity supplied, but more product
would be available.

The long run is defined as the time required for all factors of production
to be replaced or replicated. In other words, physical constraints that are
long lived like buildings and land are removed. In the long run it is possible
to duplicate all the existing production and more. The supply of most goods
is elastic in the long run. In this diagram the long run supply curve is drawn
with some upward slope. This means that not all factors of production
are unconstrained, and that as demand increases for some of these limiting
factors of production, their prices get bid up. An easy example is land which
is fixed in supply. If more land is required to increase supply, assuming all
other uses stay constant, it will cost more to replicate the existing production
and so the long run supply curve is upward sloping.

Modal Supply Characteristics

Costs are generally borne individually by transportation firms, but the modal supply response depends on the structure of market. The number and size of competitors is an important determinant of market supply. This in turn is a function of costs and economies of size, network, scope, and other topics covered in Chapter 5. The supply responses for each of the major modes are considered in turn.

(1) Ocean shipping

Tramp shipping deals with port-to-port ocean transport (usually dry bulk cargo) at rates negotiated between the shipper and the vessel owner. This contrasts with the fixed route and scheduling found in the liner shipping trade, e.g., container ships.[1] The tramp shipping market is extremely competitive because the ship owners usually own no more than a few ships and these owners are geographically dispersed. With many suppliers providing similar goods or services along with many demanders wishing to purchase those items, the market is competitive. No firm by itself feels the need to lower its price because it would diminish profits and, as well, it would not wish to raise price because that would entice customers to use rival firms.

As described earlier the price elasticity of supply is dependent upon, among other things, the length of time the firm has to adjust to market changes. The distinction between the short run and the long run in ocean shipping is important because the lead-time involved in bringing a new vessel on line can be 18 months to two years. New vessels will only be added to the fleet if the owner is convinced of favorable and long lasting shipping rates. The firm and the industry will reach a capacity constraint due to the fixed supply of vessels at a given time. The supply curve for the firm and the industry in these circumstances is given in Figure 6.2.

---

[1]Liner shipping involves the movement of many goods on a given vessel while bulk shipping handles larger individual cargos. Bulk carriers are more prone to tramping when they travel from port-to-port to fill their holds while liner carriers, with their consolidation staff, can afford to offer greater speed and reliability. A detailed analysis is provided in Stopford, M. *Maritime Economics*. New York: Routledge, 1997.

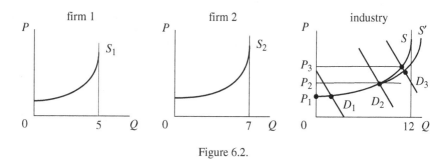

Figure 6.2.

The industry supply curve is the horizontal summation of the supply curves for the firms. In the diagram, only two are shown for clarity but the reality is that there will be many due to the competitive nature of this industry. The flat portion of the supply curve indicates that supply is readily forthcoming because these "low" rates do not induce the firms to reach fleet capacity. Vessels out of each fleet will only be used as they are needed because a firm wishes to reach as close to capacity as possible on each ship at the margin. In the panel depicting the industry it can be seen that the demand expansion from D_1 to D_2 produces little change in price (or shipping rate) because the industry has a lot of available capacity. As industry capacity is approached, prices rise sharply as seen from the D_2 to D_3 shift. If the change in rates over time, due to demand curve shifts, are not considered by firms to be too erratic and a clear upward trend is discerned by them, ships will be added to their fleets and the supply curve will expand outward in the long run from S to S' as shown.

Figure 6.3 illustrates the historic pattern of ocean freight rates. As a derived demand, ocean shipping rates rise and fall with the cycles of world economic growth. However, it is the supply response of the industry that causes ship owners to experience long periods of low returns, punctuated by short periods of very high profits.[2]

At low prices the supply curve is price-elastic over a considerable region of output. This is explained by the lack of alternative uses for the fixed capital and the strategies employed by ship owners during periods of low prices. A ship owner has two options: reduce variable costs or

---

[2]Actual ocean freight rates are available from the Baltic Exchange Dry Index, http://investmenttools.com/futures/bdi_baltic_ dry_index.htm.

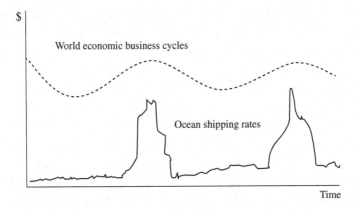

Figure 6.3. Pattern of economic cycles and ocean freight rates.

decommission the ship and try to avoid all variable costs. In a buyer's market, the sellers' opportunity costs are low. The ship owner could choose to accelerate scheduled maintenance thereby having the ship out of service when rates are low. Alternatively, the ship may sail at a slow speed, which conserves fuel, and call at more ports in search of cargo. If the ship owner decides to "mothball" the ship, other costs must be considered. The owner must pay docking fees to a port and may have to buy out the labor contracts of the crew members. Costs will be incurred to decommission the ship, and yet more again to get it ready for sailing when the situation becomes favorable. As a result, ship owners are reluctant to exit the market and would rather accept low returns.

The difference between Figures 4.5 and 6.2 should be kept in mind. Figure 4.5 discussed the applicability of constant returns to scale (a long run concept) to the tramp shipping industry. As such, changes to the fleet are made under a time frame where owners have a lot of time to make decisions. This is the elastic portion of the vessel supply curve. The fleet size is fixed while it is the decision to merely deploy a given vessel that is dependent upon the shipping rate. As the capacity becomes more constraining for a given fleet, the supply curve becomes non-flat and more inelastic.

The finances of the container shipping lines bear some resemblance to bulk shipping with regard to the vessels, but their economics are more complicated. In addition to ships, the container lines own fleets of ISO containers (boxes). Total container numbers are easily triple the number of containers on the sea at any point in time. Some shipping lines also own other land-based assets, like container terminals and truck chassis for containers. Unlike the bulk ships that operate on a charter basis, the container shipping lines offer scheduled services at fixed ports of call.

There is less competition amongst the container ship owners than is observed in the bulk carriers. Industry consolidation has decreased the number of container shipping lines[3] and many companies belong to organized cartels, called *shipping conferences*. Whereas the bulk shipping segment is characterized by years of stable freight rates punctuated by periods of volatile price movements, the container shipping segment has experienced years of steadily declining freight rates in accord with the increasing efficiencies of larger post-Panamax container ships and general network economies.

The lack of freight rate volatility can be attributed to *self-regulation* of the container shipping lines through the shipping conferences. The conferences publish minimum freight rates and try to prevent "price wars" during cycles of low demand. The economics of cartels is illustrated in Figure 6.4. On the left is a representative firm. Alone they would have to settle for a price P' that is determined by the industry supply and demand. The industry supply curve is depicted as the cumulative marginal cost (MC) curves of the firms. As a cartel, the group can reduce supply to Q_m and force prices up to P_m. This is the price where industry profits are maximized (MR = MC). Each cartel member is allocated a quota share of the reduced output. The hatched area on the left identifies the additional profit obtained by the cartel member.

There are four conditions for a cartel to be successful. First, the number of firms must be few in order to organize and operate the organization. If the numbers are too large, some firms may try to be free-riders. Second, the industry demand must be inelastic, otherwise industry revenues cannot be increased by reducing supply. Third, the output of the firms must be easily

---

[3]The 10 largest container shipping lines represent 53.6% of the world market share. The top 20 shipping lines account for 76.9% (*Journal of Commerce*, Vol. 6, No. 26 (2005)). Although this would not appear highly as concentrated as airlines or railways, the shipping conferences can exert considerable pressure to support freight rates and in some traffic lanes individual carriers have a larger market share than the average concentration of the industry would suggest.

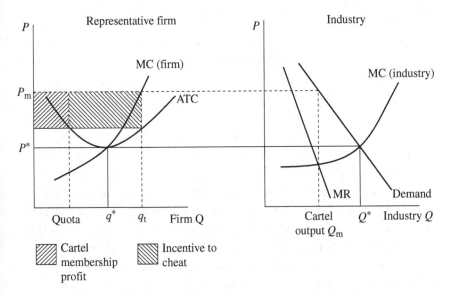

Figure 6.4. Cartel model.

monitored to be sure that no firms are cheating. Poor enforcement of the quotas is a dilemma for industries where it is easy to hide output. Finally, there must be no close substitutes that can erode the cartel's demand.

A problem for most cartels, other than they are generally illegal in most countries, is the temptation to cheat. The hatched area on the right in Figure 6.4 indicates the extra profit for the representative firm, if they did not have to obey the quota. Of course if firms are allowed to cheat, the unity of the cartel soon breaks down.

Unlike most cartels that are unstable and subject to anti-combines legislation, international shipping conferences have been long lived, and given exemption from national competition oversight. Ironically, the durability of the shipping conferences is likely attributable to their weakness as a cartel. The conferences have no ability to raise rates and cannot prevent independent operators from entering the market. Generally, they are viewed as adding greater stability to the market, and as such they are tolerated.[4]

---

[4]An EU-funded independent, five-person economics team from Erasmus University found that liner conferences do not have the power of price setting normally associated with cartels, and that they do reduce the volatility of ocean container freight rates. European Commission

(2) Trucking

A supply curve can also be based on an institutional setting; that is, the interplay between industry and government can have implications for how the industry adjusts quantity supplied to a change in price. An example of this type of supply response can be given with respect to the trucking industry in terms of its activity within either a regime of governmental regulation or one of deregulation. The supply curves that result are "kinked" in shape as seen in Figure 6.5. The heavily shaded upper portion (EAB) represents the expansion/contraction path that occurs in a regulatory regime, while the lower kinked supply (FAC) is that for a deregulated industry.

What we have here are really two straight-line supply curves of different steepness and price-elasticities. The steeper supply curve is a short to medium run supply response of the trucking industry and the flatter curve represents the long run supply response. The trucking industry operates as if it has a kinked supply curve because the demand for trucking services is cyclical by nature. If the economy experiences a recession (expansion) it is guaranteed that the demand for trucking services will decline (expand). In order to understand how government regulations affect the supply response in trucking, we need to review the mechanism that was used to control its inherent instability.

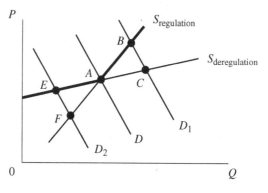

Figure 6.5.

Review of International Liner Shipping Competition and Regulation. November 12, 2003. Available at the EU website.

The trucking industry is volatile by nature in that, as compared to rail, air and ocean vessel shipping, it is an industry that does not require much capital expenditure to enter. The regulatory system that was imposed on the trucking industry in North America from the 1930s until the 1980s was based on a desire to treat all the modes of transport fairly and to discourage what were considered to be *destructive competitive* practices.[5]

One of the impacts of regulation was that it encouraged the growth of fewer, larger trucking firms behind a significant barrier to entry. In order for a new entrant to obtain an "operating authority", which is a license to conduct specific for-hire services in a set geographic area, the new carrier had to prove that their service would be in the public interest. In practice this meant that the new trucking firm had to solicit shippers to come before a quasi-judicial proceeding to testify that they needed the new trucking firm because the service they were receiving was inadequate. Under the "public convenience and necessity test", the incumbent trucking firms only had to prove that they were already providing enough service for the application to be rejected.

Needless to say, few new truck operating authorities were granted. Trucking firms became larger by buying up their competitors and amalgamating operating authorities. Consequently, the larger companies could afford a bevy of lawyers to defend their quasi-monopolies against the application of new entrants for a competing operating authority. Of course the regulated trucking industry provided an opportunity for organized labor to extract part of the excess profit created by the protected market in the form of higher wages and benefits.

After the regulatory system was abandoned in the 1980s, the new entry test became "fit, willing, and able". In essence anyone who could demonstrate the financial wherewithal to buy and insure a truck was granted a license to take any freight anywhere within the country. Many of the large trucking firms fell into bankruptcy because of the intense competition

---

[5]A detailed discussion of the impact of regulations on the economics of the trucking industry is provided by Felton, John Richard and Anderson, Dale G. (eds.). *Regulation and Deregulation of the Motor Carrier Industry.* Ames, Iowa: Iowa State University Press, 1989.

provided by a flood of lower cost, non-unionized, small carriers that entered the market.[6]

Assume that the cyclically-adjusted demand curve D in Figure 6.5 is taken to be permanent as far as the industry is concerned. The analysis begins with both the regulated and the deregulated industry at point A that represents the position in which the industry is expected to remain in the long run. First, we will consider a temporary expansion in the market for trucking services as seen by the demand curve shifting cyclically from its permanent position at D to D_1 (an economic boom period). Under a regulatory regime, the government-granted operating authorities prevent new firms from entering the industry to compete with the established trucking firms. They are able to raise their shipping rates faster than they provide extra services as is seen on the steep part of the supply curve to point B. Regulatory protection allows the established firms to upwardly co-ordinate their rates, while adding some new capacity.

In a deregulated regime the trucking industry will provide more services at lower rates during a boom period. Compare point B with point C on the deregulated supply curve. The reason is because, without the governmental red-tape restricting operating licenses, new firms can quickly enter the industry and existing firms can purchase more trucks to put on the road. Such competition keeps transport prices from rising quickly, as compared to the regulated industry because the expansion path follows the flatter, long run supply response.

A temporary demand contraction is represented by the shift in the demand curve D_2 (a recessionary period). Under the regulatory regime the decline in rates is slower than the drop in services provided. The regulated industry contracts along the flatter long run supply curve to point E. The large regulated firms can easily scale back their operations by removing a portion of their fleet from service and ride-out the recession because they only have a few competitors who are also content to park a few trucks if they

---

[6]In the U.S.A., deregulation of trucking was squarely aimed at removing the power of the Teamsters Union. It was estimated that the trucking unions added over $5 billion annually to the cost of moving goods. In this regard, deregulation has worked very well. Only the large LTL carriers remain heavily unionized. The implication for the model is that the deregulated kinked supply curve should be separated and moved down to allow for the lower cost base of the deregulated trucking industry. This is not done for the sake of clarity in exposition.

see their competitors doing the same. In contrast, the trucking firms within a deregulated regime face a large drop in rates during a recession because of fierce competition for survival amongst many small carriers (i.e., one truck owner-operators).

Compare point E with point F. The small carriers have an incentive to hope that they can survive long enough to live through the recession as long as the freight rates remain above their average variable costs. The firms "loss minimize" by staying in business as long as they can make a contribution towards their fixed costs. This leads to competitive price-cutting along with the provision of more services than would be provided by the regulated industry because they are contracting down the steeper short run supply curve.[7] If this "temporary contraction turns out to be permanent, the final equilibrium of the deregulated market could rest at E which is the long run supply curve for the trucking industry. The reason is that enough small carriers would be forced out of the market and the reduction of competition would force prices up to this new long run equilibrium.

(3) Passenger bus, marine and airline tour operators

The package air charters, bus charters, and ocean cruise operators attempt to compete for the primary demand for transportation through product differentiation. Tour promoters can offer different hotel and entertainment choices, feature special scenery, or promise dissimilar experiences in an attempt to attract buyers. Firms that engage in non-price competition through product differentiation on the basis of advertising, packaging, warranties, special discounts, or bundling are known as *monopolistically competitive* firms. The supply of the charter tour industry is characterized by monopolistic competition.

The model of a representative package tour operator is presented in Figure 6.6. Monopolistically competitive firms are prone to *excess capacity*.

---

[7] This model is explored in greater detail in Prentice, B. "The Stability/Efficiency Trade-Off: Policy Implications for For-Hire Trucking." *Canadian Transportation Research Forum: Proceedings* (1994): 494–507. It is worth noting that the small independent truck driver has a lot in common with a farmer. The tractor-trailer can represent a significant proportion of the trucker's wealth, as well as his source of income. Given that the truck, like a farm, is partly financed, if the trucker exists the industry he not only loses his job but also the down payment or asset value accumulated in the truck. As a result, the trucker like a farmer will endure significant periods of low income operations in expectation of better times.

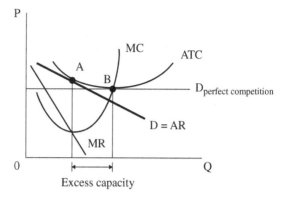

Figure 6.6.

The long run equilibrium of such a firm occurs at point A, where the marginal revenue (MR) equals their MC. A competitive equilibrium is at point B. The difference in output is the excess capacity of the firm. Consumers who are patient can take advantage of the chronic excess capacity in the tour industry. Waiting until near the time of departure to book a tour, or selecting travel times over holiday periods, like Christmas, can lead to deep discount prices because tour operators attempt to fill empty seats.

Monopolistically competitive firms possess a slight degree of market power because of non-price competition and product differentiation as shown by the downward sloping demand curve. The more differentiated the firm's product, the more price-inelastic will be its demand curve. Firms have an incentive to enter the industry until all profits, as given by the representative firm, are driven down to zero. Firm entry, in an attempt to mimic the product of rivals, serves to add more price elasticity to the firm's demand until a point such as A is achieved.

The supply function for each monopolistically competitive firm is represented by their MC curve. It may not be technically correct to aggregate the provision of differentiated products into a supply curve, but the differentiation in tourist supply may be no greater than for manufactured products, like automobiles or other consumer goods.

(4) Pipelines, railways and airlines

Supply functions for the pipelines, railways and scheduled airline industries do not readily exist even on a theoretical basis. Such industries are not marked by competition in the way an economist would strictly classify it. A competitive industry is characterized by a uniform product being produced by many firms for many consumers with all parties operating with near-perfect information and no *barriers to entry* and exit being in place. Rail and air do not fit this profile to the extent that the North American air and rail industries have relatively few players. If a competitive environment occurred in such an industry it would be taken as temporary due to a jockeying for market position.

A supply curve is a one-to-one correspondence between price and quantity supplied and because a variety of prices is possible for any given quantity of rail or air services provided, no supply curve exists. This phenomenon is best seen for pipelines and railways in the light of the *monopoly model* to be presented in Chapter 7. The behavior of the aviation industry may be viewed in terms of competition with hub-and-spoke networks.

The large "full service" airlines establish routes through hub airports in order to take advantage of cost savings. However, there is another phenomenon that may be at work. Airline analysts have examined the existence and non-existence of the so-called *S-curve*. The hypothesis is that a carrier that manages to dominate a hub market in terms of capacity and frequency will capture a disproportionate share of passenger and/or cargo traffic. For example, if the dominant carrier supplies 60% of the available flights, it may receive 70% of the total passengers/cargo available. In this way, the end result of competition is an air hub that tends to be dominated by only one carrier.

Figure 6.7 shows the S-curve phenomenon. The 45-degree line, by construction, shows all points where flight share equals traffic share. Notice that the S-curve passes through the 45-degree line at a total flight share of x. Any carrier with a higher flight share than x would receive a traffic share that would be greater. Of course, to the left of x, a carrier with a smaller flight share would receive an even smaller traffic share.

What are the implications of the S-curve, if it exists? On the supply side there would be an incentive for a carrier either to add more spokes to its hub airport or to operate more frequently along a given spoke. Doing so will allow it to pick up increasing traffic amounts and erode a competitor's market share. In this way a single carrier can dominate the hub.

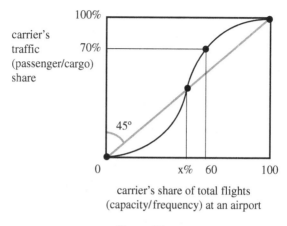

Figure 6.7.

Business travelers welcome more frequency and generally pay a premium above the casual traveler. The probability of obtaining a seat at a desirable departure time would seem highest for the carrier with the greatest frequency. From the demand side, the S-curve implies that the dominant carrier is the first one to be considered by business travelers in terms of their travel plans. Consequently, the dominant carrier also receives the lion's share of the higher air fares.

Of course, before a carrier succeeded in dominating the hub, competition among the carriers in the interim would lead to over scheduling and overcapacity as the fight for domination waged. The hub could face a significant congestion problem as well, especially at the most desirable arrival and departure times. Thus, if the end result was domination coupled with the social costs of hub congestion and destructive competition beforehand, the S-curve hypothesis would make the case for entry regulation and strict control of landing rights at airports. In this way, the government or airport authority could merely establish a dominant firm without going through a competition leading, ultimately, to it.

Is the S-curve theory valid? Opponents have an intuitive criticism. Consider an airline facing losses due to under capacity of usage meaning that it found itself to the left of point *x* in Figure 6.5. The S-curve hypothesis would dictate that it simply attempt to expand capacity. The solution needed to fill empty seats or cargo space is to supply more seats or cargo space.

The theory presupposes that demand will flow to supply by way of a lemming effect and capacity will be utilized. This is a large assumption to make. Airlines with smaller flight shares may engage in advertising to attract customers. And in hubs that have, say, three or four carriers with around 20–25% market share, there is no reason to think that one carrier with the biggest share in that range will have an extra control over demand.

Transport Modes: A Comparison

Figure 6.8 provides a comparison of industry structure. The structure of competition in the transportation industry structure is greatly affected by the ratio of fixed to variable costs. The breakdown of fixed and variable costs for each mode is approximated. In general the higher the percentage of costs that are fixed, the less competition is found across the modes. Part of the reason for this is the barrier to entry. Pipeline construction costs can measure in the billions, whereas tractor-trailers can be acquired for $100,000.

Industrial structure by mode

	Fixed cost	Variable cost	Level of competition	Modal nature of supply curve
Truck	5 20%	1 80%	1 many	defined: LR & SR
Marine	4 40%	2 60%	2 numerous	defined: LR & SR
Air	3 50%	3 50%	3 few	reaction function
Rail	2 60%	4 40%	4 few/regional	reaction function or undefined (monopoly)
Pipeline	1 80%	5 20%	5 none	undefined (monopoly) or LRMC*

1 = highest/most   LR = long run   * long run marginal cost (LRMC) holds under
5 = lowest/least   SR = short run   government induced MC pricing.

N.B. The percentage breakdown of cost shares are estimates at best since the issue is empirical.

Figure 6.8.

An important point that should be highlighted by this table is that one cannot simply take the managerial practices of one mode of transport and apply them to another. The economics are too divergent. It is interesting to note that lateral transfers of management between the various modes of transport have not been frequent. Once someone starts a career in one mode of transport, generally they will not move to one that is radically different. Some shifting does occur between rail and truck modes, but it is less frequent to see people reallocate between air, marine and surface modes of transport.

Note that the category of supply applicable to the rail and air modes is a *reaction function*. Technically, a reaction function is not a supply function per se but rather a quantity-supply response to the actual (or expected) action of a competitor. This is a quantity-supply response to another firm's quantity-supply in contrast to a supply function, which is a quantity-supply response to, among other things, a market price for the firm's output. Reaction functions are used in markets dominated by a few players — so-called oligopoly markets. Oligopoly models are complex by construction and will not be explored here; suffice it to say that one of its primary tools — game theory — will be touched upon in Chapter 14. Industries that seem to gravitate between periods of price wars and a dividing up of the market among its member firms usually indicate oligopolistic behavior.

Figure 6.9 provides an attribute breakdown by mode. Bear in mind that a low score should not be construed as necessarily a sign of one mode's

	Speed	Availability	Dependability	Capability	Frequency
Truck	2	1	2	3	2
Marine	4	4	4	1	5
Air	1	3	5	4	3
Rail	3	2	3	2	4
Pipeline	5	5	1	5	1

1 = best

Figure 6.9. Modal attributes.

efficiency gain over another's. Time, geography, government regulation as well as intermodal competition can skew a shipper's choice to use any one of these modes.

A missing piece in this matrix is intermodal transport. Containerization has become the fastest growing component of transportation in the last two decades. Where would you rank the attributes of intermodal containers in this chart?

Keywords

barriers to entry	monopoly model	shipping conferences
excess capacity	price elasticity of supply	S-curve
monopolistically competitive	reaction function	tramp shipping
	self-regulation	

Exercises

1. The taxi industry is characterized by constant returns to scale. The only aspect that exhibits some network economies is in the dispatch of rides. However as the cost of communications has declined, even this benefit of larger organizations has diminished. Nonetheless in most taxi markets the industry still operates under a regulated cartel system, in which a government agency limits the number of licenses and sets taxi fares.

    Draw and explain an appropriate economic model(s) that illustrate(s) the manner in which the taxi industry operates as a regulated cartel.

    If the government regulation were removed, and the laws permitted a private cartel to operated, explain why the taxi cartel would be stable or unstable and fail.

2. The truckload carrier industry is very competitive and efficient. The number of trucks increases rapidly during expansionary periods, but during recessions truck numbers contract very slowly.

    Draw and explain an appropriate economic model(s) that illustrate(s) the nature of the truckload supply that explains this behavior.

    In your discussion of the economic model(s), explain the managerial options open to an owner-operator, and to trucking companies that they work for, when the economy enters a prolonged recession like the one being experienced at the moment.

3. Every year the opportunity arises to buy deeply discounted vacation packages to the southern sun spots. Excess capacity that is chronic in this industry permits flexible buyers to get great deals, if they are willing to fly at the "last minute".

   Draw and explain an appropriate economic model(s) that illustrate(s) why the individual firm in the packaged tour industry has chronic excess capacity.

   Explain how firms in industries like tourist charters compete for market share and the advantage it gives them.

4. The International Association of Bulk Marine Carriers (tramp steamers) is unhappy with the current pattern of the boom and bust price cycles in their industry. They want to form a "shipping conference" like the liner carriers (container ships) to set prices and output. They have asked you to examine the feasibility of forming a cartel, given that international law does not prevent them from creating such organizations.

   Draw an appropriate economic model(s) and explain whether or not, this industry has the conditions for a cartel organization to be a successful.

   The bulk marine carriers' customers are raw material shippers (minerals, coal, grain, etc.) that experience demand shifts as the world economy expands and contracts. Why would this make a cartel more difficult to manage?

5. Dry bulk marine carriers (tramp steamers) can experience long periods of stable, but low prices, punctuated by short periods of rapidly increasing prices.

   Draw and explain an appropriate economic model(s) that illustrate(s) how the nature of marine carrier supply causes this price pattern and why it persists.

   Discuss the managerial options open to ship owners to deal with periods of high and low prices in your explanation of the economic model(s).

6. The distribution of passengers between competing airlines is not equal to the number of flights they offer. This is particularly true at hub airports where the passenger traffic share of the main carrier is even greater than its share of flights.

Use an appropriate economic model(s) to describe the observed phenomena and explain why this occurs.

The airline industry is does not have defined supply curves. Instead each airline adjusts its prices and service offerings based on the actions of its competitor. Explain why the airline industry operates this way.

7. The transportation system is built on five modal transport systems (air, rail, truck, ship and pipeline). Each mode of transport has unique characteristics that give it a comparative advantage for certain applications.

Complete table by ranking these modes from best to worst, with 1 = best. Explain why you have organized the modes of transport like this, and justify your answer. Start by defining the economic concept on the left first.

Explain why the combination of modes, or inter-modal transport, is often necessary, usually lower in cost and more desirable than a single mode of transport.

Concept mode	TL trucking	Bulk marine	Pass. air	Freight rail	Liquid pipeline
Economies of size					
Level of competition					
Network economies					
Economies of traffic density					

8. The elasticity of supply has an important impact on the response of transportation prices given shifts in demand that can occur during the business cycle.

Explain the behavior of the bulk (tramp) ocean shipping freight rates (how prices change) when the business cycle goes from boom to bust. Illustrate your answer with an appropriate diagram, or diagrams.

Explain why the freight rates in the truckload trucking industry behave differently than bulk ocean shipping rates when the business cycle goes from boom to bust. Illustrate your answer with an appropriate diagram, or diagrams.

9. Network economies can lead to increasing economies of scale in transportation.

Explain why modes of transport that have increasing network economies become concentrated in the hands of a few large competitors; whereas modes of transportation with constant economies of scale have many firms of different sizes competing together successfully. Use an appropriate model or models to illustrate your arguments.

Chapter 7

Markets and Competition in Transportation

The previous chapters discussed supply and demand in detail and it is the coming together of these in the marketplace that allows the price of the good or service in question to be determined. This interplay, however, needs to be elaborated upon more fully because the nature of the market itself will affect how demand and supply behave.

The nature of the market is the result of the way the key players react. The government exercises a certain degree of control over the supply and demand process through *property rights* and contract enforcement to regulate firm entry and exit from production. The firms within the industry may compete to varying degrees with each other. Consumer demand may or may not be uniform in that it may be broken into subgroups by the seller. The pricing processes found in the two polar opposites of industrial structure — *perfect competition* and monopoly — are the focus of this section.

Allocative and Productive Efficiency Perfect Competition

It has been alluded to in previous chapters that competition leads to efficiency. Of course, no details have yet been provided; indeed the specifics of what is meant by the word "efficiency" have not yet been introduced. When we speak of economic efficiency we speak of two sub-components; specifically, *productive efficiency* and *allocative efficiency*. Each is discussed in turn. Figure 7.1 provides a diagrammatic explanation. The price-quantity combination of $P*$ and $Q*$ is both productively and allocatively efficient.

Productive efficiency simply means that the production process used by the firm is the one that allows it to produce any and all units of a good or service at least-cost. The combination of factors of production chosen

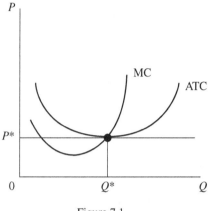

Figure 7.1.

cannot be altered in such a way as to allow the same unit(s) of the good or service to be produced at a lower cost. The firm that achieves productive efficiency will have a plant size in which minimum point of its average total cost (ATC) function equals the price of its output. In this way, the firm will be making neither *economic profit*, nor loss. The firm will be earning a normal return and charging the lowest sustainable price in the long run. While economic losses may be tolerated in the short run, as we will see, they cannot be tolerated in the long run because the firm would have the option of closing down and eliminating the loss.[1]

Allocative efficiency is achieved when the firm allocates factors of production such that only goods and services that are actually desired by consumers are produced. More specifically, priority in the allocation of factors goes only to those goods and services most wanted by consumers. In this way supply of goods corresponds to a demand for those same goods and thus we have a market for transactions. This aspect of efficiency is related to the concept of *consumer sovereignty* whereby consumer demand is the signal for supply to respond, and not the other way around. The old phrase

---

[1] It should be noted that economic profit and accounting "profit" are different. The accountant calculates profit by deducting expenses and depreciation from sales. This could be called "botton-line" profit. Economists allow for compensation to all factors of production including the implicit costs of ownership and unpaid labor. If any revenue exists after all input costs have been fully accounted for, this is referred to as "economic profit", or "rent". These rents are the economic return that the entrepreneur earns for bearing risk.

"the customer is always right" has a ring of truth to it. Safety standards on automobiles increased greatly during the 1970s not in response to manufacturer desires but due to consumer desires. If consumers did not desire the change they would not have purchased the safer cars.

A firm that achieves allocative efficiency sets the price of its output at the point equal to the marginal cost (MC) of the last unit produced. Why? If $P > $ MC at the current unit, resources are under-allocated because the revenue gained, through the price (P), from that unit is greater than the cost of producing it as represented by MC. When that unit is produced the next unit's MC will be higher once diminishing returns set in. Thus, a firm will continue to produce goods with $P > $ MC until MC rises to where $P = $ MC. Similarly, if $P < $ MC an over-allocation of resources occurs because the revenue gained from that unit (i.e., P) is less than the cost of producing it as given by MC. Thus, production would be cut back to where $P = $ MC.

Perfect Competition

The reason why economists look upon competition as being important to the economy is because its absolute form — the perfectly competitive model — is capable of achieving both allocative and productive efficiency. That point will be made once the assumptions of perfect competition are laid out.

In the perfectly competitive model there are a large number of both suppliers of, and demanders for, a standardized good. In this sense a demander does not care from which firm the good is purchased and because the good is identical, firms feel no need to engage in non-price competition such as advertising or discounts. As there are many suppliers, a firm is a "price taker" in that no one firm, or group of firms, could influence the market price because their output would be such a small amount of the total. A firm will be able to sell all that it can supply at the market price because there are many demanders. Another assumption is freedom of entry and exit, a long run assumption highlighting the lack of barriers to the market — legal, technical, or financial — that would stop a firm from selling its output if it were able to produce it. A final assumption is that of uniform information meaning that no supplier or demander has an informational advantage over another which serves to keep all participants in each group on a level playing field.

The absolute form of perfect competition has very strong assumptions, but cases can be found in transportation that come close to meeting this ideal. An example in North America is the drayage truckers who move containers to and from the port terminals. The barriers to entry are low. Operators can buy used highway tractors at depreciated prices and the container chassis are provided by the terminal. As a result, anyone with an appropriate driver's license and a down payment on a truck tractor can enter the market. The service is standardized (one driver/one truck) and uniform, cell phones provide communications, the operators are price-takers and, consequently, competition is intense.

All firms in the perfect competition model take the price of the output (P) to be given and constant. Total revenue (TR) is defined as the price of the output (P) multiplied by the quantity sold (Q). Figure 7.2 illustrates the firm's total revenues, average and marginal revenues as a function of output Q.

In the first panel, with TR $= P \times$ Q, we see that if $Q = 0$, TR $= 0$. When an extra unit is sold TR rises by the sale price (P). From the TR curve, the average revenue (AR) and marginal revenue (MR) curves can be

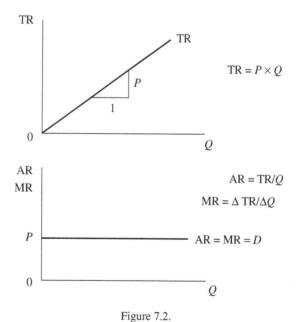

Figure 7.2.

derived which both equal *P*, as seen in the second panel. Because the firm is assumed to be able to sell all of its output at the market price, this price line is also the demand curve (*D*) for the firm. It should be noticed that the demand curve is perfectly price-elastic.

The typical assumption for all firms in all types of markets is that they wish to maximize total profits. Normal profits are defined as the difference between TR and total cost. In order to determine the profit maximizing level of output for the perfectly competitive firm, the firm's costs must be compared with its revenues.

Figure 7.3 illustrates the case of economic profits. The total cost function (TC) has the same shape as developed in Chapter 3 and is applicable to all types of firms because costs are based strictly on technology (or productivity) and not market structure for output. The profit maximizing quantity is *Q**. In the first panel *Q** comes about as the quantity where TR is most above TC leading to, of course, the highest total profit. In the second panel, *Q** is seen to be the quantity where marginal revenue (MR) equals MC. When MR = MC the revenue gained from the last unit produced is exactly equal to the cost in producing it. If the firm went beyond *Q**, MR < MC would result and production should be cut back. If the firm produced

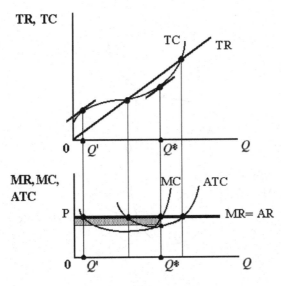

Figure 7.3.

an amount slightly less than Q^*, MR > MC would result and production should be expanded.

Technically, the profit maximizing rule is to have MR = MC as long as MC is rising because we see from the second panel that MR = MC at two quantities, Q^* and Q'. The reason why Q' would not be chosen is that, by looking at the corresponding quantity in the first panel, TR is as much below TC as is possible. In other words, Q' is the output where losses are maximized! At Q^*, AR exceeds ATC so that economic profits are seen in the second panel to be equal to the shaded area. In the perfectly competitive model economic profits cannot persist for long.

If all firms expand to take advantage of the opportunities, the market price could fall as illustrated by TR$'$ in Figure 7.4. The new point Q' is the breakeven output that has no economic profits, but the firms continue to earn normal profits.

If for some reason the market contracted and prices fell further due to a change in, say, consumer tastes, the firm could move from a breakeven position to negative profits (i.e., losses). To see this, consider Figure 7.5.

As the price of the good falls in the marketplace, TR pivots downward as shown by TR$'$ which can be compared to TR in Figures 7.3 and 7.4.

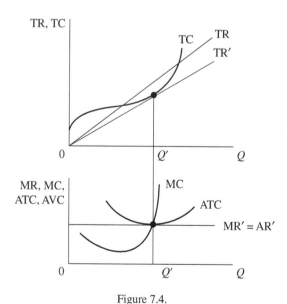

Figure 7.4.

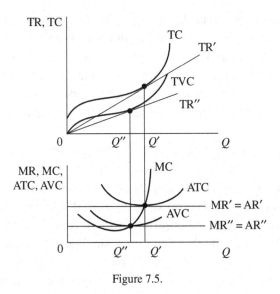

Figure 7.5.

With TR′, TC is everywhere above it except at Q' where TR = TC and the firm is earning normal profits. This can be confirmed in the lower panel where MR′ = MC at the point where they both cross the ATC curve. Thus MR′ = MC = ATC. If MR = AR in this model, it must be the case that ATC = AR which is identical to saying TR = TC.

If the price fell further, losses would occur and TR would continue to pivot down. At TR″, where it just touches the total variable cost function; the firm is at the shut-down point. Its revenue can barely pay its variable costs (labor) let alone its fixed costs (capital). This is why the short run supply curve for the perfectly competitive firm is the portion of the MC curve above the point where it intersects the average variable cost (AVC) curve.

In the long run, when all firms can adjust their capital as well as labor, and firms can enter or exit the industry, the only viable equilibrium for all firms is where they only make normal economic profits. The reason for this is because if one or more firms were making economic profits in the long run it would signal other firms to enter the industry. More firms in the industry will serve to lower the market price of the output because of the larger supply with a given demand, thereby removing any economic profits. Likewise, if some firms made losses in the long run those firms would be better off leaving the industry. When firms leave, the fall in supply with a given demand will serve to raise the price of the output, which eventually stops firms from exiting. In the perfect competition model, the exit of firms would reduce total supply until prices again returned to TR'. This is based on the assumption of a great number of buyers in the market, each of which has no ability to influence the price (individually). This is not necessarily observed in practice.

Returning to our example of the drayage truck drivers, there are relatively few port terminals and none of the buyers have any incentive to raise prices as long as the drayage service continues to be provided. Over time inflation can erode prices, such that TR' can pivot down to TR''. This has happened on several occasions with the result that virtually all the drayage truckers reach the shut-down point simultaneously, creating a mass exodus from the industry and great disruption at the ports.[2] Economists refer to this market failure as destructive competition. Although this is a rare phenomenon, it can occur when a highly competitive market serves a concentrated oligoposony.

In the perfect competition model the output of all firms in the industry sums to create the industry supply curve as illustrated in Figure 7.6. It should be noticed that zero economic profit fulfills the conditions for economic efficiency. First, the firms always set output where MR = MC and because P = MR in perfect competition, P = MC which is the requirement of allocative efficiency. The industry diagram shows the interaction of simple

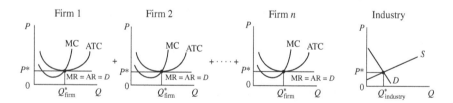

Figure 7.6.

---

[2]A description of the drayage industry and recommendations for regulatory change is presented in *Review of the Vancouver Container Trucking Regulation.* (Regulations Amending the Port Authorities Operations Regulations, July 31, 2007) Report to the Minister of Transport, Infrastructure and Communities, Transport Canada July 2009 http://dtci.ca/wp-content/uploads/2010/09/regulations.pdf.

supply and demand leading to an equilibrium price (P^*) that the firms take as given. As long as industry supply and demand stay constant, P^* will remain likewise. The fact that supply equals demand at the industry level also indicates allocative efficiency. Because of zero long run profits as shown by AR = ATC, firms will neither enter nor exit the industry. Notice, however, that Q^* for the firms exists at the minimum point on the ATC curve. This means that output is produced at least-cost, which indicates productive efficiency is taking place.[3]

The efficient allocation of resources through the market is further illustrated in Figure 7.7. This diagram illustrates the three distinct divisions of the market based on marginal pricing. The top shaded area is the *consumer surplus.* Only the marginal consumer, or in this case the last consumer, values the product or service at its actual market price. Other consumers are willing to pay more than the actual price, but do not have to do so. The difference between the maximum prices that consumers are willing to pay and the actual market price is the consumer surplus.

Producer surplus has an equivalent interpretation from the seller's point of view. The shaded area shows the amount that individual producers would be willing to accept below the market price that is the minimum that the marginal producer would accept to remain in production. Producer surplus consists of economic rents accruing to input owners and gross profits accruing to firms. As an example, image farmers that own land of different productive qualities. The most fertile land earns the most rent because with the same inputs, it yields a larger harvest. The marginal producer is likely located on the least fertile land. If prices drop, the marginal producer would

---

[3]Zero economic profit is not akin to simple (accounting) profit being zero. In the common, man-on-the-street usage of the word, zero profit implies that the firm made no money at all. Zero economic profit, on the other hand, means that all factors of production received an efficient payment for their services that will equal the precise opportunity costs of those services. Wages for workers, rent for landowners, interest for capital owners, and a normal profit for the entrepreneur means that no member of the firm loses out in pay. And if research and development (R&D) were a part of the legitimate production efforts on the part of all firms in the model, those efforts would have been paid for as well. Technically though, the perfectly competitive model is not usually adapted to allow for the growth effects that R&D would bring. It is far simpler to leave the model as static. Indeed, in a static model, if all members of the firm receive sufficient pay, any excess profits beyond that must be looked upon as useless from the firm's, and from the economy's, vantage points.

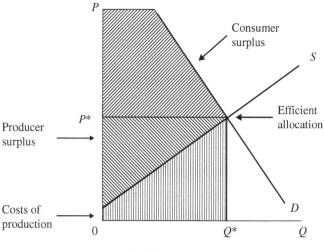

Figure 7.7.

have to cease production, but the farmer on the best land would simply earn less rent and would continue to produce at the new lower market price. The costs of production are the factors that are consumed in the production of the quantity Q^*. This is a measure of the real resources consumed.

Monopoly

The polar opposite of the perfectly competitive model is the monopoly model where instead of many firms there is only one firm — the monopolist. Monopoly power comes from barriers to entry that stop other firms from competing with the monopoly. These barriers can be natural or governmental. "Natural barriers" involve such things as a firm having sole ownership of a critical resource for the production process or a firm possessing large economies of scale.[4] Typically, such enterprises have very high capital costs such that the ATCs are declining throughout the relevant demand. As the firm expands its sales its costs keep falling. Thus competing firms keep merging until only one is left. Utilities like gas, electrical and water distribution are typically cited as examples of natural monopolies.

---

[4]Not everyone agrees that natural monopolies exist. For example, see DiLorenzo, Thomas J. "The Myth of Natural Monopoly." *Review of Austrian Economics* Vol. 9, No. 2 (1996), 43–58.

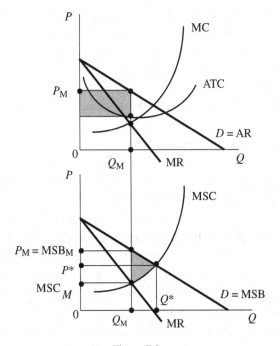

Figure 7.8.

Governmental barriers that create monopolies involve patent protec-tion, licenses, or patronage.[5] Of course, businesses also tried to create cartels before anti-combines legislation made this illegal. A famous example is the Standard Oil Company created by John D. Rockefeller. Unlike a natural monopoly, the ATC curves of these artificial monopolies are upward sloping. As illustrated in Figure 7.8, the monopolist restricts output to force up prices such that they can maximize profits. This contrasts with the perfectly competitive firm that takes the price set in the industry as given. As a result, the monopolist does not bring about the efficiency found in perfect competition.

The monopolist, as shown in the first panel, finds the quantity where MR = MC as would a perfectly competitive firm. But, unlike the perfectly

---

[5]In some cases, a government monopoly may be in the form of a cartel that has many firms, but operates under output quotas and regulated prices. Taxi services are in many cities operate on this basis.

competitive firm, the monopolist is able to charge the highest price consumers are willing to pay for that quantity. Thus, the price–quantity combination chosen is P_M and Q_M. As seen in the figure, this monopolist is making an economic profit equal to the shaded rectangle. So long as AR exceeds ATC at the monopolist's chosen quantity, economic profits will occur. Note that nothing stops the monopolist from making positive economic profits in the short run or long run because there are no competitive forces to drive them down to zero.

A monopolist will never achieve economic efficiency in the way all perfectly competitive firms would. The social loss due to monopolization is shown in the second panel of Figure 7.8. In this case, we wish to show the loss of efficiency as far as society is concerned. To do this requires a couple of assumptions. First, the demand curve is looked upon as the marginal social benefit (MSB) received from the various output levels. Second, the cost to the firm is assumed to cover all societal costs in using the resources for production meaning that the MC is now the marginal social cost (MSC). These two assumptions imply that either no *externalities* exist or, if they do, they have all been internalized either through government regulation or *Coasian bargaining*. These topics are addressed in Chapter 8.

In the second panel, it is seen that the chosen quantity, Q_M, occurs where the MSB of the next unit exceeds its MSC. That unit, if produced, yields a net benefit to society. The range of output where MSB > MSC is between Q_M and Q^* meaning that the latter is the socially optimal quantity to produce because MSB = MSC. The price that should be charged for Q^* is P^* because that would mean that the price charged for the last unit exactly corresponded to the cost to society of producing it (i.e., MSC) and the benefit to society in consuming it (i.e., MSB). The shaded area highlights the value of all those quantities where MSB > MSC and represents the efficiency or welfare loss due to monopolization. It should also be noticed that, as compared to the socially optimal price–quantity combination (P^*, Q^*), the monopolist restricts the quantity and raises its price. Of course, the monopolist would have no incentive to achieve the socially optimal solution because he prefers the privately optimal solution as shown in the first panel of Figure 7.8. The monopolist would have to be forced by the government to set (P^*, Q^*) or else be taken over and nationalized by the government.

Keywords

allocative efficiency   economic profit   producer surplus
consumer sovereignty   externalities   productive efficiency
consumer surplus   perfect competition   property rights

Exercises

1. In highly competitive markets, businesses like trucking companies are price takers and have very similar costs.

   During recessionary periods, prices can fall to the place where it no longer makes sense to continue, and companies will stop operations. Draw and explain an appropriate economic model(s) that illustrate(s) how highly competitive businesses, like truckload truckers could reach this point. The application of monopoly theory also depends on the validity of the assumptions. While monopolies created by governmental barriers, like patent laws, may fit most of the assumptions, for many forms of transportation local monopolies are more likely to be observed than total monopolies. The reason is intermodal competition. Pipelines have to compete with railways, and railways have to compete with trucks and barges. Nonetheless, a coal mine served by a single railway could face a local monopoly, or be a *captive shipper*.

   Even in the case of captive shippers, the railway may not be able to extract the full degree of its potential economic profits because of product competition. If freight rates are too high, the coal mine could become uncompetitive with alternative sources of supply. As world markets become more integrated, competition is evolving into one supply chain versus another. This reality has tempered the need for governments to intervene on behalf of society to correct for welfare losses associated with monopoly power.

   Economists like competitive markets like trucking, because they generate productive and allocative efficiency. Explain what is meant by these concepts.

2. Canada has thousands of large and small trucking companies, but only two national railways (i.e., CN Rail and CP Rail).

   Draw and use appropriate model(s) to explain how competition affects allocative and productive efficiency in trucking and rail.

What could the government do to obtain allocative or productive efficiency in the railway industry, and what would be the benefit?

3. The railways have monopoly power, at least in some parts of their network. The government recognizes that letting the railway operate as a monopoly achieves neither allocative efficiency, nor productive efficiency. They would like to enforce MC pricing, but are loath to begin subsidizing the railway.

Draw and explain an appropriate model(s) that illustrates the efficiency problem, and outline the options that may be open to the government.

Explain the method for dealing with the lack of rail competition in Canada where we have two railways serving most urban centers.

Chapter 8

Externalities, Public Supply and Marginal Cost Pricing

The history of transportation is replete with public policy swings between periods of economic regulation, subsidies and other interventions, and periods of *laissez faire competition*. Unlike production processes that can be designed to maximize efficiency, transportation supply is a combination of private sector and public sector investments. In general the public sector provides the long lived fixed infrastructure, while the private sector provides the mobile assets that can be quickly depreciated.

Some factors of production are treated as if their supply is infinite and they have a zero price. Anyone is welcome to use as much of these inputs as they wish with no concern about the future or the consumption of any other individual. Although the situation is changing, until recent times, this is how clean air and water were used in production processes. Evidence of climate change and the visible deterioration of fresh water lakes and ground water have forced society to reassess how public goods are used that are not part of the firm's ordinary accounting.

The full costs of transportation are not borne by the private sector. The transportation industry accounts for approximately 25% of all Greenhouse Gas (GHG) emissions that impact air quality and potentially climate change. In addition, the by-products of transportation supply can include noise, water pollution, vibration, visual intrusion and vehicle crash victims.[1] This chapter discusses these external costs and public intervention in the supply of transportation. The principles of marginal cost pricing are also reviewed in the context of transportation provision.

---

[1] A discussion of the full costs of transportation is provided in Gillen *et al.* "Trying to Put the "Full" in the Full Costs of Transport." *Canadian Transportation Research Forum, Annual Proceedings*, Vol. 41 (2006), 433–447.

Social Costs and Benefits

All of the costs discussed so far have been internal to the firm except for the external costs that lead to economies of scale, but even these are costs that are related to other firms within the industry or to the infrastructure upon which the industry relies. There are however, a whole set of costs of production that the firm(s) may not even be aware of. The distinction here is that the costs looked at so far have been private costs and the remaining set of costs to be examined is known as external costs. Because these costs of a firm's production derive from external sources beyond the industry, they are referred to as externalities. An externality occurs when the actions of one or more persons or firms have an indirect effect on the well-being of another person or firm and this indirect effect is not transmitted through the price mechanism (i.e., the private market).

An economist is interested in the valuation of externalities because they help one define the true social costs and true social benefits of production over the whole of society. Figure 8.1 presents the model of marginal social costs (MSCs) and benefits. The MSC are the sum of the marginal private costs (MPC) and the external costs that result from human activity. The MPC can be interpreted as a "renaming" of the supply curve. Similarly, the marginal private benefits (MPB) can be interpreted as a "renaming" of

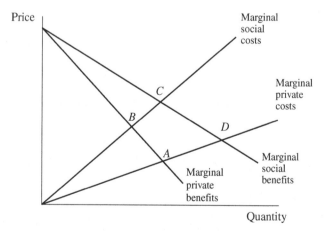

Figure 8.1.

the demand curve. The marginal social benefits (MSB) are the sum of the MPB and any positive externalities.

If there are neither positive, nor negative externalities the optimal position for the economy would be at **A** where MPC = MPB, our familiar equilibrium of supply and demand.

If negative externalities are created by this activity, but no positive externalities, then the optimal equilibrium shifts to point B, where MSC = MPB. This means that the price of the activity should rise (through taxes or other means), and the quantity produced and consumed should fall.

If only positive externalities are produced, the incentives of the private market may be insufficient to produce at the optimal point **D**, where MPC = MSB. A public contribution may be warranted in the form of a subsidy or infrastructure provision to more output at a higher price.

If both positive and negative externalities exist, they may be offsetting, such that a point **C** becomes the equilibrium where MSC = MSB. In practice, many forms of transport operate with both positive and negative externalities.

Let us examine the type of negative externalities that create a difference in the social costs of production versus the private cost whereby the former exceeds the latter. Examples of negative externalities in a transportation context, include: the effect of the noise from airplanes that create a nuisance for homeowners that may live close to the airport; rush hour motorists that create road congestion that delays truck shipping thereby adding to the latter's costs; a railway that decides to close down unprofitable branch lines with the result that towns along those lines face increased costs in using alternative bulk shipping and travel modes; and a ship captain that decides to flush out his ballast tanks and leaves a slick of diesel fuel on the ocean. In general, the creators of the negative externality do not have any malicious intent. The costs they impose on some other part of society are an unintended by-product of their economic activity.

When a positive externality results the social benefits of production may exceed private benefits. We are not as likely to recognize the positive externalities of transport, but some do exist. Examples of positive externalities would include: a lowering of bus fares leading to more bus usage and less congestion for cars that remain on the road; the introduction of mandatory seatbelt usage reducing the number of accident injuries thereby allowing government to lower taxes earmarked for public health care (note that this effect ignores the *moral hazard* problem to be covered in Chapter 14); the building of a new airport facility leading to the improvement in business prospects for all the firms in the area; and the increased national security that results from better transportation infrastructure to move emergency services and armed forces for disaster relief. Some positive externalities exist as an unintended side-benefit of another activity, but unlike negative externalities, there is a role for public intervention to enhance output beyond the activity that the private market would naturally provide.

The essence of externalities is that their creator does not include them in his calculation of the costs and benefits of production because such costs and benefits are not built into the price system. The trucking firm does not charge motorists on the highway for the costs of shipping delays meaning that the motorists have no incentive to consider the full social cost of their action. Certainly the motorists calculate the cost of their fuel while idling on the crowded roadway and consider the opportunity cost of the time delay; but all of these are only the private costs. The negative externality goes un-priced. Similarly, a mining company that contemplates building the new port in a remote area does not go to the existing communities in the area demanding a contribution to its costs because they would have better access to emergency supplies. Because of the futility in doing this, the mining company does not consider the extra social benefits created by the port; they would only think of the return to their investment in building the docks, which yield a private benefit. The problem, then, is to get the externality creators to consider the full social costs (benefits) of the negative (positive) externalities they create.

Taking the social cost aspects of negative externalities into account, some recommendations can be brought forward. If the negative externality means that an individual or firm is imposing a cost on society and is not considering that cost as a legitimate cost of operation, the government can create the incentive for the individual or firm to take into account that cost over and above the private costs. Consider automobile use in a residential area. The private cost is the fuel, time, insurance and maintenance costs while the extra costs to form the remainder of the social costs are borne by the residents in the form of air and noise pollution.

The government may come to realize that because motorists do not take full account of the costs of driving, a tax should be imposed on motorists. The tax may be levied on fuel or may be in the form of a surcharge levied on insurance premiums or licenses. In any case, the optimal levy is equal to the monetary cost of the negative effects of driving that the residents are suffering. Of course, the government assessing the proper value for these items is not easy.[2] Suffice it to say, a tax of some kind will lead to a lesser amount of driving thus leading to an elimination somewhat of the negative externality. Figure 8.2 shows this result in diagram form.

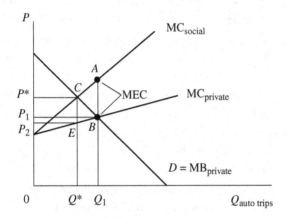

Figure 8.2.

---

[2]While assessing the value of these external costs is not easy, the tax or surcharge levy is not straightforward either. The tax or surcharge must only hit the externality creator. Certainly rural drivers are lesser creators of the external costs of driving than are urban drivers. In this way, the optimal levy should not be uniform across all drivers.

The external costs may be constant over all marginal users, in which case a unit-tax or surcharge is reasonable. However, the external costs may rise with each marginal creator (as shown in Figure 8.2) in which case either a tax on value (*ad valorem*) or graduated user fee may be desirable. Still, if the amount of driving were the true indicator of its external costs, a fuel tax would be superior to a surcharge on insurance premiums or licenses. Of course, road tolls are directly related to the amount of driving as well and represent a user-fee alternative to fuel taxes. In fact, a toll may take into account such things as the number of passengers in the car — an incentive for car-pooling. Such an incentive is not as easily created by a fuel tax. A toll officer at the tollbooth can assess several attributes of the vehicles gaining admittance to the road while a tax at the pump is essentially blind.

The demand curve is the MPB that motorists receive from taking various numbers of trips down the road in question over a specific period of time (say, per year). It is called the MPB because it represents the monetary value of each extra trip taken by the motorist. And the curve is downward sloping due to the concept of *diminishing marginal utility* meaning that the first trip is more valuable than the second, which is more valuable than the third, etc. The motorist, taking only the private costs of his actions into account, faces the MPC curve and it is upward sloping because we can consider the motorist to be facing higher maintenance and insurance costs for each extra trip taken. The market mechanism leads to an amount of trips equal to Q_1 at a cost of P_1 to the motorist. But, if the motorist were to consider the further social costs for each trip taken, the marginal cost curve would shift upward to the position of the MSC curve. These extra or marginal external costs (MEC) to society amount to the monetary difference between A and B at the privately chosen quantity Q_1.

If the government imposed a tax or user fee equal to the difference between these two curves at any other quantity, the motorist would end up choosing the quantity Q^* at a cost of P^* which happens to be the socially optimal quantity. At that point the MSC of the last trip chosen equals its marginal benefit and there is no reason to deviate from that point. In this sense we see how the government can solve the externality problem. It is also worth noting that the government collects a tax equal to P^*CEP_2 that can be used to mitigate the harmful the harmful effects of the negative externality and the *deadweight welfare loss* represented by the area ABC.

One of the problems inherent in public action is the question of whether a negative externality is real or merely pecuniary. While trucks and cars share the roadway it is a matter of context to properly define the type of externality that is taking place. If one considers the movement cars and trucks to be part of different market transactions then each vehicle-type's presence on the roadway acts as a third-party with respect to the other meaning that congestion caused by trucks is indeed a negative real externality as far as car travel is concerned, and vice versa. If one wishes to consider the relevant market to be the services of the roadway itself then indeed both cars and trucks are part of the same market meaning that the effect of congestion from one vehicle-type to another is not a true externality but rather a *pecuniary externality*. In that sense, each is not really a third party to the other and there is no deadweight loss.[3]

To make the distinction between real and pecuniary externalities clearer consider that a line of cars ahead of another at a toll gate is a source of a negative pecuniary externality for the latter because of the delay caused while, in contrast, a delay caused by a flock of ducks crossing the road would be a source of a negative real externality.

Governments have difficulty in properly assessing the value of real externalities in order to levy an appropriate tax. The government may not be as effective in finding out the position of the MSC curve as would be the residents themselves. Sometimes it is possible for the private market to solve the externality problem. This is the essence of the *Coase Theorem*, which specifies that a market to solve the externality problem may in fact exist.[4]

What is required for the private solution to the externality problem is: (1) property rights are well-defined; (2) transactions costs involved in negotiating a solution are nonexistent; (3) the number of players involved in the negotiation is not too large. If these three points are satisfied, we can return to the previous example and Figure 8.2 to see how the Coase Theorem may apply. Let us say that the residents have the legal right to clean air and no noise. Because the motorist would be violating that right the residents would charge him the monetary value of that cost given the number of trips he chooses. Thus, the motorist is charged an amount equal to the line segment AB (which was exactly equal to the tax that the government would have charged). The driver would respond by cutting back his trips until the MSC equaled the marginal benefit leading again to the optimal number of trips (Q^*). He cuts back because he would not pay this charge on Q_1 because his total cost (inclusive of the charge), AQ_1, exceeds his benefit, BQ_1.

---

[3]The wear-and-tear on the common roadway, potentially affecting the maintenance costs of car owners when they happen to use that road, may be taken to be another negative pecuniary externality caused by all road users on themselves.

[4]A straightforward yet thorough discussion of what the Coase Theorem means for economic theory is found in: Coase, R. *The Firm, the Market and the Law*. Chicago: University of Chicago Press, 1990. Suffice it to say that Coase's analysis is far richer than the simple Coase Theorem to which he is often associated.

But, there is an important twist that the Coase Theorem brings about: suppose that the motorist now has the right to use the road as he wishes. In this case, the residents could pay the motorist an amount up to the value of line segment AB at his privately chosen quantity so as not to take that marginal trip, Q_1. Would the motorist accept that "bribe"? Only if that amount exceeded his net benefit from taking the Q_1^{th} trip. And it does. The motorist's net benefit at Q_1 is the difference between his MPCs and benefits. Because that difference is zero, any bribe will induce him to forego that trip. A bribe will be forthcoming until the quantity of trips drop to the optimal level ($Q*$). Notice that under the Coase Theorem, property rights, while being well-defined, need not be allocated to any particular person or group for the optimal result to occur. Having property rights well-defined simply creates an anchor upon which the negotiation process may take place.

Bear in mind that the Coase Theorem is an abstraction from reality in that, in the real world, the number of affected residents may be so large as to make negotiation very time consuming; in fact, the arrangement of the negotiation process is a transaction cost that is likely to be substantial. These points, however, do not mean that a private solution is impossible; it just means that the initial allocation of property rights will be pivotal and that the process will be more complex.

Public Supply

The previous section showed that the government might be able to correct the externality problem and allow a socially optimal result to occur. The issue of government presence and intervention in any industry is important because the government does not have to play by the same rules as do private firms. A public solution to motorists' externalities is "road pricing". With the advance of electronics, passive toll collectors can be set up to manage specific links in a network, or a geographically defined area. Conceptually, these tolls can be applied on a continuously changing pattern to charge for the supply of cars in excess of $Q*$ (in Figure 8.2). These ideas have generally been resisted by politicians because new taxes are seldom popular.[5]

---

[5]The toll system that was enacted by the City of London to manage traffic in their central business district is an interesting example that is being watched internationally.

The government, due to its power to tax and, in the case of the federal government, to print money means it need not worry about going bankrupt or having to turn a profit. The goal of a private firm is, we assume, simple profit maximization in which sense we assume that firms are interested in achieving efficiency first and foremost. It may be surprising but government's goal in engaging in the provision of goods and services is not just for the attainment of efficiency; rather, a conflicting goal of equity or fairness to society at large is its other desire. Of course, the definition of fairness is a value judgment and fairness is gained at the expense of efficiency and vice versa.

In the transportation industry, government's presence is seen in the form of: Taxes levied on the providers and users of transport services; regulations designed to control how the services are provided; provision of certain transportation infrastructure through public works projects; and direct ownership of certain transportation facilities. There is a public and private sector mix in transportation in the sense that, for example, private trucking firms and bus companies use publicly provided and maintained road systems and private airlines make use of public airspace. Is there an optimal public and private sector mix? An attempt to answer this question is provided in Chapter 13.

The government may regulate or take over an industry if evidence of either destructive competition or monopolization can be found. Of course, some governments as a matter of national pride wish to maintain control of "key" sectors for political gain; but the era of nationalization of industries is long-gone. Nevertheless, most urban transit bus systems in North America continue to be operated as public monopolies. The rationale for government oversight of monopolies was presented in Chapter 7.

Under destructive competition firms may be cutting corners in their production processes in order to undercut their competitors by offering lower prices. Of course, there are two effects to this strategy: (1) the quality of the product may be curtailed to the point of it being hazardous; and (2) this drive to undercut means that only the leanest and most aggressive firms will survive, which leaves the industry with only a few firms that may wish to begin to raise prices as would a monopoly. Such an industry would lead to instability with respect to employment in the remaining firms. The government could forestall these consequences by regulating the industry with specific standards that put a floor on quality levels and requiring the application of operating licenses that grant entry only to firms that can show evidence that they are serious contenders in the market and not so-called "fly-by-night" operations.

The government is also required to provide public goods because the marketplace will not properly price such non-excludable goods. Airspace is definitely a public good and it is probably a good thing that parcels of airspace are not auctioned off to private airlines. While the government does not actually provide the airspace, it does set regulations as to how aircraft are to conduct themselves during flight.

Private firms could provide certain infrastructure such as roads, if they could charge user fees in the form of a toll and make road access excludable. The owners of the road would need enough traffic to give them the necessary toll revenue to achieve a positive return on their investment. This might be feasible for major highway segments, but tolls would not support the cost of lightly-used rural roads. The benefit of a viable agricultural sector justifies the public provision of these roadways.

Marginal and Average Cost Pricing

It was shown in the previous chapter that a monopoly would not achieve economic efficiency if it acted based on private initiative. The second panel of Figure 7.8 showed that the socially optimal situation was where MSB = MSC and while it is quite true, one may notice that allocative efficiency is achieved because the price is equated with the marginal cost; but productive efficiency is not unless the ATC curve crosses right through the point where MSB and MSC intersect. In fact, if ATC happened to be above that intersection point the monopolist would be making a loss.

This becomes an issue for the government that needs to live with natural monopolies, like public utilities, because this is the only way of creating the industry. For example, it would make no sense to have three sets of electrical transmission systems serving the same area, just for the sake of competition.[6] So the question becomes one of regulating a natural

---

[6]It is worth noting that "natural barriers" that create such monopolies are subject to change as technology advances. For example, telephone systems were considered to be natural monopolies prior to wireless cellphone technology emerged. While the network benefits

monopoly so that either: (1) a socially optimal solution is reached; or (2) the monopolist is given a "fair return". The choice one makes in this regard highlights the difference between marginal cost pricing and *average cost pricing*.

Marginal cost pricing involves the setting of price equal to the MSC of provision for the last unit provided. In the second panel of Figure 7.8, $P*$ is the price set in this regard when the firm is a monopoly. A way to establish the societal gains that accrue when a monopoly is required is to mandate marginal cost pricing. $P*$ in Figure 8.3 represents the regulated marginal cost price forced on the monopoly. For ease in labeling, the MSC curve is drawn as a horizontal line indicating, of course, the presence of scale economies associated with a natural monopoly.

The unregulated firm wishes to maximize its profits, while the government that either owns the monopoly or regulates it would rather maximize *total social welfare* (TSW) defined as:

$$\text{TSW} = \text{TR} + \text{CS} - \text{TSC}, \qquad (8.1)$$

where TR = total revenue; CS = consumer surplus; and TSC = total social cost.

Thus, TSW at the chosen price and quantity is the total social benefits accruing to the firm and the consumers minus the cost to society in producing that quantity. Marginal cost pricing serves to maximize TSW. The first panel of Figure 8.3 shows that, by plugging in the appropriate values, TSW under monopoly pricing is:

$$P_M b Q_M 0 + ab P_M - P^* d Q_M 0 = abd P^*.$$

While under marginal cost pricing TSW is:

$$P^* c Q^* 0 + ac P^* - P^* c Q^* 0 = ac P^*.$$

---

of cellphone company towers do limit the number of competitors, multiple companies can operate competitively. Similarly, the railways were monopolies when they first emerged, and even with multiple rail companies, the railway would still have parts of its network in which it enjoyed an absolute monopoly of service. With the advent of tractor-trailer trucks and paved highways, intermodal competition reduced the number of shippers for which the railway was the only choice. Consequently, it is debatable to what degree the railways can still be considered natural monopolies, except for a few captive shippers, usually raw material producers like coal and grain.

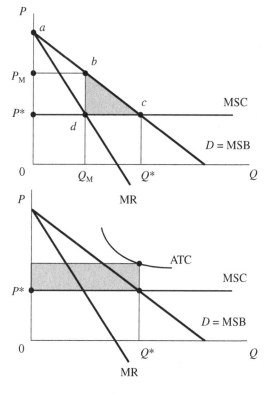

Figure 8.3.

The TSW is higher under marginal cost pricing by (*bcd*) which is the welfare loss due to monopoly already discussed. The second panel in Figure 8.3 shows what the average total cost curve would look like under economies of scale. It can be seen that the monopoly would suffer a loss equal to the shaded area if marginal cost pricing were used. In other words, what is socially optimal is not privately feasible in this case. The government would have to either subsidize the firm or nationalize it and use general tax revenues to cover the loss.

Let us suppose that the government institutes a policy of adopting marginal cost pricing. There would be a few problems to be worked out. The first is to make sure that the marginal costs used by the firm included all social costs meaning that all negative externalities must be either internalized through property rights or taxed at appropriate rates.

Another problem involves the choice between long run costs and short run costs. Should long run or short run marginal costs be used in the marginal cost pricing exercise? The problem is that the short run costs exist under a fixed capacity of production given that we assume capital to be fixed. In the long run, costs may be higher as firms bid up the cost of capital during expansions.[7] It is important to distinguish between long run and short run marginal cost pricing because all modes of transport face some capacity constraint in the short run.

It seems that short run costs exist below long run costs leading to different prices being set under marginal cost pricing. It turns out, as shown in Figure 8.4, that the market will take care of marginal cost pricing under short run and long run conditions.

$SRMC_1$ is drawn such that costs are constant up to the capacity constraint at Q_1; thereafter, costs are infinite during the short run. LRMC is drawn higher than SRMC because we are assuming that there are extra costs involved in capacity expansion. Using SRMC, marginal cost pricing

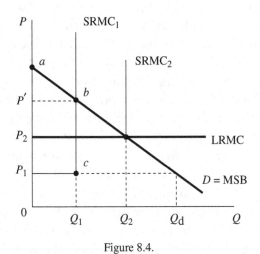

Figure 8.4.

---

[7]While "lumpiness" was discussed in Chapter 3, the further idea of a capacity constraint is something that is unique to the areas of infrastructure and transportation. As well, having SRMC< LRMC shows the typical economies of scale discussion of that chapter to be somewhat simplistic. Whereas it was shown that the optimal scale was determined at the minimum SRATC in the set, Figure 4.8 shows that the demand curve actually plays a role in the determination of optimal scale.

would dictate that a price of P_1 in the short run be charged for all output forthcoming which, of course, leads to excess demand equal to $Q_d - Q_1$. In this case price is set equal to marginal cost but note that price does not equal the MSB at Q_1. Instead, excess demand has to be gotten rid of through rationing of the output. The MSB received from Q_1 is equal to the price set at P_1'.

Comparing TSW under the two choices, using Equation (8.1), gives:

Short run MC-pricing with rationing:

$$P_1 c Q_1 0 + abc P_1 - P_1 c Q_1 0 = abc P_1.$$

Short run MC-pricing with no rationing:

$$P_1' b Q_1 0 + ab P_1' - P_1 c Q_1 0 = abc P_1.$$

TSW is identical in both cases but the no rationing result is advantageous because: (1) it allows the firm to make more revenue; (2) it allows all consumers able to obtain the Q_1 units to pay amounts closer to their MSB; (3) the consumers that would have entered the market if the price were P_1 no longer feel the need to do so; and (4) the extra revenue earned provides an incentive for firms to expand capacity in the long run.

In the long run, the firm expands output to Q_2 as given by LRMC. The price set at P_2 allows for marginal cost pricing to occur without the need for rationing. One point to note about long run marginal cost pricing is that, while LRMC is technologically fixed, the optimal quantity is thus demand determined in which case indivisibilities (or lumpiness) in such things as ocean vessel capacity or airport size may not allow Q_2 to be reached exactly. Thus, the firm and/or government have to decide whether the sub-optimality is lessened by over-capacity or under-capacity in the long run.

A further case of marginal cost pricing for consideration involves the situation where capacity is not continuously used. The indivisibilities in the capacity infrastructure are compounded by peak and off-peak utilization. This makes the provision of infrastructure similar to the joint product problem. This case is certainly true with respect to transport equipment such as railcar and trailer fleets as well as terminal and port facilities. Suppose that LRMC indicates a particular capacity (Q^*) that is not technically possible; rather available capacity choices involve ones that are either slightly greater

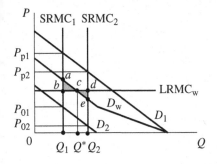 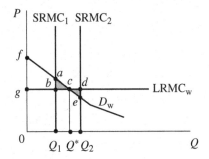

Figure 8.5.

(Q_2) or slightly smaller (Q_1). The question becomes whether to over-provide or under-provide. The first panel in Figure 8.5 illustrates the problem.

The peak (D_1) and off-peak (D_2) demand curves are averaged according to their share of utilization to form the *weighted demand curve* D_w. If the area of triangle *abc* is greater than that for triangle *cde* then capacity Q_2 is preferred to Q_1. The second panel of Figure 8.4 shows why. The area *fcg* is the consumer surplus that accrues if Q^* capacity occurred; but because it cannot, consumer surplus for the lesser Q_1 amounts to *fabg* which thus foregoes *abc* while consumer surplus for the greater Q_2 amounts to *fcg–cde*. The *cde* portion is subtracted because in the range of Q^* to Q_2, LRMC exceeds the marginal benefits as given by D_w meaning that consumers face a negative surplus in that range. Producer surplus is zero because LRMC is a horizontal line. Thus, if *abc* > *cde* then the consumer surplus foregone at Q_1 exceeds the negative surplus that must be sustained at Q_2 meaning the latter is a more efficient capacity level than is the former.

The change in prices evident in the first panel of Figure 8.5 suggests the cost of providing the greater social benefit. Prices fall in both the peak and off-peak periods. The lost revenue in the peak appears to be made up in the additional volume of passengers. In the off-peak however, the lower prices are firmly in the inelastic portion of the demand curve, and total revenue would be lower at the higher capacity level. This could be less than the variable costs of production such that in the off-peak the operator will choose to charge a higher price, like P_{01} and idle capacity equal to Q_2-Q_1. This topic is revisited in Chapter 9.

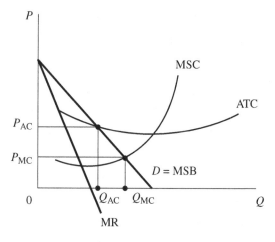

Figure 8.6.

If for some reason the government wishes to regulate the monopoly but not wish it to make losses due to, perhaps, political difficulties involved in extra taxation to pay for subsidies, a compromise in the form of average cost pricing may be possible. In this situation the firm is allowed to make a "fair return" in that it makes zero economic profits. Remember that zero economic profit means that there is merely no excess over and above the payments to the factors of production used — a firm does not suffer when they are zero. Figure 8.6 shows how average cost pricing works.

Price P_{AC} along with output Q_{AC} gives the firm this "fair return" but social optimality is not achieved, as it would be under marginal cost pricing (P_{MC}). Between Q_{AC} and the larger quantity produced under marginal cost pricing, Q_{MC}, MSB > MSC meaning that some consumers are willing to pay more than the cost of provision of the extra output but they are priced out of the market.

As it happens, even a compromise between MC- and AC-pricing exists in that the firm may institute a two-part pricing policy. The important point is that the loss that would otherwise occur from MC-pricing, if the firm faces falling average costs, will be covered by some of the consumers as opposed to government. Instituting two prices for the same good is a form of *price discrimination* of which more will be said in Chapter 10. An example of two-part pricing is shown in Figure 8.7.

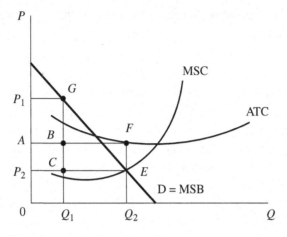

Figure 8.7.

The lower MC-price of P_2 is charged to the "marginal users" while the higher price of P_1 is charged to those consumers with higher willingness to pay. The high price payers subsidize the firm so that it may charge a low price to the marginal users. These marginal users demand (Q_2-Q_1), which generates a loss of BCEF. The profit the firm receives from the high price set up to the Q_1 quantity is P_1GBA. This is so because the average total cost of the entire output provided (Q_2) is given by point A and AB$Q_1$0 is the total cost of the Q_1 portion of this total quantity and P_1G$Q_1$0 is the corresponding total revenue leaving the above noted profit.

The trick for the regulator, who allows for this pricing policy, is to make sure that the firm sets Q_1 such that the P_1GBA profits do not more than cover the BCEF losses. As well, the firm has to be able to split up its set of consumers that demand its output into high and low demanders. In other words, the high price can be charged to users with relatively price-inelastic demands because the percentage fall in their quantity demanded is compensated by a larger percentage rise in the price meaning that total revenue rises. The transport firm has to figure out which group of users is the more dependent upon its services, but also bear in mind who has the ability to pay. In this regard, a railway may charge lower prices per weight class to bulk shippers and save the higher charges for manufactured goods shippers; and airlines may charge higher prices to business flyers and lower ones to casual flyers.

Keywords

average cost pricing	diminishing marginal	moral hazard
Coase Theorem	utility	pecuniary externality
Coasian bargaining	laissez faire	price discrimination
deadweight welfare	competition	total social welfare
loss	monopoly	weighted demand curve

Exercises

1. An individual can use the court system to obtain compensation from a neighbor, if the neighbor's actions cause a loss in their property value. For example, if the neighbor constructs a new building that blocks the entrance to their property. However, individuals cannot use the court system for compensation for damages suffered from the air pollution created by passing cars.

   Draw a model of the impact of air pollution caused by cars and trucks, and explain why the government must play a role in defending individuals from this loss of air quality.

   Explain why it may be unnecessary for the government to be involved with the problems of traffic congestion that car and truck drivers impose on each other.

2. Setting prices equal to marginal cost is necessary to achieve allocative efficiency. This result is obtained in highly competitive markets, but in some cases where natural monopolies or other market failures exist, the government must use regulatory powers to set prices.

   Draw and explain an appropriate model(s) that illustrates the problems with implementing marginal cost pricing for regulated industries.

   Explain the other options that are open to governments when marginal cost pricing is not feasible.

3. The use of an automobile is paid for by the individual owners. In addition to these private costs, automobiles also create noise and air quality externalities. Environmentalists would like a carbon tax to be imposed

on fossil fuel consumption to reduce air pollution and slow climate change.

Draw and explain an appropriate model(s) that illustrates the rationale for imposing an additional charge on car drivers, and illustrate how large this carbon tax would have to be to arrive at a social optimum.

Explain how a change in the price of gasoline (up or down) would have an impact, if any, on the optimal value of the carbon tax.

Chapter 9

Spatial and Temporal Pricing in Transportation

Pricing in transportation is complex because the market is influenced by differences in time, location and cargo value. In addition, transport services are capital intensive, energy dependent and offered in a less than perfectly competitive market. As a result, freight rates vary between the maximum value of the service provided and the minimum cost of providing the service. Value of service pricing is often referred to as "charging what the market will bear". This can also be thought of as demand-based pricing, and applies in situations in which the carrier enjoys a "seller's market". Sometimes, however, the carrier faces a "buyer's market" in which freight rates are depressed by a surfeit of vehicle supply. The question then becomes how much of the carrier's costs can be obtained from the market. Such freight rates can range from fully allocated costs to just "out-of-pocket" costs.

The factors of production influencing the costs of transportation service have been discussed. This chapter considers the demand side of transportation pricing in which conditions of space and time determine carrier strategies.

Fronthaul and Backhaul Pricing

Practically all transportation services provided by the various modes require the operator and/or his equipment to return to the point of origin. While passenger travel usually requires round trips, the transport of freight does not. Convention labels the direction of trade with the greater derived demand as the fronthaul; the direction with the lesser volume of trade is the backhaul. The carrier is forced to consider the nature of a secondary backhaul market.

In the transport of freight, carriers try to find shipments to haul back to their point of origin, or the next destination on their route, as opposed to returning empty. In the absence of a backhaul, the fronthaul shipper must absorb the entire round trip costs. The availability of a backhaul shipper may reduce the costs of the fronthaul shipper, but not necessarily. It depends on the backhaul shipper's contribution to the costs incurred by the carrier in sustaining empty backhaul movements. If such a shipment exists, and the terms of its transport are agreeable to both shipper and carrier, it is an efficient use of resources. This section develops an economic model of backhaul pricing that explains the shares of the round-trip paid by the origin and destination shippers.

In Figure 9.1, the interregional model (from Chapter 3) is expanded to consider reciprocal trade. Region A is the exporter of product we now label as f and the importer of a product b. Region B is its sole trading partner. The excess supply and demand curves trace out a derived demand for the movement of product b in the opposite direction of product f. The question arises: will the freight rate to carry products from A to B equal the freight rate to carry products from B to A? Inspection of the diagram would suggest that this is not the case. The derived demand for transporting b to A is less than the derived demand for transporting f to B. Assuming products f and

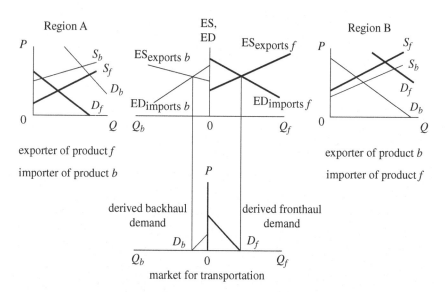

Figure 9.1.

b can use the same means of transport, more vehicles will be required to ship product f from A to B, than to ship product b from B to A.

The fronthaul movement of a vehicle leads to one, and only one, backhaul movement. The fronthaul is always assumed to be full; the backhaul may or may not be an empty haul along the return path. The production of a round trip is an example of what an economist calls *joint production* because the proportion of these two hauls are fixed at one to one. We can now return to the interregional trade model and consider the backhaul demand in this market.

For convenience, the fronthaul and backhaul derived demand curves in the lower section of Figure 9.1 are drawn on the same graph in Figure 9.2. The fronthaul demand (D_f) is assumed to exceed the backhaul demand (D_b) because the former represents the primary market for freight transport as far as the carrier is concerned. It is also the case that the backhaul demand is more price-elastic than is the fronthaul demand for any given price because the former curve is always below the latter; and this holds no matter what the relative slopes between the two curves might be.

Given a joint production process, a joint demand curve (D_{f+b}) can be formed by vertically summing the two demand curves. The reason for summing vertically is because, for each round trip, the marginal willingness to pay for it is the sum of those willingnesses on the part of both the fronthaul

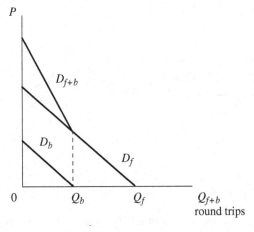

Figure 9.2.

and the backhaul shippers. As seen in the diagram, the joint demand curve is kinked at a quantity corresponding to the maximum quantity in the backhaul demand.

A balance in two-way traffic along a trade route can be skewed by the composition of trade goods. Some products require highly specialized equipment (i.e., refrigerated vehicles, logging trailers, etc.) such that the items to be imported back to the origin may not be conducive to the equipment used on the fronthaul export trip. An example of this is the bulk handling of raw materials like grain, potash and coal. Rail cars generally return empty. Similarly, many bulk ocean carriers travel one way carrying only water ballast.

The model presented in Figure 9.3 assumes a vehicle that has the ability to find loads to carry in both directions. The model shows that some of the fronthaul and backhaul costs of transport may be separated.[1] The marginal costs are taken to be constant for simplicity. Notice that the marginal cost of the fronthaul plus empty backhaul (MC_{f+be}) is distinct from the marginal cost of the loaded backhaul (MC_{bl}).

What would be included in the loaded backhaul costs? Certainly, a loaded vehicle would experience a bit more wear and tear, some extra fuel consumption and additional loading/unloading time, but the greatest

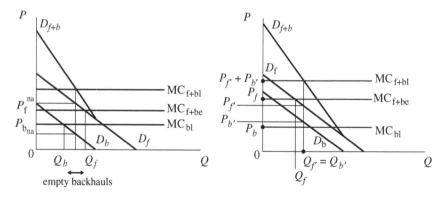

Figure 9.3.

---

[1]This section follows the analysis of: Felton, J. "Impact of ICC Rate Regulation upon Truck Back Hauls." *Journal of Transport Economics and Policy*, Vol. 15, No. 3 (1981), 253–267.

expenses are likely the opportunities foregone and the stand-by costs. If a backhaul load is not immediately available the vehicle and the operator have to wait. The owner may incur out-of-pocket costs for driver meals and accommodation during the dwell time as well as marketing costs to find a return load. The opportunity cost is the alternative use of the vehicle to obtain a higher paying fronthaul load. The time that the vehicle is waiting for a low paying backhaul could be used to return home and pick up another fronthaul load.

The joint demand (D_{f+b}) is the vertical sum of the marginal willingness to pay of the two sets of shippers and this is compared to the total marginal costs of the loaded round trip (MC_{f+bl}). From this joint quantity, the optimal prices for each leg of the trip may be determined by the individual demand curves. The first panel shows that empty backhauls occur because the fronthaul quantity (Q_f) exceeds the loaded backhaul quantity (Q_b).

The marginal cost of the fronthaul and backhaul loaded cannot be divided between the two markets on the basis of their joint demand because of competition. The freight rate required for the fronthaul to compensate for the low rate available for this quantity of loaded returns is not applicable (na). Carriers can obtain a freight rate P_f from the fronthaul market that is equal to the marginal cost of carrying the fronthaul and returning with an empty backhaul (MC_{f+be}). Open competition in the market will force the price down to P_f and Q_f trucks will make the trip.

Similarly, the jointly determined backhaul rate is not applicable (na) because it lies below the marginal costs of taking a backhaul loaded (MC_{bl}). For these backhaul loads, carriers demand at least P_b to offset their marginal costs. Consequently, some carriers will simply take P_f and return empty. The balance of trade is the key to this problem. The traffic flows are too imbalanced for the freight rates to be determined on the basis of the joint demand. The demand for the fronthaul is too strong relative to the backhaul demand.

The second panel illustrates a situation in which the traffic flow is more balanced. In this case, the demand for the backhaul D_b is much closer to the fronthaul demand D_f. Loaded backhaul rates, as determined by the backhaul demand ensure that there are no empty backhauls. In fact competition on the backhaul traffic lane bids up the prices of available trucks from P_b that just covers the marginal cost of the loaded backhaul to P'_b. The quantity of fronthauls and loaded backhauls are equal at Q_f. With the stronger backhaul demand, no carrier can obtain the rate needed to cover the costs of a one way trip (MC_{f+be}) and return empty. The fronthaul rates are bid down from P_f to P'_f.

The second panel illustrates the point that as the traffic lane becomes more balanced, the backhaul shippers begin to carry a larger share of the round-trip costs. Part of the costs of the fronthaul is now being borne by the backhaul shippers because a greater joint quantity is forthcoming and yet nothing has changed in the fronthaul market. By definition, however, the backhaul shippers still pay less than the fronthaul shippers.

It is worth noting that this analysis only deals with the private costs of the carriers and ignores any negative externalities associated with a greater number of empty trucks on the road. Society would gain if an increase in total loaded vehicle-miles occurred. The reduced cost of transport, through a reduction in empty backhauls, would encourage specialization through trade, while fewer vehicles would reduce congestion and air pollution. An empty truck, for example, burns about 95% of the fuel used by a full truck. Filling empty trucks would have a minor impact on air pollution and presumably decrease congestion and traffic accidents.

This model assumes perfect information such that every available truck can locate a waiting load. In reality, more empty trucks return than is necessary to serve the fronthaul demand.[2] Another problem is regulation.

Full exploitation of backhaul markets may be prevented by governmental regulations. Private trucking, where the shipper owns his own truck(s), can fall into this category. Private deliveries are permitted to various destinations but the private carrier license has less flexibility than a for-hire carrier to solicit independent shipments on the backhaul. Another example occurs in international or transborder markets in terms of restrictions on *cabotage*. Cabotage involves the shipping of goods by a foreign carrier solely within the domestic territory of the host country and raises the issue

---

[2]This is another case in which communications and transportation are complementary. Internet services that have emerged since 1990 assist shippers and carriers to locate each other, or to take advantage of brokerage services to book loads. Similarly, satellite linked vehicles can be re-directed more quickly to the source of a backhaul load.

of domestic job protection and other political hot buttons.[3] Of course, an increase in cabotage possibilities would allow the foreign carrier to engage in more activities on the backhaul out of the country in question.

In practice trucking companies often try to avoid a low paying backhaul traffic lane by using a triangular route in which they can obtain better paying loads on three legs of the trip. In the United States, geography and population provides many opportunities for triangular routings, but in Canada the population centers are strung out along the U.S. border. Triangular routes are possible if they include a cross-border Canada–U.S. shipment. Cabotage restrictions limit this option in many transborder markets, but some routes are available. Figure 9.4 illustrates a common example in which Canadian truckers take loads from the Prairies to the U.S. Midwest, then pick up the U.S. loads bound to southern Ontario where they can pick up a load for the return trip to western Canada.

The triangular route allows the Canadian carriers to avoid the western Canada to Ontario traffic lane that is a chronic backhaul market. The Winnipeg to Chicago traffic lane also faces backhaul rates, but it is shorter

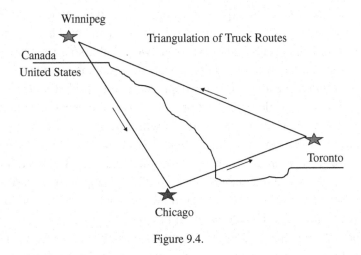

Figure 9.4.

---

[3]Cabotage activities in ocean vessel, airline and trucking activities by foreign carriers are highly regulated by all governments, ostensibly to protect domestic carriers. Stephen Blank and Barry E. Prentice provide a current status of cabotage in North America in "NAFTA at 20: Time to Open the Internal Borders of North America to Cabotage." in *Research in Transportation Business & Management.* 2015.

and the rates are higher than they are north of the Great Lakes. A similar triangular route operates from Canada's Maritime Provinces. Truckers carry seafood and potatoes south to New York, then pick up loads of dry goods and travel northwest to Toronto or Montreal, and finally an eastbound trip back to the Maritimes.

Peak Load Pricing

When demand for a good or service is not uniform over time *peak load pricing* may be used. It is easy to see how the provision of transportation is subject to the peak load problem: urban travel by all modes is subject to daily "rush hours"; and airline usage is higher during special holidays (e.g., Christmas) and the summer months as opposed to autumn and winter giving it what is called seasonality in demand. Of course, all modes of transport face, to varying degrees, peaks and troughs in demand over time due to the cyclical nature of the economy; however, peak load pricing is used in the situation where the variation in demand is systematic on a daily, monthly, or seasonal basis as can be seen from the two examples cited above. Differing time-based demand curves (peak and non-peak) can be modeled similarly to location-based differences such as the fronthaul and backhaul demands.

The problem of peak loads arises from two possible sources. A transport service is supported by public and/or private infrastructure with investments related therein that cannot be easily deployed when a peak disappears; that is, supply is indivisible over short time periods while demand certainly is not. Certain fixed costs in the short run will have to be lived with by the firm during the peak and off-peak periods.[4] Another source of the peak load problem occurs when a particular conveyance (e.g., bus, truck, etc.) faces an unexpected surge in demand. For example, a bumper crop harvest that demands well above average number of rail cars, or a special event, like the Olympics that doubles the demand for urban transport.

Faces an unexpected surge in demand. For example, a bumper crop harvest that demands well above average number of rail cars, or a special event, like the Olympics that doubles the demand for urban transport.

---

[4]When farmers complain, the railways are fond of reminding them that they would not build a church to hold the entire congregation for the Easter service.

Customer Service and Capacity Management given a Seasonal Demand Pattern

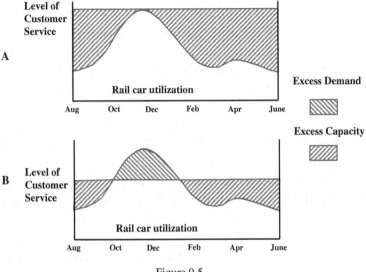

Figure 9.5.

The economic dilemma created by the peak demand is the trade-off between capacity management and customer service. The greater the difference between the peak and the off-peak demand, the more difficult it is to manage the capacity of the supply chain, or deliver consistent levels of customer service. Figure 9.5 presents a model of two levels of customer service and capacity utilization. These diagrams illustrate the seasonal demand pattern for the crop year that begins in August and terminates in July. In model A, capacity is established so that customer service is maximized and consistent throughout the year. However, this also maximizes the cost. The more equipment and crews that are dedicated to serve the peak demand, the more idle equipment and crews remain under-utilized during the balance of the year. The cost of this unused capacity must be financed year-round.

In model B, the capacity is set to meet a "high average demand".[5] During the peak period some shippers receive a lower level of customer service than is experienced by off-peak shippers. However, spreading out

---

[5]The high average demand could represent the mean expected demand plus one standard deviation.

the peak also lowers the cost of providing the service. The quality of customer service that shippers are willing to pay for, and the level of customer service that carriers can afford to offer, is found by the interaction of supply and demand. Typically, the capacity is set to serve a "high average demand" rather than the maximum possible peak demand because shippers are prepared to trade-off a lower level of customer service for a lower price.

The situation becomes more complicated if government regulation or company policy administers a fixed price that ignores market demand. In this case, some method of rationing the scarce supply during the peak period must be used. One option is to offer service on a first-come, first-served allocation basis.

The dilemma posed by ignoring the peak load is illustrated in Figure 9.6. The peak and the off-peak demands are distinct. The administered price is such that during the peak period demand greatly exceeds current capacity. Of course the excess demand leads to continuous complaints from users regarding the fairness of the system and its impact on their efficiency.

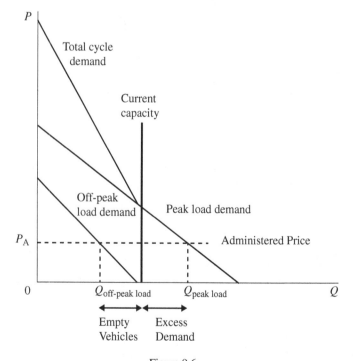

Figure 9.6.

During the off-peak period, the administered price is higher than the equilibrium market clearing price, which in this case would be zero. Consequently, the operator is left with empty vehicles that are parked, or otherwise under-utilized. Now the operator may be criticized for being inefficient. The first-come, first-served allocation policy has another chronic problem that is referred to as "phantom orders". Given that users learn that they may be short of service in the peak load period, they have an incentive to over-order to ensure that they get a sufficient share in the inevitable rationing of supply. The phantom orders provide a misleading signal to the operators regarding the true market demand, and inject a further element of unfairness for those who do not play this game.

The other method of dealing with the peak load demand problem is to use the pricing mechanism to allocate supply.[6] Prices that vary with time periods help moderate the effects of time-dependent demand and allow for the optimal use of a given level of capacity. The economics of using prices to allocate the peak load is illustrated in Figure 9.7.

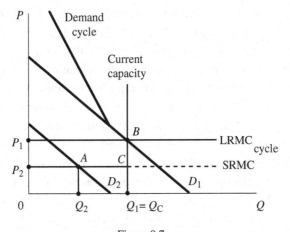

Figure 9.7.

---

[6]Many examples of the two alternatives can be found in transportation. At some airports the power of regulations is used to ration the allocation of passenger loading gates. Typically these airport gates are assigned to the airlines based on past activity. Other airports use an auction system to determine gate access.

Quantity (Q) may be passengers over a specific period of time to be moved by a fleet of buses or airplanes. Let demand curve D_1 represent the (higher) peak demand for the transport service and D_2 represent the (lower) off-peak demand. The capacity maintenance cost per unit is CB meaning that capacity is divisible so that any size can be chosen at this constant cost in the long run. In the short run, the operating cost per unit of a given and fixed level of capacity is CQ_c (assuming Q_c was the current capacity). Of course, any lesser unit of $Q < Q_c$ would operate at a total cost of BQ_c as well.

It turns out that the optimal result is for peak users to pay P_1 for Q_1 while off-peak users should pay only P_2 for Q_2. Notice that the higher price is being charged to the set of users with a more price-inelastic demand. The reason that peak users absorb the entire P_1BQ_10 cost is because the current capacity of Q_c was constructed to meet their high demand. The fact that this chosen capacity level has a cost exactly equal to the peak users' willingness to pay means that P_1 is, in effect, the LRMC of providing the service. Off-peak users face only the operating cost of a given level of capacity (P_2AQ_20) because they never approach the capacity constraint. In effect, they pay the SRMC of providing the cyclical services which is equal to P_2. Of course, the SRMC would only be effective to the left of the capacity constraint. Once at the capacity constraint SRMC would become vertical.

If the off-peak demand increased so much so that it shifted beyond point C in Figure 9.7, the off-peak users could not be accommodated beyond Q_c and a case is made for the off-peak users to share some of the capacity maintenance costs. This situation is depicted in Figure 9.8.

Assume for simplicity that the peak and off-peak periods are divided into 12 hours per day each. Think of costs A and B, which exist 24 hours each day, to have to be optimally divided between the two sets of demanders, D_1 and D_2, whose usage's occur during two separate 12 hour durations. The LRMC are decomposed into the investment required to maintain the given capacity (B) and the operating costs (A).

With each peak and off-peak period being of equal duration, the two demand curves may be summed vertically in order to obtain the joint demand curve showing the total willingness to pay for a given level of capacity. Because the question concerns the optimal division of B between the two sets of users, things are made more convenient by letting operating

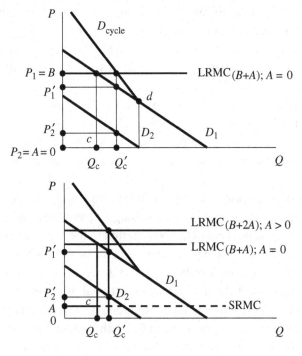

Figure 9.8.

costs (A) be zero. In order to facilitate comparison, point (c) from Figure 9.6 has been appropriately positioned and labeled in Figure 9.7. The optimal capacity with the higher off-peak demand is now higher at Q'_c with peak users paying a lower price of P'_1 and off-peak users paying a higher price of P'_2. And because:

$$(P'_1 + P'_2) = (A + B); \quad A = 0. \tag{9.1}$$

Marginal benefits equal marginal costs meaning that optimality has occurred. Social optimality, of course, would occur if social costs and benefits were built into the cost curves and demand curves. Now, if positive operating costs occur (i.e., $A > 0$), the total of these, given the two sets of users for the 24 hour day, amounts to $2A$ giving a grand total for all costs of $(2A + B)$. So with $A > 0$, Equation (9.1) becomes:

$$(P'_1 + P'_2) = (2A + B), \quad \text{or} \quad (P'_1 - A) + (P'_2 - A) = B. \tag{9.2}$$

It is important to follow this reasoning clearly. The joint demand curve is, in effect, a 2-period demand curve; therefore, it must only be compared to a 2-period LRMC. The 2-period LRMC is the sum of the costs facing the two demand groups for the full cycle: A for the off-peak and $(A + B)$ for the peak. The second panel of Figure 9.7 shows the optimal prices when $A > 0$ occurs. Also, by comparing Figures 9.6 and 9.7, if the horizontal line at $P_1 = B$ intersects D_1 to the right of point d, in the first panel of Figure 9.7, then peak users must pay all of B as they do in Figure 9.6 because the off-peak users are no longer demanding a capacity amount.

The optimal peakload pricing solution implies that no seats are left empty. Off-peak users are able and willing to pay above the SRMC and high prices restrict demand in the peak period to the available space. It has been assumed that the two demand curves in the peak load pricing problem were independent of one another. In the real world a change in the peak price (P_1) may affect the preferences of off-peak users meaning demand curve D_2 shifts in response. Such a result requires that the analyst estimate the cross-price elasticities of demand for both peak and off-peak users so that a measure of the demand curve shift may be had. Certainly with a user's gravitation between peak and off-peak use depending upon the set prices, it becomes harder for a firm to break the set of users into these two groups. Some light will be shed on this matter in Chapter 10 dealing with price discrimination. Demand dependency of this sort would serve to complicate the model further.

The LRMC is neither visible, nor easily measured in practice. Fortunately, if the market has sufficient competition, it is possible to approximate this theoretical result with an auction market. The railways in the U.S. and Canada are using such an auction system to allocate rail cars. Shippers can bid for rail cars on a guaranteed reservation system that has performance penalties for both the shipper and carrier.[7]

---

[7]Burlington Northern Santa Fe offers a Certificate of Transportation program, the Union Pacific has a Car Supply Voucher program and Canadian Pacific Railway has its PERX program. Each program has its unique features, but operates on the basis of guaranteed car placement service at prices that are set through an auction that allows part of the fleet capacity to be allocated based on shipper demand. The remaining fleet capacity is allocated to dedicated shuttle or cycle train service and to general tariff/distribution service. General

Appendix

Weighted demand curves

Where peak and off-peak demands exist over non-equal durations a weighted demand curve (D_w) must be calculated.[8] A weighted demand of two curves with two equal durations in Figure A.1.

The weighted demand is simply the sum of the willingnesses to pay at each quantity with weights of (1/2) assigned to D_1 and D_2. The optimal capacity is determined where the weighted demanded curve intersects the weighted LRMC; that is, $(1/2)(B + A)$ is the weighted average of the applicable cost to any one of the two sets of users.

If one wishes to specify a case where, for example, peak use lasts for 2/3rds of the time period while off-peak use lasts the remaining 1/3rd, a new weighted demand curve must be calculated; from that point the analysis is identical to the above.

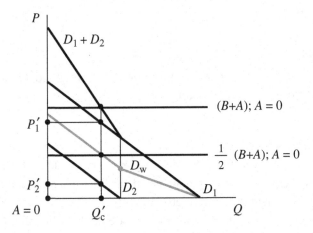

Figure A.1.

---

tariff/distribution cars are still allocated, for the most part, on a first-come-first-served basis, however these shippers bear the most risk of car availability during the peak demand period.
[8]The seminal article showing this technique is: Williamson, O. "Peak-Load Pricing and Optimal Capacity under Indivisibility Constraints." *American Economic Review*, Vol. 56 (1966), 810–827.

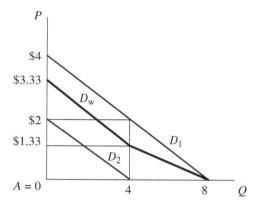

Finding the peak and off-peak prices requires the inclusion of the weighted LRMC which is $(1/2)(A + B)$ when $A = 0$. Of course, as in Figure 9.6, its value will still be $(1/2)(A + B)$ because the average of the weights is $[(1/3)+(2/3)]/2 = (1/2)$; indeed $(1/2)(A + B)$ is the case for all possible peak and off-peak weights because there are only two and they both sum to 1.

Keywords

cabotage	peak load pricing	weighted demand curve
joint production	two-part tariff	

Exercises

1. The Alberta Government decides to give every resident of the province another cheque for $400 to share the oil wealth. Most people are expected to spend this windfall gain pretty quickly.

   Draw and explain an appropriate model(s) that illustrates the impact on the demand for the transport of imported goods to Alberta that would result from this "generosity".

   Would this growth in imports have any impact on Alberta exports? Explain the conditions under which this might occur.

2. China is the world's foremost manufacturer of consumer goods. They are exported in intermodal sea containers (20-foot and 40-foot). The

demand for container transportation from China to North America greatly exceeds the return movement. Half of all the containers come back to China empty.

Draw and explain an appropriate model(s) that illustrates the nature of transport demand for containers on the Pacific routes between China and North America.

Explain the economics of the model(s) and why the number of empty containers returning to China will likely fall as the value of the Chinese Renminbi rises in value relative to the U.S. dollar.

3. Restrictions on cabotage in the U.S. mean that if a Canadian truck takes a load to the U.S., and cannot find a return load to Canada, they have to return empty. Canadian truckers are prohibited from carrying loads with both a U.S. origin and destination. Canada imposes reciprocal restrictions on U.S. carriers with respect to cross-border trucking.

Draw an appropriate model(s) to explain how the removal of these restrictions would affect the costs of transport between the U.S. and Canada.

Explain why the removal of this restriction might not have any effects on freight rates in some cross-border markets.

4. Canada ships frozen French fries to Mexico in refrigerated rail cars. Southbound freight rates (to Mexico) are high because 75% of the rail cars return empty. A group of Mexican frozen food processors comes forward and offers to utilize half of the refrigerated railcars that now return empty.

Draw appropriate model(s) to illustrate the before and after demand situation, assuming the railways accept the offer.

The railways have low variable costs relative to their fixed costs. How would this affect the freight rates that the railway could charge on the northbound cars from Mexico versus refrigerated trucks?

5. The most convincing economic arguments for removing cabotage barriers between the NAFTA countries (Canada, United States and Mexico) are: (1) increased efficiency, (2) expansion of trade and (3) reduction of negative externalities.

Use appropriate economic models and examples, to explain how allowing reciprocal access to the carriers of the NAFTA countries to compete in each other's domestic markets would reduce the costs of transportation and stimulate trade.

How would the extension of cabotage for all modes of transport (marine, air, rail, truck) between the NAFTA countries impact inter-modal competition and negative externalities.

6. Truckers often employ triangular routes instead of just traveling back and forth from their origin to destination on the same route.

Draw appropriate model(s) to illustrate the economic rationale for this observed behavior.

How do cabotage restrictions influence truck routing patterns between adjoining countries?

7. After the harvest begins in September, the demand for railcars to move wheat, canola and other grains increases rapidly until Christmas. Subsequently, the volume of grain shipments begins to decline, with few shipments during the summer months. Despite the large changes in the volume of grain to be moved, the railways charge the same price per ton because of the government regulation. Consequently, the railcars are rationed to shippers (grain companies) during the peak on a modified "first come, first served" basis.

Use an appropriate economic model and analysis to explain why the rationing system is subject to chronic complaints by the grain shippers about the quality of the service they receive from the railways.

The alternative to administered rationing is to deregulate the market and let the railcars be allocated according to supply and demand. Freight rates would increase with demand during the peak and decline during the off-peak. Describe the pros and cons of letting prices determine which shipper gets a railcar.

8. The automobile traffic congestion that occurs during the daily "rush hours" is a close relative of the peak-load pricing problem.

Use an appropriate model, or models, to explain how imposing road/highway tolls is like a peak-load pricing policy, while ignoring traffic congestion is similar to an administered pricing policy for roads.

Explain why highway tolls can be a socially optimal method of dealing with traffic congestion, but generally, they are unpopular.

9. Air fares in Canada and the U.S. are generally higher in the summer travel season and on special holidays than they are during the rest of the

year. It seems unfair. Just when most people wish to travel, the airlines jack up the prices.

Draw and explain an appropriate model(s) to assess the fairness and efficiency of this variable pricing policy.

Explain why the government might be reluctant to act on consumer complaints about high airfares.

Chapter 10

Product Pricing in Transportation

As we have discussed, pricing of transportation services can vary from out-of-pocket expenses (AVC) to whatever-the-market-will-bear, or value pricing. However, in some cases prices can also be paid in-kind. An example is riding a bicycle versus driving a car. The implicit value to the rider, ignoring any exercise benefit, is the difference between their out-of-pocket expenses to drive the car and the extra time spent riding the bicycle. Similarly, the intrinsic value of the time, and some share of extra operating costs, is what car drivers pay to be stuck in rush-hour traffic congestion.

Product pricing in transportation can also involve market segmentation in which different consumers may be discriminated against with higher or lower prices for the same service. Price discrimination and its counterpart yield management are commonly practiced in transportation to increase total revenues of the carriers.

Congestion Cost Pricing

Pricing under congestion costs is a relative of the peak load pricing problem. Peak load pricing involves a market that is divided, so to speak, into heavy users and light users that made their presence felt on the market over separate times. Congestion costs are a result of: (1) the *speed–flow relationship* that occurs on common traffic ways; and (2) the *speed–cost relationship* that occurs with respect to vehicle use.

These two points are related in that traffic flow relates to vehicle productivity. Lost utilization relates to opportunity cost. During traffic peaks congestion costs are highest, while during the off-peak traffic may flow smoothly with no measurable impact of congestion on utilization.

163

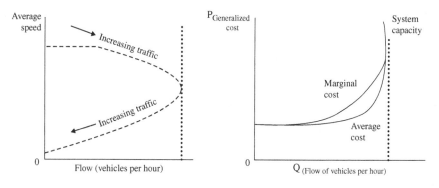

Figure 10.1.

The relationship between flow and average speed over a given traffic way is negative after a certain point.[1] The left-hand panel in Figure 10.1 illustrates a roadway with a given number of traffic lanes and a given surface quality. The flow past a certain point on the roadway must on

---

[1]A more formal presentation is given in: Vickrey, W. "Congestion Theory and Transport Investment." *American Economic Review*, Vol. 59 (1969), 251–260. When traffic volumes are between 50% and 90% of capacity, a functional form for the average delay per vehicle, written as z, is given as:

$$z = t - t_0 = (1/s) - (1/s_0) = ax^k, \tag{1}$$

where t is the actual time used in traveling a given distance; t_0 is the time required under very light traffic conditions; s is the average speed of a vehicle in the flow; a and k are constant parameters; and x is the traffic flow. An increase in flow leads to a rise in the average delay because of the increment in time needed to complete a given distance. The increase in time required arises from slower speeds; that is, if $t > t_0$ then $s < s_0$.

From the average delay per vehicle, the total delay that is spread across the given flow is zx if it is assumed that each vehicle in the flow (x) will experience the same delay (z). The change in this delay with respect to flow is written as a total derivative:

$$d(zx)/dx = z(dx/dx) + x(dz/dx) = z + x(dz/dx)$$
$$= ax^k + xakx^{k-1} = ax^k + kax^k = (1+k)z. \tag{2}$$

When the flow increases by an increment of one vehicle (dx) the total time delay across this now larger flow rises by $(1+k)z$. For every one minute of delay on the extra vehicle, the remaining ones face an average delay of k minutes. What is the value of k? Under light congestion it could be 2 meaning that the time delay varies with the square of the traffic flow based on Equation (1). Higher congestion levels mean a higher value of k.

average slow as ever more vehicles enter the road way. As the increased traffic flow on the roadway approaches system capacity, all lanes sooner or later become crowded so that drivers respond by slowing down. Note that this is an engineering relationship of speed–flow characteristics. If additional vehicles continue to enter the roadway after system capacity is reached, both the average speed and the flow past a certain point can decline further.

Of course, as speed falls: (1) the operating cost per kilometer of the vehicle rises; and (2) the time required to travel a given distance also increases which thus adds to the opportunity cost of travel. This is represented in the right-hand panel of Figure 10.1. The term *generalized costs* will be developed more fully in the text, but it includes compensation for the drivers' time (opportunity cost) as well as the out of pocket costs to operate the car. These are the private costs of congestion. Note that marginal costs (MC) and average costs do not begin to rise until there are sufficient automobiles to interact with each other. Once the traffic starts to create congestion however, the costs rise rapidly. If the traffic increase reaches the state of the lower half of the left-hand panel, then marginal and average costs would begin to rise vertically and could even curl back.

The social costs of congestion can add to the private costs. Extra pollution can be created because engines are worked rougher due to more stops-and-starts as well as more idling; and the time delay costs due to others not being able to access the road at all due to the congestion. The effects of diminished and yet more erratic traffic flows on the accident rate as well as road maintenance are not clear *a priori*.

The obvious engineering solution to a congested road is to make it wider so there are more lanes to accommodate the traffic. Practice has shown that no road building scheme has ever been able to build its way out of congestion. The reason however is quite subtle. Consider an example of the speed–flow relationship taken in the context of line-ups and through-put.[2] Imagine a line of skiers with each waiting for his turn, in a pair, to use a ski lift. With a fixed population of skiers wishing to make use of the lift

---

[2]The following example is from Schelling, T. *Micromotives and Macrobehavior*. New York: W.W. Norton and Co., 1978, which provides a splendid discussion of microeconomics and the problems of human interaction.

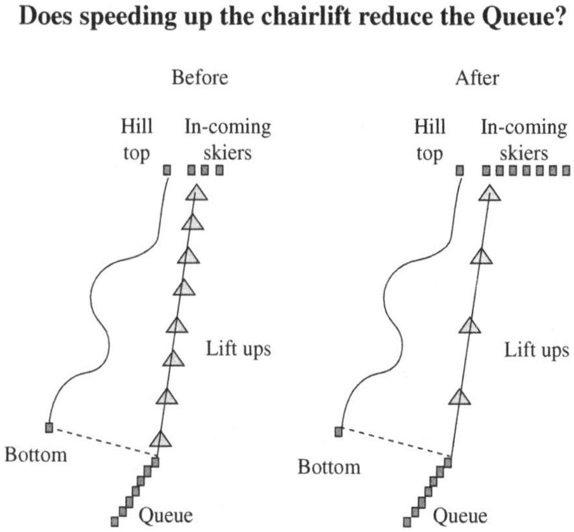

Does speeding up the chairlift reduce the Queue?

Figure 10.2.

at any given time: would it make sense, in terms of shortening line-ups, to increase the speed of the ski lift? No it would not. In fact, the paradox is that speeding up the lift would serve to make the line-up longer.

Let us consider why. Assume that it takes a fixed amount of time for one pair of skiers to position themselves after the preceding pair has been carried off. This is illustrated in Figure 10.2. It can be concluded that the load rate is independent of the speed of the ski lift. Of course, one might even argue that the increased speed of the lift forces pairs to more carefully prepare for lift-off meaning that load time may perhaps increase but this effect will be ignored. The unload rate would also be constant and equal to the load rate as well. The fixed population is divided into three groups: (1) the lift-ups, (2) the in-coming skiers, and (3) the queue. There will thus be a circular flow of activity.

With the load and unload rates constant, and the in-coming ski time being independent of how fast was the lift to the top, the same amount of skiers load onto and off the lift over any given time irrespective of the lift's speed. Subtracting the fixed number of people in the ski phase from the fixed total number of people in all three phases leaves the number of people in the other two phases unchanged. But carrying time on the lift is reduced because the lift is moving people to the top faster and, given that loading/unloading time is constant, chairs in use are spaced farther apart. With the same number of people skiing down but less on the lift at any instant in time, the only place where the balance resides would be in a now longer line-up. In summary, speeding the lift serves only to reduce lift-up time but does not reduce the delay.

Consider the implications of the above example. If only a portion of a notoriously congested roadway is widened, will total congestion along it be reduced? No. One bottleneck is eliminated and the traffic merely speeds up until it runs into the next one along the narrower portion of the roadway ahead. In fact, that bottleneck, just like the line-up for the ski lift, will be even more congested than before because more traffic is able to get to it faster. The ski process, as a closed system, implies that the "price" is paid on the lift process while the downhill process is "free".

A somewhat artificial congestion problem occurs in the form of drivers who gawk at accident scenes as they pass by. Presumably these drivers slow down as they observe the accident. In this way, an accident in the southbound lane can slow up traffic even in the northbound lane. The act of gawking may take only seconds, but the line up in order to get to do it may take several minutes to clear through. For some drivers the accident may be cleared away by the time they reach the point of viewing it but that is the chance they take. These people, in a perverse sense, lose out but there is no way to ensure that they get the same "privilege" as did the earlier gawkers short of turning the accident into a shrine. The earlier gawkers imposed an external cost on everyone behind them that the former required not to consider.

Finally, consider an obstruction (e.g., a garbage can) along a busy roadway that forces drivers to slow down and proceed around it. There is no incentive for any one driver to pull to the side and remove it from either a private or social point of view. In the private sense, he endured the line up until reaching it and will resume normal speed once he has gone around it no matter if he moves it or not. In the social sense, his removal of the obstruction creates a benefit to the other drivers for which he is not compensated. So why do some people in the real world perform these acts of kindness? It would be for non-monetary reasons such as altruism or a belief in the "golden rule". Perhaps, to reverse the onus, it may be asked:

how many drivers would tip this altruist by, say, throwing him a penny, as they passed by?

Consider a related example. A car is proceeding through peak load traffic along a multi-lane expressway. The driver notices his particular lane to be the slowest and decides at that moment to switch lanes. Is this a good strategy for dealing with peak load congestion? The answer is more likely to be no. Lane switching cannot guarantee the driver the shortest possible drive time; in fact, specifically switching lanes due to the one in question slowing relative to the others may be suboptimal because of similarly slowed-up drivers getting the same idea. When enough drivers make the change to the other lane, it will slow while the previously slowed-up lane will begin to speed up.

The problem facing the driver in question is to calculate the difference between the marginal benefit of the lane change with the MC. If he perceives it to be positive then, for him, a lane change would be warranted. The costs would be such things as the extra care needed for the change as well as the potential for an accident while the benefits would be the perceived time savings. Notice that this calculation involves the driver's perceived costs and benefits meaning what he calculates may or may not be borne out by what actually will happen when in that other lane. A good additive in his calculation would be his perception as to whether or not the other drivers in his lane ahead of him have decided to switch. Our driver would not want to be that one marginal driver who succeeds in merely slowing up the other lane to a time amount equal to that of the lane he just switched out of. Only those marginal switchers before him would have realized a time gain. The equilibrium of this system will be achieved when all lanes are moving at equal speeds.

When an airport runway is congested there are three possible forms of cost involved: (1) time delays in take-off and landing could create a time loss for passengers; (2) the operating cost of the airplanes could increase because of additional idling time on the runway and possibly circling the runway awaiting clearance; and (3) an airline, in response, may increase the size of its fleet serving the airport. The third point needs more explanation: with increased congestion the number of completed trips per time period, by a given fleet size, declines meaning that fleet revenue per time period also drops. To arrest the fall in revenues an extra airplane could be added in order to increase the number of trips completed by the airline. Of course, a negative externality has occurred in that this airline has just further increased the congestion costs faced by the other airlines, as well as perhaps itself, in using the airport.

The decision of the airline to increase its fleet is conditioned upon the marginal revenue (MR) earned by the fleet, as contributed by this extra airplane, exceeding the MC of that airplane inclusive of the further congestion it creates. However, the fleet revenue would surely increase if the extra airplane could be employed at a different, non-congested airport. Again, a distinction may be made between a pecuniary externality and a real externality. If one considers every airplane to be part of the same market then congestion is merely a pecuniary externality and is the price that must be accepted by the user. But if each vehicle is considered part of a separate market transaction then congestion is a real externality that needs to be accounted for. The choice is subjective.

A pecuniary externality does not remove the government from playing a valuable role in the market. Consider the following illustration of the congestion cost problem shown in Figure 10.3. Congestion sets in, in this case, at a flow quantity of vehicles per time period of Q_1 and the problem worsens as quantity increases further. With higher congestion resulting from an extra vehicle on a roadway, for example, speed falls so that the generalized cost per trip rises as each new car enters the road. As such,

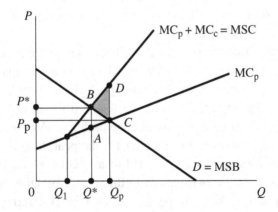

Figure 10.3.

the average cost for all cars already on the road will also rise which is the source of congestion as a negative externality. At equilibrium for the existing road capacity and traffic flow, the pecuniary cost is DC. Given that cost, automobile drivers might be pleased to pay a toll equal to BA, and travel the road with less congestion.

Without consideration of congestion costs the private market would settle at a price of P_p and a quantity of Q_p. With congestion costs properly considered the optimal price and quantity would be P^* and Q^*, respectively. Beyond Q^*, the congestion-inclusive MC of the trip exceeds the marginal social benefit of the trip to the drivers. If these costs of the activities of one driver on the rest are not considered then a tax (or road toll) of size AB on the $Q^{*\text{th}}$ car upon entering the roadway as well as similar taxes on each previous car would force the private MC function (MC_p) to increase in line with the congestion-inclusive MC (MC_p+MC_c).

The net social benefit from the reduction in traffic flow from Q_p down to Q^* comes from the reduction in operating cost (Q^*BDQ_p) while a loss in benefits comes from those marginal drivers between Q_p and Q^* that would have used the roadway (Q^*BCQ_p). Thus, the net social gain owing to the traffic reduction is the shaded area BCD.

In the case of the airline example cited above, a private airline operating with the others at a total flow of Q^*, but not itself affected by the congestion it creates, would wish to add an extra airplane to its fleet because MSB > MC_p when that extra airplane is added. If the airline itself does not feel a cost of congestion equal to AB or, equivalently, the government does not assess a tax due to the problem it creates for the others then this airline would add that extra airplane.

It is possible that the peak load problem and the congestion problem may occur on the same traffic way; that is, the roadway may always be congested but it is even more so during peak time. To properly price in this situation a two-part tariff would be required which is really nothing more than a tax to account for two separate problems. A charge per vehicle per peak/off-peak is needed to account for the peak load problem and a charge per distance traveled is needed to account for congestion build-up. A fuel tax is not an optimal tax in this regard because, while it may account for distance, it is not peak/off-peak related. Parking charges as well are not optimal here because these charges may be levied differently for peak/off-peak time periods but cannot account for distance traveled in order to reach the parking spot.

On toll roads the peak problem can be taxed on a time-related basis and by accounting for entry and exiting points the distance problem can be taxed. The congestion tax would be paid upon exit with a ticket marked with the point of entry. In this regard, toll roads can simultaneously, and optimally, solve the congestion and peak load problems.[3] In terms of a toll system leading into and out of a popular area, the toll need only be charged in one direction because people will already be "captured" going in the other. In other words it does not make sense to queue people twice if the same cash amount can be collected from queuing them once.

Price Discrimination

The peak load pricing problem showed how optimal pricing of transport services occurs when the peak and off-peak users could be separated from each other in terms of their separate demand curves. This is the pricing of a joint product because the peak service cannot be supplied without also providing the off-peak service. When a firm is able to separate out its consumers into various demand classes and charge different prices for the same service at the same time, it engages in price discrimination. While the term may sound negative, economically speaking it merely implies that firms have an incentive to charge different prices to different classes of consumer and thereby transfer some of their consumer surplus to themselves. Of course, a firm needs market power in order to do this, which is why the types of firms that engage in price discrimination are not perfectly competitive firms.

In order to charge different prices for the identical product (size, quality, etc.), three conditions must exist for a price discrimination policy to be

---

[3]An optimal toll, while being an efficient way to price congested roads, is by no means easy to implement. If congestion caused by vehicles varies from day-to-day, or hour-to-hour, so must the charge. Electronic tagging is now possible so the problem of toll booths is avoided and charges may be modified on the fly so to speak. The greater barrier is political. Governments have shown great reluctance to utilize tolls to manage congestion because they fear a backlash at the next election. The success of the congestion tolls in London are being watched closely and may embolden civic leaders in other jurisdictions to experiment with some form of tolling to reduce traffic congestion.

effective. First, the different market segments must exist (i.e., they must have different demand characteristics). Second, an effective means of identifying the groups must be available and enforceable. Third, the groups must be unable to conduct arbitrage (i.e., the group paying a lower price cannot be allowed to transfer or sell its "privilege" to the group that is paying a higher price).

Second degree price discrimination

Second degree price discrimination is a weak form because the conditions for market segmentation are incomplete. Different consumer demands are known to exist, but the group members are impossible to identify directly. Consequently, firms have to rely on some method of self-identification. An example of second degree price discrimination is to offer quantity discounts on purchases. Lower prices induce those that would otherwise not enter the market to buy the good or service. The effect is shown in Figure 10.4.

If a uniform price were efficiently set, the result would be a price of P_3 with a quantity of Q_3 sold. A consumer surplus of ABP_3 exists. But if the firm were to charge three different prices for that total quantity, it would capture an amount of the consumer surplus equal to the shaded area. In effect, Q_1 sells for the highest price of P_1; $(Q_2 - Q_1)$ is discounted to a

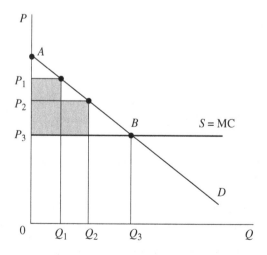

Figure 10.4.

price of P_2; and $(Q_3 - Q_2)$ is sold "at cost" with a price of P_3. A common example of second degree price discrimination is the marketing of table potatoes. The price of potatoes in a 5 pound bag is often double the price per pound in a larger 20 pound bag. The sellers discriminate against small families and anyone without a place to store potatoes.[4]

Less-than-truckload carriers price their services in this manner. They have discrete weight categories that offer lower prices per pound as the shipments increase in size. Once the shipments size exceeds half a truckload, their rates approach the truckload rate. Another example is the purchase of a flight pass on the airlines. Some airlines offer passes of 30 or more flights for a fixed fee that is lower than the average price of purchasing single tickets.

Third degree price discrimination

If the firm faces the entire market demand for the product, or if a small group of firms can cooperate effectively, the market demand may be broken into various classes of demanders. Certainly, in urban transit there are travelers of different ages and income levels; airline travel is made up of business and casual travelers; and the truck and rail modes face bulk and manufactured goods' shipments. To the extent that these classes of demanders are different, their willingness to pay for services may be different which is why their demands may be distinct. Assuming the firm, or group of firms, acts as a monopoly, pricing under price discrimination occurs as illustrated in Figure 10.5.

The market is broken into two demand sub-components, D_1 and D_2 with each having its own MR curve. The MC curve establishes cost for both sub-markets. The profit maximizing firm will set the optimal quantity (Q^*)

---

[4]The demand for the 20 pound bag of potatoes can also be viewed as an "all-or-nothing" demand curve that lies to the right of the normal demand. At the lower price, consumers are offered all or nothing. Whether they consume the potatoes is irrelevant to the seller. The seller is happy to remove this perishable inventory from the market. Another example of second degree price discrimination is the sale of season tickets to sporting events. Arena owners know that some seats may otherwise go empty, so they are willing to discount the price for the larger quantity in order to capture more consumer surplus from the walk-up ticket buyers.

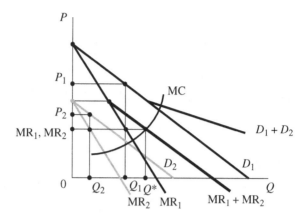

Figure 10.5.

where MC equals the horizontal sum of the two MR curves $(MR_1 + MR_2)$.[5] As well, the last unit sold in each market (Q_1 and Q_2) will each bring in the same MR. Note that $(Q_1 + Q_2) = Q^*$. If, for example, MR_1 exceeded MR_2 then the firm's revenue would rise by selling more of the good to class 1 and less to class 2.

From the individual quantities the individual prices for classes 1 and 2 are obtained by setting price equal to the corresponding point on the specific demand curves. Notice that the price charged is higher for the more price-inelastic class of demanders (class 1). A general result is that the price set under price discrimination should be inversely related to the price elasticity of demand if the firm wishes to maximize profits. This is known as third degree price discrimination. Intuitively, if facing two classes of demander the higher price should be set where the premium in price is not offset by a greater percentage fall in the quantity demanded thus leading to a fall in revenue, which is, by definition, where demand is more price-inelastic. For a proof of this result, see the appendix at the end of this chapter.

---

[5]One should note the difference in procedure used here as compared to peak load pricing. Under peak load pricing the joint demand was compared with a vertically summed LRMC because the capacity quantity was, in effect, jointly supplied meaning that a vertical sum gives the total of the LRMCs of supplying that capacity facing the two demand classes over the two time periods. But in the present case the firm wishes to supply different quantities to the two demand classes over the same time period. To establish the total of the MR that accrue to the firm, these curves must be added horizontally.

Even when groups can be identified that have different price elasticities, segmentation into subcomponents is not always easy. Firms have devised ingenious ways for the classes to reveal themselves. Suppose, for example, an airline realizes that its passengers consist of two distinct groups: business travelers and casual/vacation travelers. The airline knows that business travelers appreciate the speed factor allowed by air travel and thus anticipates that this group has a more price-inelastic demand and, under price discrimination, should be charged a higher price for tickets. The problem is that simply asking a ticket purchaser if his flight is business or casual, and charging him more if he reveals that it is the former, will not work for long because business travelers would eventually catch on and claim to be casual travelers.

A way around this problem is to raise prices for everyone and deflate the casual travelers' price by offering them a cut rate if they meet certain conditions. Until the advent of the discount air carriers, the large airlines would advertise cut rates on round trip ticket purchases that include a Saturday night stay. This was effective because the casual traveler is more apt to stay over a weekend than is a business traveler who usually requires stays that occur only over the weekdays. The airlines also observed that employees might demand that they receive pay for the extra time if their employer wanted them to use a cut rate ticket. The competition from domestic discount airlines destroyed this form of airline price discrimination because they began offering low fares for everyone, including the price-inelastic business travelers. However, the "Saturday night" pricing system can still be observed in intercontinental flights.

Of course, price discrimination in the airlines did not disappear; the airlines just became more creative. Now groups are separated on the basis of time penalties and perks. In addition the airlines are loading on a complete menu of charges for features of the trip that used to be free. For example, charges are imposed to reserve seats, for meals and for baggage. The "a la carte" offering of services that were previously incorporated into the ticket has made elements of their pricing strategy comport with third degree price discrimination. The need for this approach has been reinforced by Internet booking that increased the transparency of price competition because a customer can easily compare the offerings of each airline with a few clicks of the fingers.

First degree price discrimination

First degree price discrimination requires monopoly power and involves charging every user his maximum willingness to pay. First degree price discrimination is also called *Ramsey pricing*. Ramsey's rule[6] assumes that the monopolist is constrained by regulations to zero economic profits and prices are set according to the inverse of the individual's price elasticity of demand. The more inelastic the demand, the higher the markup charged. In this case, an efficient result occurs because the entire consumer surplus is appropriated by the monopoly that can set production according to long run marginal cost (LRMC) and avoid welfare loss commonly associated with monopolies.

Paradoxically, natural monopolies are inefficient unless they can indeed perfectly price discriminate. Figure 10.6 presents the natural monopoly model. A key condition of a natural monopoly is that the long run average total costs (LRATC) are declining throughout the relevant demand. Why? Because if the LRATC continually falls as the firm gets larger, the leading firm can keep buying its competitors and achieving lower costs until only one firm, the monopoly remains.

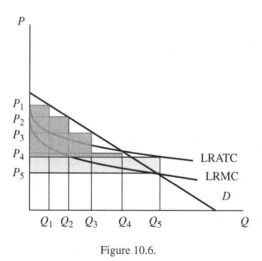

Figure 10.6.

[6]Ramsey, Frank. "A Contribution to the Theory of Taxation." *Economic Journal*, Vol. 37 (1927), 47–61.

The intersection of the LRMC curve and the demand to the right of the LRATC/demand intersection means that the monopoly cannot be profitable and achieve allocative efficiency, too. If the natural monopoly is forced to offer the quantity Q_5 at the price P_5 then the monopoly will suffer losses equal to the light shaded area between the LRATC and its revenues at the LRMC. Ramsey pricing by the monopoly extracts a different price from each of the four other users. Each price is determined according to the buyer's price elasticity of demand. Price discrimination transfers the consumer surplus represented by the dark shaded areas to the monopoly. The gains from price discrimination cross-subsidize the losses inherent in providing the optimal quantity. If the pricing yields a zero economic profit for the monopoly, then it is optimal.

In the case of a multi-product firm, the Ramsey rule requires that the prices of the firm's outputs are changed such that all prices are changed proportionately. Assume that a railway has two products bulk railcars (A) and container service (B), and that the quantities are produced under MC pricing QA^{MC} and QB^{MC}. Ramsey prices charged for A and B, at quantities QA and QB produced, should yield a zero economic profit. This requires that if any changes occur, $QA^{MC}/QB^{MC} = QA/QB$. If the demand for bulk shipping (product A) is more inelastic than containers (product B), then a change in prices require a greater increase for bulk rail cars relative to their MC. Many problems confront Ramsey pricing in practice, not the least of which is accurately estimating the elasticity of demand.

Ramsey pricing has been used for marine and rail transportation. The arguments for price discrimination in transportation are strong, but not always intuitive. One of the interesting paradoxes is where society may be better off if the railway price discriminates with respect to distance because of intermodal competition. Friedman (1988) put forward this case for a railway in competition with a river route.[7] In this case, cities located on the river have a choice of barges or railway, while cities away from the river must depend solely on the railway. Understandably shippers located

---

[7]Friedman, David D. "In Defense of the Long-haul/Short-haul Discrimination." *The Bell Journal of Economics*, Vol. 10, No. 2 (Autumn 1979). Copyright 1979, American Telephone and Telegraph Company. Also available at http://www.daviddfriedman.com/Academic/Long_haul_Short_Haul/Long_haul_Sht_Hl.html.

in the intermediate locations away from the river could feel that they are over-paying when the rate per mile on the short haul is higher than the per mile rate on the long haul to a river competitive city. However, the cost of railway infrastructure is such that without price discrimination the railway's revenues might be insufficient to justify the track investment rail for service to the intermediate locations that are not on the river. This example of intermodal competition is explored further in Chapter 11.

In practice, first degree price discrimination is rare, usually frowned upon and sometimes illegal. An example of perfect price discrimination would be a ticket scalper holding a separate auction for each of his tickets. If such a thing were not illegal, a scalper would have an incentive to buy all of the tickets at the posted price and auction them off on the Internet. Still, there is no efficiency loss; just a large gain for a scalper.

Another example of first degree price discrimination is the pricing policies of drug companies. Interestingly, advances in communications, and specifically the Internet, have undermined the market power of these large corporations. In the case of the drug companies, first degree price discrimination is country based. The citizens of higher income countries, like the United States, are charged more for the same pharmaceuticals as citizens of poorer African countries. The ability of consumers to obtain drugs across borders through Internet-pharmacies is challenging the power of the drug countries to exercise their form of Ramsey pricing.

In summary, first and second degree price discrimination are related because they involve a single market demand curve. First degree price discrimination is an attempt to capture the entire consumer surplus with different prices set over multiple buyers of the same or similar amounts of a good or service. Second degree price discrimination is more ham-handed in that only some of the consumer surplus is captured because the seller is only able to price discriminate in terms of different lots of the good or service along a single market demand curve. Finally, third degree price discrimination occurs when the seller is able to divide the consumers into distinct sub-markets and set a unique price for each of them.

Yield management

Yield management is used to set prices by the airlines in order to maximize revenues. Yield management is not pure price discrimination, to the extent that the product may have differences in quality that are only a bit more costly to produce. An example is airlines that offer a first class section with roomier seats, a hot meal and some complementary alcoholic beverages. They know that higher income passengers can be attracted to buy the much more expensive first class seats more by snob appeal than real value.

The airlines also know that groups of passengers have difference demand elasticities (business versus leisure travelers), but they cannot identify the members of each group at the time of booking. They can separate the groups to some extent by imposing or waiving change fees. However, the greatest difference is the flexibility of travel time. Leisure travelers can and do plan their trip months ahead, while business travelers may have to make their decision to travel at the last minute. This also includes flexibility in the return date. A business person may wish to cut short or extend their trip depending on the opportunity presented, whereas a leisure traveler is more likely to have fixed travel plans.

The airlines try to extract the maximum amount that each traveler is willing to pay by continuous changing prices as the date of departure approaches. As the date of the flight approaches, fares rise because the airlines know that business people are more likely to travel at the last minute and will pay more. To prevent early booking by business people and switching at the last moment, the airlines impose significant penalties to changes in low cost tickets. Figure 10.7 illustrates the yield management system of the airlines that is built into their reservation system.[8] The airlines employ computer algorithms to manage the number of seats available at each price according to the number of fares booked. The expected bookings are based on the historical pattern for each origin–destination pair. The actual bookings are observed in real time.

The airline might expect to have one-third of their seats sold three weeks prior to departure, but if this point is not reached, the computer will automatically lower fares and keep fares low until the actual bookings catch up with the expected. Conversely, if this point is already reached four weeks ahead, the fares will increase until the actual and expected coincide. Of course, the computer is programmed to raise fares as the date of departure

---

[8]A good description of how the airlines use yield management to set airline ticket prices is provided in the book by Tretheway, Michael and Oum, Tae. *Airline Economics: Foundations for Strategy and Policy.* Canada: Centre for Transportation Studies, University of British Columbia, 1992.

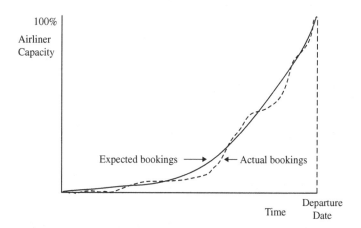

Figure 10.7. Airline ticket sales yield management system.

approaches because they know that business travelers are more likely to book tickets at the higher prices during the week prior to departure.

Yield management is also used by the package tour operators, hotels and increasingly the railroads. The cruise line reservation system can close out and open space. For example, the reservation system could close out the second class service and offer only first and third classes to the public. At two weeks before departure, seats in the second class may re-open and seats in the third class may close if they have now passed their historic pattern of sales. By raising and lowering space availability, the carrier can reduce shifting between class categories and force more passengers to accept the higher priced fares, while maximizing capacity.

Even if demand can be successfully separated, there is no guarantee that consumers will not "downgrade" their preferences. If the cross-price elasticity of demand is high then a small price decrease in a lower class may lead to substitution by consumers into that class and away from the higher class. Consider a split into three classes as shown in Figure 10.8. Each class has its own MC of provision. This could involve separate types of accommodation as found on airplanes, trains or cruise ships. The operators can impose "change fees" to prevent passengers from exchanging tickets for less expensive options.

A price of P_1 retains for the high end users a consumer surplus of ACP_1 when they consume Q_1. It is assumed that the number of switchers is small enough so that shifts in D_1 and D_2 are insignificant. But the price of P_2

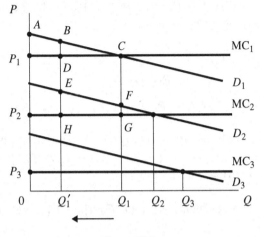

Figure 10.8.

for middle end users may entice, as shown in the figure, $Q_1 - Q'_1$ of the high end users to switch to the middle end thereby receiving a surplus of EFGH instead of BCD. Even though EFGH > BCD it is not certain that this switch will occur. If it did then revenue to the firm would certainly fall. The tendency to switch is based on the cross-price elasticities. Prices must be set so that high end users reveal themselves as such.

Appendix

Price discrimination

Under price discrimination, price is inversely related to the price elasticity of demand. First it must be shown that $MR = P[1+(1/E_d)]$ where E_d is the price elasticity of demand.

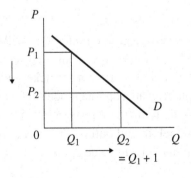

In general, we have $MR = P + Q\Delta P$ for a 1-unit change in quantity; for an indefinite change, ΔQ, we have:

$$MR = (\Delta TR/\Delta Q) = (TR_2 - TR_1)/\Delta Q = (P_2 Q_2 - P_1 Q_1)/\Delta Q$$
$$= [P_2(Q_1 + \Delta Q) - P_1 Q_1]/\Delta Q$$
$$= (P_2 Q_1 + P_2\Delta Q - P_1 Q_1)/\Delta Q = (Q_1\Delta P/\Delta Q) + P_2.$$

In other words, $MR = P + (\Delta PQ/\Delta Q)$; and multiplying the 2nd term by $(P/P) = 1$ gives: $MR = P + (\Delta P/\Delta Q)(P/P)(Q/1) = P[1 + (\Delta P/\Delta Q)(Q/P)] = P[1 + (1/E_d)]$.

Now if $MR_1 = MR_2$ then $P_1[1 + (1/E_{d1})] = P_2[1 + (1/E_{d2})]$.   (A.1)

But if demand 1 were more price-inelastic than demand 2, the result would be $|E_{d1}| < |E_{d2}|$ or, because price elasticity for a non-Giffen good is a negative number, $E_{d1} > E_{d2}$ meaning:

$$[1 + (1/E_{d1})] < [1 + (1/E_{d2})].   \text{(A.2)}$$

To see this let $E_{d1} = -1$ and $E_{d2} = -2$ which then gives, from Equation (2), $[1 + (1/-1)] < [1 + (1/-2)]$ or $0 < 0.5$. Now, if Equation (A.1) is to hold given Equation (A.2), we need $P_1 > P_2$. Thus, the more price-inelastic good should receive the higher price.

Keywords

backhaul	peak load pricing	speed–flow relationship
fronthaul	Ramsey pricing	two-part tariff
generalized cost	speed–cost relationship	yield management

Exercises

1. A city announces a new cash fare policy that will force all passengers to pay the same $2.25 cash fare. Students and senior citizens would no longer enjoy discounted rates, except for tickets and passes.

   Draw and explain an appropriate model(s) that illustrates why a one fare policy is unlikely to increase revenues.

   Explain the model(s), and outline the pricing rules for a monopoly like Transit to maximize its revenues.

2. Most people do not like to fly at midnight (the "red-eye" flights) or at 6:00 a.m. (the "early-bird" flights). The airlines offer their lowest fares to passengers that will travel at these times.

What is the logic for the airline to charge low prices for travelers at the beginning and the end of the day? The "red-eye" and "early-bird" air fares to some major airport hubs are so low that the airlines cannot cover their full costs. Explain the economic logic and draw appropriate economic model(s) to illustrate your answer.

Can you explain an operational reason why the airlines might offer these flights to their airport hubs?

3. Construction of the new airport terminal has gone way over budget and the Airport Authority needs every dollar it can get to pay its debt. They have asked your advice on a pricing strategy for parking at the airport. They know there are three types of parking users: (1) Short-term users, who come to the airport to drop off or pick up passengers and stay for two hours or less; (2) Business travelers, who are away for one to four days; and (3) Leisure travelers that need parking for a week or more.

Use the model below to explain how and why the airport could maximize its parking revenue by charging difference prices to each group of users.

The Airport is considering an increase in their parking lot capacity to earn more money. How would you go about determining whether an investment in more parking is a wise decision?

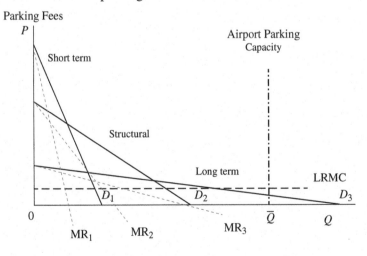

4. Yield management and price discrimination are both designed to increase revenues by charging different customers higher or lower prices.

   Draw and explain an appropriate model(s) that illustrates how yield management could be used to increase revenues for the airlines.

   Explain the difference between yield management and price discrimination, and the conditions required to use these methods.

5. Railways have a more or less fixed capacity in the short run. They use freight rates to ration space and determine their revenues. These freight rates differ by the class of goods carried. Goods that have a more inelastic demand get charged more than products that have weaker, more elastic demands, even if they move an identical distance and occupy the same space on the train.

   Draw and explain an appropriate model(s) that illustrates the benefits to the railway of this pricing strategy.

   Explain the conditions necessary to make such a pricing strategy work, the rule for optimizing the results and why results are beneficial to the railway, and to society, as well.

Chapter 11

Transportation, Investment and Generalized Cost

The analysis of the market for transportation services has ignored much of the details accounting for the infrastructure upon which these services are provided. The previous chapter began to make endogenous the capacity aspects of transportation infrastructure but that was as far as it went. The decision to invest in the provision of infrastructure is the first physical building block in the transportation process. This chapter looks at the criteria upon which that investment decision is made.

Cost–Benefit Analysis (CBA) and Investment in Infrastructure

Roads and rail lines are inputs to the provision of surface transport; ports, canals, and lighthouses are inputs to water vessel transport; airport terminals, runways, and air traffic control are the inputs for air transport. All of these inputs may take years to complete and, when constructed, provide a stream of benefits to the owners and to society at large for many years thereafter. If the projected benefits received from an investment outweigh its projected costs then a projected gain can be expected and the investment may be considered favorably. Abstracting for now from the question of just who receives the benefits and who pays the cost, Cost–Benefit Analysis (CBA) is a technique that can be used to strictly determine the favorability of an investment. While the requirements of CBA are specific, real world applications rarely fulfill them without qualification thus making its use in decision-making more of an art than a science.

It is worth noting that all the transportation infrastructure examples mentioned above are taxpayer funded. They are also long-lived and fixed in place, unlike the mobile, short-lived assets of private transportation firms,[1] e.g., trucks and airplanes. The private firm is assumed to have one goad, profit, and to be the sole "user" of the resulting investment. The firm only considers its own revenue increase/cost saving and expenditures in the investment decision. Either the opportunity meets some after-tax investment criteria of the private CBA, or it is not considered.

A social CBA considers a much larger set of criteria that consider societal benefits, like safety, aesthetics and mobility. The government does not have to make a profit or worry about paying taxes. Consequently, the metrics for a social CBA are different than the CBA of a private firm. However, many more worthy projects with political support are always available than the resources of the treasury can fund. In this regard, a CBA is not just used to quantify infrastructure projects, but to rank projects for funding in terms of priority and importance.

The steps involved in CBA are: (1) list all of the costs and benefits associated with the entire life of the project inclusive of the opportunity costs and any positive and negative externalities; (2) monetize all of the costs and benefits; and (3) discount to the PV all costs and benefits that are flows over time by use of an appropriate rate of discount. If the sum of the discounted benefits exceeds the total discounted costs, then the investment is deemed to qualify for consideration. Each of these steps will be explained in greater detail below.

When putting together a list of costs and benefits to be had from a given project it is important not to double count any of them. For example, in the beautification of a vacant lot that involves setting up a park, the value of the surrounding houses may increase due to their proximity of access to it. Counting the access value of the park as well as the increase in housing values would be double counting. One must choose to count one or the other.

In some sense the costs of the project are easier to enumerate properly than are the benefits. Certainly the presence of negative (positive) externalities makes the enumeration of costs (benefits) difficult in their own right but let us ignore these external effects for the moment. Costs are easier to see because expenditure required to undertake a project means that specific factors of production are used up over a specific period of time.

---

[1]The freight railways and pipelines are exceptions because they provide their own infrastructure privately.

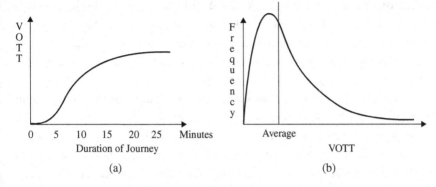

Figure 11.1.

In many social CBAs, monetary costs (benefits) may not be possible to obtain directly. In these situations, a subjective social value is employed, known as a *shadow price*. An example is the value of travel time (VOTT) savings, which is often the largest single benefit of transportation infrastructure investments. Estimating an appropriate VOTT confronts two problems. First, the VOTT is likely to vary with the length of the journey. Second, the VOTT is likely to vary amongst individual transport users. These two concepts are illustrated in Figure 11.1 as hypothetical response curves and population distributions.

Figure 11.1(a) postulates a small benefit for a short period that rises rapidly before easing off to a lower rate of increase. This S-shaped curve is difficult to verify but is generally accepted in the literature. Distance elasticities, which relate a 1% increase in distance to the corresponding increase in the VOTT, are estimated to lie between 0.25 and 0.35 for trips beyond 10 minutes.[2]

Figure 11.1(b) illustrates the second problem that is finding an average VOTT to use for the benefit calculation. The distribution of the VOTT could be skewed to the left by income because the low-income population is greater than the number of high-income people. This is a particularly important consideration if a toll is contemplated to finance the new

---

[2]Waters, William. "Issues in Valuing Travel Time for Calculating the Total Social Costs of Transportation." *Canadian Transportation Research Forum*. Proceedings Issue: 43rd Annual Meeting (2008): 60–71.

infrastructure improvement because the willingness to pay for time savings could be easily over-estimated. In practice, analysts often choose a proxy for the value of time, like the minimum wage rate, or an average industrial wage rate. Although choosing shadow prices in this manner risks over-valuation, giving time saving a zero-value would likely be worse.

Benefits can be a bit trickier in that the planner should only count those benefits that add economic value as opposed to a benefit created by merely redistributing wealth to this project away from somewhere else. In a sense there is a jurisdictional context to the list of benefits that should be a caveat in the mind of anyone assessing the merits of a CBA report. Ideally, the economist wishes to see benefits that add to total global wealth, meaning that a project whose benefit in one region occurred at an equal monetary expense of another would not be labeled a benefit because wealth was merely redistributed. This point also highlights the difference between private CBA and social CBA.

Consider the following examples. Suppose that widening a highway leads to an increase in profits to firms along this highway. Is this a benefit of the project? If the project were financed out of general income tax revenue then this increase in profits has to be weighed against the loss in income experienced by those in other jurisdictions with no access to the highway and yet helped to finance it. Thus, the benefit would be somewhat less than total firm profits. But if the economy is experiencing full employment and no further increase to national income is occurring then all increases in income (in this case business profits) to the jurisdiction are merely redistributed from others and no economy-wide benefit occurs when the wider highway adds to firm profitability.

Another case would be where one airport emerges as a major transport hub at the expense of others. Businesses at or near the hub airport certainly gain but this benefit must be tempered by the losses in business that occur at the other airports as a result. If the hub airport is expanded in size to create greater ease of arrival and departure in the midst of increased traffic, the specifics leading to that are indeed a benefit because new value was created. If the airport owners use some of their funds to install more vending machines, for example, the revenues generated from them are not a benefit of the airport because nothing has been done here to increase the hub value of the airport and, furthermore, the presence of this airport does not make the economy physically better at producing snacks for vending machines. Snacks bought at this airport are merely transfers to its users at the expense of other users elsewhere on a one-to-one basis.

Finally, consider a project that uses labor that would otherwise be unemployed. The unemployment insurance benefits that are not paid out by the government do not enter the CBA framework because they were strictly a transfer. The tricky part is the proper labeling of the workers' wages. Their wages in the project would be a cost to their employer but they are creating wealth and would otherwise be idle. Consequently, social CBA would take these wages as the shadow price indicating the benefit to society in creating jobs.

It must also be borne in mind that the list of costs and benefits is subjective. Consider the highway widening project again. Travel time is saved. How should this benefit be measured? In terms of increased output of all businesses that are accessed from the highway? This would indicate that there is a bias in favor of work meaning that the value of the highway comes from getting to work faster and thus increasing productivity. Perhaps the travel benefits should instead be measured in terms of leisure. The reduced crowding of the highway may lead to a greater desire for recreation instead of a greater desire to get to work faster. This would require attempting to value the benefits received from more trips to the countryside. Of course, the bias in favor of work or leisure is important because a unit of leisure is taken at the expense of a unit of work and vice versa. In terms of costs, the wider highway presumably will lead to more pollution in the surrounding area. How should this cost be measured? It could be measured in terms of increased morbidity/mortality or environmental damage or both. But only the cost of the damage shown to be specifically caused by the highway pollution must be estimated and the task is not easy.

In monetizing costs and benefits the planner needs to capture the social value of these costs and benefits for social CBA. In private CBA they need only be specific to the supplier and demander. The discussion above reveals the difficulty in doing this. While the accounting for externalities and the valuing of goods and services not sold in markets are the two most difficult aspects, there are certain distortions even in marketable goods and services that must be considered. Government activity in the form of taxes, subsidies and regulation are a source of distortions in that all applicable taxes must be subtracted from the market price paid in order to remove the distortion caused by firms passing some or all of the tax onto consumers.

A tax on the project distorts its true social cost and the revenue from the tax is merely transferred to another concern. Similarly, if the government subsidized an airline to give it an incentive to use a particular airport in order to ensure its hub status, this effect gets built into the airline's demand curve or MSB for the use of that airport. Consequently, the MSB should be adjusted downward to account for its propping up due to government subsidization. The subsidy on the project came from money collected from another concern. Thus, if the market is subject to a tax or subsidy, that market, under most cases, has a distorted price that will not represent the opportunity cost of the factors of production which could have been used in other markets where taxes and subsidies are not used. The effects of redistribution of wealth due to government intervention must be removed.

Another source of distortion comes from market monopolization. Recall that monopoly pricing is not socially efficient in that the price is set by the monopolist to be above MSC. If, for example, the inputs used in the widening of a highway were bought from a monopoly supplier, should those prices be taken at market value or should a lower, shadow price be used indicating the lower MSC of the inputs? The market price would be used as a measure of cost if the input demand for the project did not alter the total amount of the factor available in the economy but merely transferred some of it away from other firms that would use it. In this case the market price is the true opportunity cost of the input.

If the input demand for the project means that more will be made available to the economy by the monopoly provider of the inputs, then the shadow price would have to be adjusted downward in the accounting of costs because only the MSCs of those extra factors used is the opportunity cost, not the actual price paid. That is, if the inputs in question are manufactured (i.e., not primary inputs) then lower-end inputs diverted into production of these higher-end inputs would have been priced elsewhere at their MSC presumably because they would have been sold in competitive markets. When there is a captive demander, the supply price contains a premium equal to the per unit monopoly profit that is not part of the social cost of those factors that might have been used in markets where monopolization is not possible. In a sense the monopoly price works like a tax on consumers with revenues going to a monopolist instead of a government.

Safety is another difficult topic for calculating a social CBA of transportation projects. How does one put a value on saving a life by removing a dangerous curve? If asked, most individuals would claim the value of their life to be infinite. But, if infinite values are included as benefits, then every project meets the CBA criteria. In practice a subjective value, like $6.3 million, is included for every life potentially saved.[3]

Another aspect of the monetization problem comes in the form of properly accounting for flows of costs and benefits over time. In order to convert a flow of costs and benefits into an equivalent present value (PV), the flows must be discounted. To see this consider that $1 received in the future is worth the equivalent of somewhat less than $1 received today. Why? Because of the opportunity for an investor to obtain compound interest on his investments. If the rate of interest per year is 10% then $1 received next year is worth, in today's money, the amount that needs to be invested today in order to get a total of $1 next year. That amount is approximately $0.91. Because the monetary value of the flows in costs relative to benefits in specific years need not be uniform, discounting these flows to their PV equivalents allows for them to be properly compared so as to determine if net benefits are in fact occurring.

The relationship between the PV of a flow and its future value (FV) in any given year and discount (interest) rate (r) is represented in the equations in Figure 11.2. Note that in this example the discount rate is 5%, rather than 10% as above. With a lower discount rate, the present value of a dollar is greater at $0.9524. This is an important point in CBA calculations. The higher the discount rate, the lower the value of benefits returned in future years.

In the example above, it is seen that the PV of $100 to be received as either a cost or a benefit at the beginning of next year is equivalent to $95.24

---

[3] Some authors treat he idea of using some statistical value for life with great disdain. See Lisa Heinzerling and Frank Ackerman *PRICING THE PRICELESS: Cost-Benefit Analysis of Environmental Protection*. Georgetown Environmental Law and Policy Institute, Georgetown University Law Center. 2002. http://www.ase.tufts.edu/gdae/publications/C-B%20pamphlet%20final.pdf

$$PV = \sum_{i=1}^{n} \frac{FV_i}{(1+r)^i} \qquad \text{where:}$$

PV = present value
FV = future value
r = rate of discount
n = life of investment
i = year

$$\text{e.g.,} \quad PV = \frac{\$100}{(1+0.05)^1} = \$95.24$$

NPV = net present value

$$NPV = \sum_{i=1}^{n} \frac{B_i - C_i}{(1+r)^i} - k \qquad \text{where:}$$

B_i = benefit
C_i = cost
k = initial cost

NPV ≥ 0 for a project to be accepted.

Figure 11.2.

received today when the rate of discount is 5%. It is the case that the higher is the rate of discount (r) the lower is the PV of the cost or benefit flow because, with the rate of return greater, the lesser amount of present money is needed to achieve future money. Thus, the choice of r is very important. If it is too high the PV of a benefit flow for a project may be too low given up front costs, while a choice of r that is too low would have the opposite effect. In the construction of transportation infrastructure it is usually the case that most of the costs are up-front while benefits need time before they kick in.

There are some points to consider when choosing the "appropriate" rate of discount. The rate should reflect the opportunity cost of the money used for finance in terms of the rate of return on the next best alternative. The starting point is to look at the prevailing rates of interest available in the economy and remove the inflation premium to arrive at a "real" rate of interest.[4] For example, if the nominal rate of interest was 8%, and the rate of inflation was 3%, the real rate of interest would be set at 5%. Depending

---

[4]If a nominal rate of interest is used without adjusting for the inflation premium, the discount rate will be higher. This would bias the calculation against projects that pay more of their returns later in the project life. In order to provide the same answer as the "real" rate of interest, all costs and benefits would have to be increased by the expected rate of inflation,

on the duration of the cost and benefit flow, a long-term or short-term rate may provide the appropriate benchmark interest rate. The advantage of using a real rate of interest is that one does not have to increase the value of the streams of costs and benefits into the future by the expected rate of inflation. This could involve predicting the rate of inflation 20 years into the future. The risk of miscalculation is much less if the effects of inflation are excluded.

The effect of taxation on investment complicates the problem for a private CBA. Suppose a firm in the private sector undertakes the project; this demonstrates that business profits are desired. These profits are subject to taxation at a rate of, say, 50% meaning that the firm will retain only one-half of these profits. Assume that the firm wished to borrow the money under a prevailing interest rate of, say, 8% to undertake investment in the project, and they calculated the inflate rate at 3% to yield a real discount rate of 5%. However, the firm would require a before-tax real rate of return on the project of at least 10% for the investment to be viable. This point is made in Figure 11.3. The tax distorts the applicable interest rate as seen by the borrower (10% + inflation) and as received by the lender (5% + inflation).

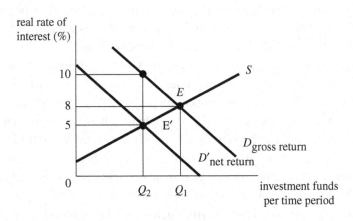

Figure 11.3.

---

before being discounted. It is much easier to simply treat all future costs and returns as if they are spent or received in deflated dollars.

If $1 is borrowed for a one-year term then $1.05 (deflated) must be paid back in one year's time. So if $1.10 is earned on the project (a 10% real rate of return), one-half of the $0.10 profit is paid in taxes leaving the required $1.05 to pay off the loan. Without taxes on profits, the equilibrium rate of interest is 8% and the project's return equals the interest rate payable to the savers who lent the funds. With a 50% tax on investment, the demand curve for investment funds (D) shifts leftward because the true (net) return to investors is now lower due to government taxation. The new equilibrium at E' indicates an after-tax rate of interest of 5% plus inflation while the before-tax rate is 10% plus inflation.[5]

In terms of accounting for the social value of borrowed funds, is the appropriate real rate of discount 5% or 10%? The answer depends on what these funds would have otherwise been used for. If they had been invested elsewhere the required gross return of 10% would be the opportunity cost of these funds. If instead these funds were used for consumption (and thus not saved) the opportunity cost would be the return to savings, which is 5%. Once a market rate is decided upon and the tax distortion removed, the proper social rate of discount will likely be lower than the one chosen in private CBA thus reflecting the societal gains that accrue beyond the ones that a private firm considers. With a lower rate of discount, the higher the PV of any future benefits will be relative to up-front costs and the likelier it is that the project will be accepted. In this sense we see that private CBA and social CBA can lead to different recommendations.

Three final points by way of criticism of CBA may be made. First, CBA accounts for net benefit flows but does not account for just who benefits and who bears the costs of infrastructure projects. A net benefit for society at large may still leave a set of losers behind. Those planners that wish to temper the strict efficiency of CBA with a subjective form of equity would need to add weights to particular costs and benefits. For example, the benefits of constructing a seaport in an economically depressed region may be subjectively given more weight relative to costs than they would in a region experiencing rapid growth. Such a decision is based on the value judgments of the planner.

---

[5]Technically this tax is *ad valorem* with the effect being that the net return demand curve will be flatter than the gross demand curve. The analysis, however, would be unchanged.

Second, political aspects may interfere with the acceptability of a project undertaken in the public sector even if it shows a positive net PV. The project may be so capital-intensive that the up-front costs lead to negative net benefits in the early life of the project, but once the project is completed and the only costs are maintenance-related the net benefits become positive. For budgetary reasons, governments may approve of projects that provide quicker returns especially if an election were near. In the crudest sense a government may be biased against long-term projects because the net benefits may accrue to other elected governments. One government pays the cost and the other reaps the benefit.

The third criticism is the determination of the salvage value of a project at the end of the discount period. After about 20 years of discounting, the PV of any further stream of benefits approaches zero very quickly. So, how should the remaining value of an infrastructure be calculated that has a useful life of 40 years or more? This is an important problem for bridges, power dams, railway cars and pipelines. A standing bridge could be worth its replacement cost, less some allowance for its shorter remaining life. At the same time, a great deal of technical change can occur over a 20-year period. The remaining asset may be worth much less than one designed to meet the modern demand.[6] The calculation of salvage value requires judgment on the part of the analyst, which further removes CBA from science to art.

A problem with any CBA is dynamic adjustment; things change after the decisions have been made. Consider the example in Figure 11.4 which shows the welfare effects presumed to take place under a project that proposes to widen a stretch of crowded highway. Under such widening, travel costs in the form of time and fuel costs to all current users will be expected to fall. As well, any extra (i.e., marginal) users will be encouraged to use the wider highway and will thus benefit from the lower travel costs; and this increased usage can be assumed to be built into the actual width decision made by the planner.

---

[6]An example of such technical change has occurred in covered hopper cars. Before the 100 ton hopper cars were half way through their useful service life of 40+ years, a more efficient 110 ton covered hopper car was introduced. The new cars reduced the salvage value of all the existing 100 ton cars because any attempt to sell a used car was met with a discount based on the productivity of the 110 ton railcar.

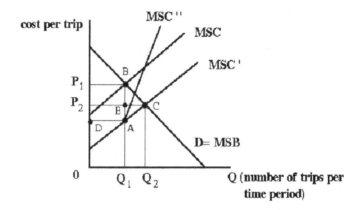

Figure 11.4.

Remember that the marginal social cost (MSC) includes all social costs such as an increase in pollution net of any reduction elsewhere due to traffic filtering to this highway and away from any other. The fact that it is upward sloping indicates that crowding does occur at the margin. Before the project is undertaken the efficient user charge is given by the social cost per unit of current highway usage in equilibrium, which is P_1 under a usage per time period of Q_1.

A lower MSC could be expected to come about under the wider highway because of the travel cost savings. This leads to a social cost per unit of P_2 with a usage of Q_2. With the wider highway in place the cost saving to the Q_1^{th} user is P_1BAD (the increase in his consumer surplus). Of course, this assumes that he is being charged only the MSC of providing the road for him and not the P_2 charge applied to Q_2. With a uniform charge of P_2, P_1BEP_2 is the increase in consumer surplus and P_2EAD is the increase in producer surplus. The increase in trips is $(Q_2 - Q_1)$ and there is a net social benefit in these trips equal to the consumer surplus minus the cost: Q_1BCQ_2 − Q_1ACQ_2 = ABC.

On this basis, the politicians could authorize the widening of the road, only to find that the size of ABC is considerably less than expected, once traffic adjusts to the new environment. The error could be the simplifying assumption that traffic flows are exogenous, such that infrastructure does not create an induced or derived demand. But if such a demand does in fact exist then the implication for CBA is that net benefits will be improperly estimated. As shown in Figure 11.4, instead of MSC′, the increased traffic could pivot the curve to MSC″.

The problem of working in an open system is not new. The massive building of freeways in Los Angeles from 1950 to 1980 could never solve the problem of traffic congestion. It poses what appears to be a paradox in investment decision making.[7] Consider two free-access highways that represent alternative means of travel between a suburb and the city center. Highway A is wide but winding while highway B is straight but narrow. Vehicles using A or B will be able to travel its length in t_A or t_B minutes, respectively.

Assuming that the highway is used as a means for travel and not joy-riding, it is reasonable to infer that congestion will build up on B until t_B rises to equalize at $t_0 = t_A$. Average users, in terms of travel time alone, become indifferent between A and B. The question becomes: is there a case for further infrastructure investment whereby highway B is widened? No, there is not. To see why, assume that A still has a lot of excess capacity under the current traffic flow. If B were widened so that its capacity increased, traffic flow would redistribute such that both highways maintain the very same travel times, $t_0 = t_A$. The investment is wasteful because it would create no time travel savings and therefore no benefits, when they are narrowly defined in terms of travel time. This point is made in Figure 11.5.

The first panel depicts highway B while the second depicts highway A. Quantity (Q) represents the number of vehicle trips per unit of time. The first point to note is that as long as both highways allow for free access, price (P) is more of a social cost inclusive of time than a direct charge to users. In the first panel, the widening project is designed to expand capacity from Q_B to Q'_B in order to achieve a long run equilibrium; that is, a capacity is provided where demand equals the long run marginal cost of provision. The problem is that usage along A is a function of that along B. The provision of more capacity along B shifts the demand for A's usage leftward. The demand for A is perfectly price-inelastic because the use quantity is dependent only

---

[7]This problem was first investigated by Pigou, A.C. *The Economics of Welfare*. London: MacMillan and Co, 1924.

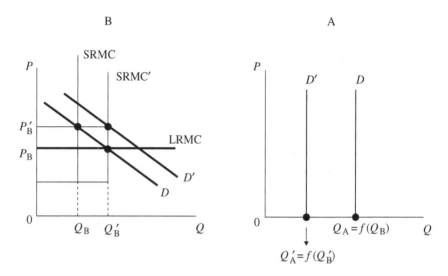

Figure 11.5.

on B's current capacity. The increased population wishing to use the now-wider B serves to shift its demand from D to exactly D' because this process will only stop once enough cars enter B to drive its (time) cost back to where it was before the widening (that is, to P'_B).

The problem here arose because both highways possessed free access. If B did, indeed, possess a toll charge of P_B, the users of A would not be so quick in changing over to B. In fact, the users of A would be all those that would not be willing to pay a toll of P_B for use of B. Notice that because $P_B < P'_B$ a time saving would occur along B if a toll were charged. This is why tolls are useful in combating the congestion problem.

Recall from Chapter 10 that there is a speed and flow relationship that is critical to the analysis of congestion costs. One could reason that such a project was not viable even before CBA were undertaken because the widening of a portion of highway serves only to push the bottleneck farther ahead along that highway. One would need to argue that the widening process would be done in stages, which means that the entire highway would eventually be widened. A separate CBA of each sub-component of the project without understanding the nature of the overall project would lead to confusion. Of course, as the ski lift example in Chapter 10 showed, an improvement to the efficiency of only a part of a closed process will not improve the efficiency of the closed process; rather, congestion over one or more other parts will be worsened. It is very important to understand the underlying process of the system under which a project is proposed before CBA is undertaken.

Finally, CBA is more of an analysis about efficiency than about equity so, in that regard, it may appear to be "heartless". Of course, a common assumption in economics is that people and firms look after their own self-interest and it is up to government to control people, firms and markets so that a social good of some sort is achieved. Would it be wrong for a car company not to recall a class of automobile that it discovered to have a potentially death-causing defect? Suppose that it undertook a private CBA and found that the probability of accidents leading to death were such that the expected cost through liability settlements were less than the cost of recall and repair. Would it still be wrong not to recall? Certainly it is privately efficient for the company not to recall and allow the deaths to occur.

Perhaps the ability of claimants to instigate class action suits allows for better coordination of their efforts so that the car company would then feel that the court settlement would be too great. Of course, this is an example of government allowing the judicial system to be more responsive to social needs. The Ford Motor Company once argued that it should not be made to undertake a U.S. national recall of 144,000 Mercury Capris that were likely to have defective windshield wipers because, by applying the U.S. government's own traffic statistics, 144,000 cars making round trips to their Ford dealer were likely to have more accidents than those that would be expected to occur with the defective parts still in circulation.[8]

Investment in transportation infrastructure can have an impact on *intermodal competition*. CBA studies are usually done as if the project is isolated from the rest of the economy. An infrastructure investment can alter the share of consumer demand between competing modes of transportation, or transport routes as described in the case of widening one of two roads,. The next section considers intermodal competition and explains the concept of generalized cost.

---

[8]This case was discussed in Rhoads, S. *The Economist's View of the World*. Cambridge: Cambridge University Press, 1985.

Intermodal Competition

Intermodal competition refers to the activities of sub-industries within the transportation industry that compete with one another. In urban transportation, cars, buses and taxis compete for the movement of people. In freight transportation, rail, trucking, barge, air, and ocean vessel shipping provide competing services. Of course, each mode of transport has a comparative advantage in certain areas and during specific seasons. For example, railway freight rates for grain to the Gulf of Mexico match barge rates when the Mississippi River is open to navigation. But when the barge season ends in the winter, rail rates for grain can double. Such freight rate fluctuations may lead to demands by shippers for government regulation. Ironically, if railway freight rates are not allowed to rise, intermodal competition may not be sustainable during the remainder of the year without a subsidy.

Consider the cost relationship between rail, intercity trucking and barge services. The rail mode faces the highest fixed cost (TFC) because the entire rail infrastructure is provided by the railway. The most expensive infrastructure component of intercity trucking is the road system, but it is shared with cars and buses and provided by the government. Fuel taxes collected from these vehicle operators are used to build and maintain the road system.

The fuel tax revenue is not necessarily earmarked for the cost of road construction and maintenance and is unlikely to reflect the full costs of use. Trucking is generally cross-subsidized by car drivers because roads could be built to much lower standards if they only had to cope with the axle weights of cars and light trucks.

The barge system has the lowest fixed cost because virtually all marine improvements and maintenance expenditures are supported by taxpayers. The variable costs for rail and barge are lower than for trucks. Consequently, each mode of transport has different total costs (TC) and comparative advantage that varies with the distance transported.

Figure 11.6 illustrates the cost of rail, truck and barge transport relative to distance traveled. In terms of costs alone, distance x is the "critical" distance whereby a shipper would be indifferent between rail and truck shipping. To the left of x trucking possesses the cost advantage while to the

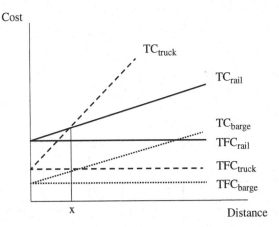

Figure 11.6.

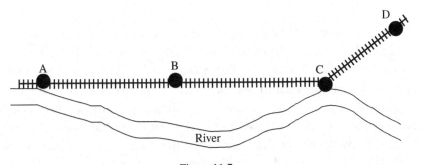

Figure 11.7.

right of x rail possesses the cost advantage. It is for these reasons that the greater the length of haul the more rail shipping is favored. Where a river route is available however, the barge can provide freight rates that are lower than either truck or rail.

Intermodal competition highlights the basic principle that the quantity of one mode of transport demanded is conditioned upon not only the user price of the mode but also the user price of the alternative modes. Such competition can lead to seeming anomalies in freight rates in which distance does not lead to higher rates. Consider the situation illustrated in Figure 11.7 in which a railway parallels a river with barge service. The cities located at A and C have access to the barge service, but cities located at B and D have to rely on the railway.

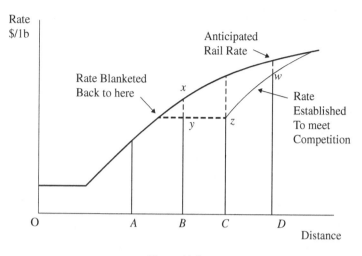

Figure 11.8.

Freight rates could be expected to increase with distance as presented in Figure 11.8 but this depends on the willingness/need for the railway to compete with the barge system. The railway may need to offer freight rates at point C that are equal to the barge rate. At points away from point C the railway might match the rates of a combined barge-truck service, or it could decide to offer a *blanket rate* from point C back to where this rate is charged by the railway. In reference to the diagram, the railway rate at point B could be charged *y* (the blanket rate) or *x* (the rising rail rate). If the rate *x* is charged, then the shippers at point B are likely to complain that they are being discriminated against because the rate *z* at point C is less even though the distance is greater.

Friedman argues that the discriminatory freight rate is not only justified, it may be necessary to make an appropriate investment decision on the railway infrastructure.[9] Figure 11.9 reproduces Friedman's model. The fixed costs are sunk and the railway freight rates are set according to the price elasticity of demand (Ramsey pricing). The dashed lines indicate the prices charged for each of the rail segments from A to B to C above the relevant variable costs: V_{AB}, V_{BC}, V_{AC}. The exception is the freight rate from A to C

---

[9]Friedman, David D. "In Defense of the Long-Haul/Short-Haul Discrimination." *The Bell Journal of Economics*, Vol. 10, No. 2 (Autumn 1979).

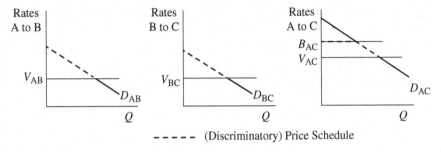

----- (Discriminatory) Price Schedule

Figure 11.9.

Source: Adapted from Friedman (1979).

that competes with the barge rate B_{AC}. If the rate B_{AC} is below the highest rate on D_{AB} or D_{BC} the railway is engaging in short haul/long haul price discrimination. The extra revenue obtained on the short haul is necessary to offset the fixed cost of providing the infrastructure to point B.

It must be kept in mind that this analysis is based on cost alone. It may be the case that shippers will be willing to pay a premium to ship by truck over distances that are less expensive by either rail or barge because of the versatility offered by trucks in terms of "right to the door" delivery, speed and other quality attributes.

A passenger or shipper wishing to make use of a particular mode will consider adding a personal valuation of these "other costs" to the user cost of the service. This total cost is known as the generalized cost and certainly exceeds the money-based user cost alone. It is for this reason that a lowering of bus fares may not induce many car users to abandon their cars for public transit because, to them, the time costs involved in public transit represents a large proportion of their generalized cost calculation. This point is further explored below.

Intermodal competition between buses and cars in an urban setting has taken the form of making certain accommodations for bus services such as express services, priority traffic lanes, and greater frequency all in an effort to lower the time cost portion of the generalized cost. In the same sense passenger rail and air competition may be looked at in the same light. Why is it that the market does not build in all opportunity costs so that the user price equals the generalized cost? The answer lies in the nature of the transportation market. As discussed in Chapter 2, transportation is by and large a means to an end and the demand for such services is a derived demand. Users in some sense do pay in-kind for their time spent in travel because they, to a degree, forego work for idle leisure. Even if all generalized costs are not directly priced the user does consider them so that, in effect, quantity demanded is more a function of generalized costs than it is of user price:

$$G_x = G(P_x; C_{1x}, \ldots, C_{nx}),\tag{11.1}$$

$$Q_{dx} = Q(G_x; G_y; G_z).\tag{11.2}$$

Equation (11.1) indicates that the generalized cost for mode x is a function of its user price (P) and a variety of opportunity costs (C) indicating, for example, time, quality, and reliability. Equation (11.2) indicates the complete demand function for mode x showing that the quantity demanded is a function not just of user price but of the generalized costs of this and all other available modes (x, y, and z).

Given that the user price is below the generalized cost consider the following example of intermodal competition. Consider two cities (A and B) that are accessible by rail, car, and air such that current passenger usage is divided among the modes. Passengers are assumed to treat all modes with some degree of substitutability. The markets for these modes are given in Figure 11.10 and note that we need not specifically refer to A and B as either origin or destination; rather it is the A–B set of modal infrastructures that are being marketed. In this sense rail passenger-kms and total car-kms may be several times larger than the number of complete A to B or B to A trips. Let an investment in high speed rail infrastructure take place such

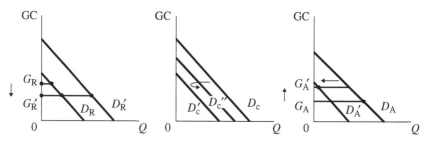

Figure 11.10.

that, upon completion, the generalized cost falls. Although the passenger fare may be higher, the greater time-savings drop the generalized cost from GR to GR′.

The quantity (Q) represents the number of trips per time period anywhere along the A to B routes. Not only does the generalized cost for rail (GR) fall, the demand curve shifts to the right because new riders are attracted to this premium rail service. Consequently, rail is substituted for these modes. Of course, this is precisely the general implication of Equation (11.2). The decrease in air travel may, however, lead to fewer flights being offered which would cause the generalized cost for air travel (G_A) to rise and reinforce the rightward shift of the demand curve for rail.

The adjustment process could have several rounds of interactions before a new equilibrium is found. For example, if the highway now becomes less congested because many drivers abandon their cars in favor of the train, the demand for cars encouraged by the faster travel time could shift the car demand back to D''_C. We may assume some rightward shift in the demand for car travel if the substitutability between air and car travel, for comparable trips, is close.

Given the extra demand for rail services, will its generalized cost go up because the new infrastructure becomes congested? If yes, then the adjustment process would continue, if no, then the market has stabilized. Note that if the investment had gone to road infrastructure instead, then the rail mode would have been affected in the way the air mode was affected in Figure 11.10. And likewise the air mode would have been affected in the way the car mode was.

Finally, consider the nature of car and bus competition for passenger travel in an urban setting using common roadways. It will be shown that the optimal modal split is either strictly bus travel or car travel with no mixture as is shown in Figure 11.11.[10]

Let the starting point be at A where all travelers use buses and there are no cars available. GC$_{bus}$, which is read from right to left in the figure, shows that there are fleet economies with respect to the generalized cost for bus use because greater usage precipitates: (1) more buses on the road leading

---

[10]This problem is presented following: Mishan (1967). "Interpretation of the Benefits of Private Transport." *Journal of Transport Economics and Policy*, Vol. 1, 184–189.

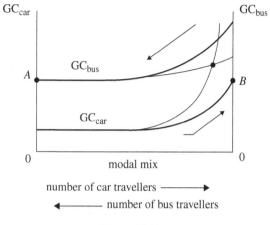

Figure 11.11.

to a fall in waiting time; and (2) speed increases due to a lesser amount of stops being made. The second point implies that either the number of passengers per bus falls as more are brought into service or the frequency of service allows passengers to sort themselves out according to their usage so that more common stops are made much in the way a rush hour bus stops more so within the central business area and a non-rush hour bus on the same route stops at major shopping centers or other businesses along the way. It is also assumed that the buses alone do not contribute to a congestion problem. GC_{car} is seen to be always below GC_{bus} because there is no wait involved in car usage and the routing is more direct.

As cars begin to be used on the roadway due to the perceived savings in generalized cost, congestion on the roadway will occur but the savings will always keep buses at a disadvantage because the car congestion affects the buses as well. The optimal solution proceeds to point B where there is no bus usage at all. Point A was optimal when no cars were available. The conclusion is that the optimal mix is an extreme solution or what is sometimes called a "corner solution".

Of course, if buses were separated into special lanes whereby they avoided the congestion due to cars it is possible that GC_{bus} would fall over the relevant range and GC_{car} would rise over the same range so that an "interior solution" came about as shown by the thinner lines in Figure 11.11. In other words, until car drivers are stalled in traffic and watching buses with empty seats passing them by, they have no incentive to switch ($GC_{bus} > GC_{car}$).

A final word on CBA and generalized cost of transportation involves the difference between projects that are economically viable (a positive CBA) and those that are financially viable to operate. The CBA of a new rapid transit system could be positive if it incorporated the value of the time savings for automobile drivers that are created by the diversion of traffic to the new mass transit system.[11] If only the fares of the transit riders are available to the rapid transit project however, it may not be possible to generate enough cash flow to finance the development and pay its operating costs. The rapid transit system creates a positive externality for car drivers that is incorporated into the CBA. If this benefit cannot be extracted directly from car users in the form of a toll, the only other option is for a transfer of funds to the mass transit providers through the tax system. This justification for the subsidization of mass transit is explored further in Chapter 13.

Keywords

blanket rate

cost–benefit analysis

intermodal competition

shadow price

Exercises

1. A Rapid Transit Task Force recommends a dedicated right-of-way (bus-only road) for rapid transit buses from the University to the Downtown. At the present, buses are mixed with cars and other traffic on the streets.

   Draw and explain an appropriate model(s) that illustrates the arguments for dedicated bus lanes.

   The other policy alternative is to impose congestion charges on car drivers to force more of them to take the street buses. Why are congestion charges likely to be less successful at reducing congestion than the construction of dedicated bus right-of-ways?

---

[11]The assignment of a value on the time savings of road users (cars and trucks) that result from proposed transit systems is fraught with mischief in CBA studies. At some value of time, any transit scheme can be made to look economic. The real value to drivers can only be assessed accurately by imposing a toll on a road system, as has been done in the center of London, England, and finding out how drivers respond.

2. Assume that the government introduces a new road pricing system for transport trucks that represents the costs of the negative externalities they create. Amongst other things, these higher road charges for trucks have an impact on intermodal competition, in particular rail and air modes.

   Draw and explain an appropriate model(s) that illustrates the economic rationale for assessing trucks with charges for their negative externalities.

   Use and appropriate economic model to explain how changing the cost of trucking is likely to impact the other competing modes of transport, like rail.

3. The economics of railways give them a cost advantage for long distances because they are very fuel efficient. Trucks are less expensive to use for short distances.

   Use an appropriate model(s) to explain and illustrate how the competitive distance of rail and truck transport would change if the cost of diesel fuel were to double in price.

   Despite the rising cost of diesel fuel since 2005, not much freight has shifted from trucks to the railways. How would you explain this observation?

4. A 50-year old bridge at the border is congested. Average crossing times are 30–45 minutes longer than necessary and excessive vehicle idling creates pollution. Government is considering a new bridge. The existing bridge is conveniently located, while the new bridge will increase driving distances by at least 15 minutes.

   Using an appropriate model(s) explain whether toll charges should be used on these bridges to manage the division of traffic over the two crossings.

   You have been hired to undertake a public benefit–cost analysis of the economic feasibility of this new bridge. Describe your method and five issues that could impact the accuracy of your work.

5. Travel time savings are often used to justify public investment in railway overpasses, bridges and rapid transit expansions.

   Use an appropriate model, or models, to explain why does the VOTT vary so much for individuals and for different situations?

   How could an under-estimate or over-estimate of the average value of time distort a public cost–benefit analysis?

6. Imagine that you have been hired to help conduct a CBA for the construction of a rapid transit system parallel to a major city street. The city is motivated by the negative externalities of cars and the social benefits of rapid transit.

   Draw appropriate models or use examples to describe the following problems associated with the calculation of a CBA for rapid transit investments: (1) Choice of the discount rate, (2) Shadow prices, (3) Double-counting of costs or benefits, (4) Salvage values, and (5) Price distortions.

   One of the risks in CBA is that forecasted events may not occur. Explain how the response of commuters could end up reducing the benefits of the investment in rapid transit envisioned by the study.

7. Construction of a high-speed passenger rail service has been proposed on the Toronto–Ottawa–Montreal route as illustrated below. Travel time would be cut in half for rail users, and the rail fares that were just a bit higher than the bus are now only a bit lower than airplane tickets.

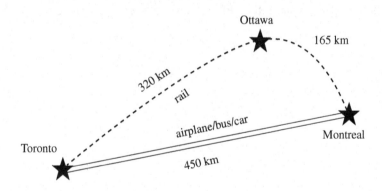

   Draw and explain an appropriate model(s) that illustrates the impact on intermodal competition if the high-speed railway is built and operated.

   The new rail service will be able to complete the Toronto–Montreal distance in 135 minutes, versus 50 minutes for the airplane, and 360 minutes on the bus or driving a car. Explain whether the bus or the airline operators have more reason for concern.

8. Normally freight rates increase with distance so that communities located farther away from the market pay more than those that are closer.

However, freight rates can be affected by the availability of infrastructure and by intermodal competition.

Draw and explain an appropriate model(s) that illustrates how the transport infrastructure can distort site prices.

Explain how intermodal competition can reduce freight costs for some locations that are farther away than those that are closer to the market.

9. Non-cash costs play an important role in the supply and demand of transportation.

Explain the concept of generalized costs and use appropriate economic models to illustrate how generalized costs affect demand in the following situations:

> Intermodal competition
>
> Road congestion
>
> Public transit

Define and explain the differences between generalized costs and externalities.

Chapter 12

Location and Land Settlement

Land settlement patterns can be viewed as the flip-side of transportation networks. Transportation infrastructure is built to serve the needs of the population, but the settlement pattern of the land is directly influenced by the cost and availability of transportation. In the settlement of the Great Plains and the Canadian Prairies, the railway preceded the pioneers. After the territory was opened, homesteaders were given free land provided they improved it within five years. The settlement spurred on by the railway created the demand for the railway's services to carry agricultural products to export markets.

Transport and settlement can happen the other way around. For example, the Yukon Territory was settled ahead of the transportation infrastructure in pursuit of the Klondike gold rush (1897); three years later the railway was completed.[1] It makes some difference whether the outbound cargo is gold or grain, but the theory of location implies simultaneous determination.

Location theory is based on price differences. In this case, market prices and transport costs determine the value of land. The first half of this chapter examines the theory of site rents and the capitalization of land. The second half considers the location of industry and the creation of gateway cities and trade corridors.

---

[1]The White Pass and Yukon Route Railway was completed in 1900 from Skagway, Alaska to White Horse, Yukon.

Site Rents

A distinction can be made between the price or value of a good determined at the physical marketplace (where the transaction takes place), and the price or value determined by the firm at the point of final production. The market price (P_M) may be looked upon as the price the consumer faces while the *site price* (P_S) indicates the value of the good before transportation to the physical market has occurred. The cone-shaped diagram on the right side of Figure 12.1 illustrates the relationship between the market price and the site price. Transport costs are assumed to be equal in all directions, but vary with distance. In this model, the Law of One Price (LOOP) reigns. Every price is related by transportation costs.

At a distance of d_1 between the production site and the physical market, the left panel of Figure 12.1 is P_{S1}. This is equal to the market price less the transport cost (T) to the market. Notice that the site price function falls at a decreasing rate with respect to distance meaning that for each extra dollar spent on transport, greater distance is possible for the next dollar spent. This is why the "footprint" of the market on the right side of Figure 12.1 expands at lower prices.

T rises at a decreasing rate with respect to distance, as shown in the second panel, is because costs related to fuel, drivers and loading/unloading for a given shipment increase with distance on a less than one-to-one basis.

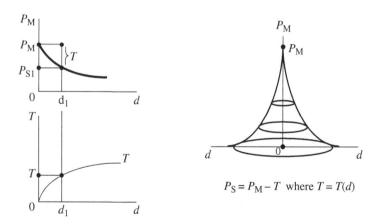

$$P_S = P_M - T \text{ where } T = T(d)$$

Figure 12.1.

A doubling of distance should not double the amount of fuel consumed because a constant idling time may be common to all trip lengths;[2]

The concept of site price is important when dealing with spatial economics (the economics of location and space). Assuming that a supplier is able to pass the entire cost of transport onto consumers, he must still pay for the initial cost of hired transport or absorb the cost as a factor of production if it is done in-house. The site price is really the value of production net of transport costs. When faced with the choice of several physical markets in which to sell, it is the site price that the supplier considers when for-hire transport is used is the one that maximizes the revenues of the firm.

In a perfectly competitive market structure, the market price for a good would be constant across all physical markets but, because the market distances vary across the firms, the site prices will differ for each physical market. The supplier would choose to ship to the market that allowed for the highest site price.

The three-dimensional space is useful in that it serves to show where firms would place themselves when faced with a multiple choice of physical markets. To make the analysis as simple as possible, consider firms deciding upon a location when there are two physical market choices as shown in Figure 12.2. The ellipses drawn indicate contour lines of all equidistant production points from the market center as given by the P_M axis. These are called *isotims*. All points along a contour line represent the collection of equivalent site prices.

In order to better grasp the spatial ordering of the firms facing differential site prices consider the right panel of Figure 12.2 which gives the top view from the peaks of the two site price cones. Point E would bisect a straight line drawn directly between markets (a) and (b) and is thus along the shortest transport route between the two. Points F and G are equidistant

---

[2]Longer distances may involve highway travel, which allows for greater fuel economy as compared to shorter-distance urban travel. Also certain aspects of a driver's wage are independent of trip length such as insurance and other employee benefits. Finally, the costs related to loading and unloading a given shipment size are common to all trips independent of length. In summary, the average total cost (ATC) of transport declines with respect to distance and this, it will be recalled, was one of the operational "economies" discussed in Chapter 5.

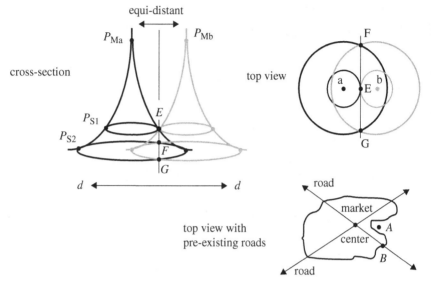

Figure 12.2.

from the two market centers. The line FEG represents the collection of all point-pairs where site prices for firms wishing to supply to both markets would be equal.

Note that the above and subsequent market comparisons are based on a strategy whereby each firm wishes to supply both physical markets efficiently. Certainly with both markets offering the same market price for each good, a firm would optimally locate at one of them and supply exclusively to it and not the other assuming, of course, that its strategy was not in fact to supply to both.

The lower panel of Figure 12.2 serves as a note of caution to the analysis. While the remainder of this section treats site prices as following concentric patterns they are only reasonable when the transport infrastructure is constant throughout the area. Certainly this may hold true for air transport or ocean vessels on the high seas but a pre-existing infrastructure of roads or rail serves to bias site prices toward specific population centers. The site price surface becomes irregular in shape. The site price at point A in the lower panel is less than that obtained at point B even though A is closer to the market center than is B. Point B is favored over point A because a road already connects it to the market center.

 In order to depart more fully from some of the confining assumptions of the perfectly competitive model, suppose that the market price in market (b) for the good were lower than in (a). Some reasons as to why this may be the case might be: a government with jurisdiction in the region of market (a) places a sales tax on the goods being sold there; or income levels are higher in (a) which serves to bid up prices in that market. How would a variety of firms wishing to supply the same good to these markets arrange themselves? Obviously it is not along a straight line, equidistant from the markets. But as LOOP holds difference in market prices must be equal to the difference in transport cost which is shown in Figure 12.3.

 Point E in this case, as compared to Figure 12.2, shows that the firms would place themselves closer to market (b) than to (a). Why? Because at the midpoint between (a) and (b) the site price earned in (a) would be

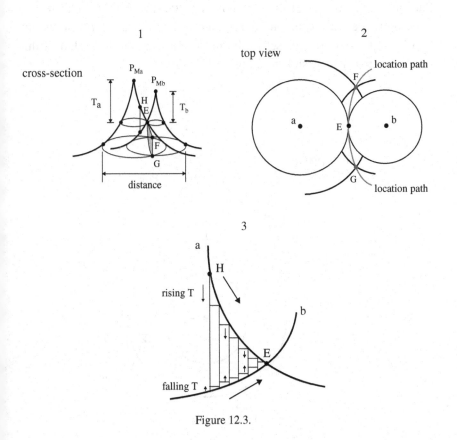

Figure 12.3.

greater than in (b) as shown by point H in the first panel of the figure. Because firms would position themselves where they would be indifferent between serving the two markets, they can afford to move closer to (b).

The third panel shows that for (a), as distance away from it increases, *T* rises (or the site price falls) by less and less while in market (b) as distance away from it decreases, *T* falls (or the site price rises) by more and more which obviously makes the case for improvements at the margin as (b) is approached. This process stops once the net returns (site prices) are equal in both markets as given by point E. The locus of the intersection points of the contour lines forms, what mathematicians call half of a hyperbola, shows the optimal locations of firms with differing site prices that wish to remain indifferent between the two markets.

The outer boundary of the shaded slice in the first panel and the dotted line in the second panel through points E, G, and F both indicate this hyperbolic location path. One final point to note is that, if P_{Mb} falls, the hyperbola locus moves closer to (b) and would begin to encircle it if this fall continued. This is shown in Figure 12.4.

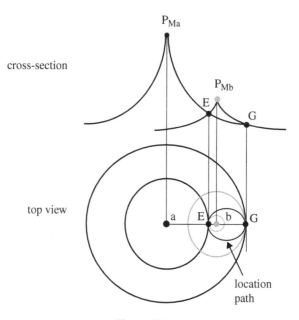

Figure 12.4.

This makes sense because once the market price in (b) falls enough to equal the site price, transport costs fall to zero because no firm would wish to incur costs that would price its output out of the market. If firms wish to supply to that market they would have to position themselves right at (b). To envision the cross section involved in Figure 12.4, picture market (b) as a small town positioned beside a large city that is market (a). At point G, the firm is indifferent whether to sell in the town or the city.

With the background behind site prices now established, the definition of *site rent* can be explored. In fact, site rent is identical to the term economic rent. Economic rent is the return that accrues to an immobile factor of production such as a parcel of land. For example, a parcel of land is obviously affixed to a portion of the earth's surface and would be available for use even if its price of usage were zero. In this way, the opportunity cost of the fixed parcel of land is zero and any positive price paid for usage is a premium above the opportunity cost, which would be characterized as economic rent. More specifically, the price paid for land is demand determined as shown in Figure 12.5.

If the demand curve were D_1, the equilibrium price for land would be zero and so would be the economic rent. If the demand curve to shifty to D_2 then the equilibrium price of P^* would be the economic rent. Notice that the demand determines the price of the land but the quantity available is constant at Q^*.

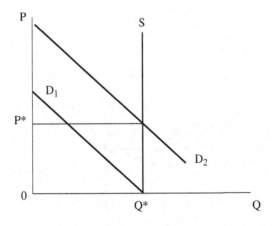

Figure 12.5.

Site rent would be defined as the maximum return to the firm for its output (site price multiplied by total output) less the total cost for all mobile factors used in the production process at the given site. Of course, this difference is the total cost of the immobile factor used in the production process assuming only normal profits prevail. Thus economic rent and site rent are synonymous. And, while land is an immobile factor, it need not be the only immobile factor at a given site; for example, plant size is taken as immobile at least in the short run.

The linkage between site rents and land values is illustrated in Figure 12.6. Consider a perfectly competitive firm facing a site price of P_s^* as shown in the upper panel of Figure 12.6, with a distance from the physical market of d^*. If someone wanted to purchase the land at location d^*, the owner would want at least the net present value of the future stream of site rents (economic rents) represented by the shaded area in the lower panel of Figure 12.6. Depending on the owner's discount rate and expectations, this would represent his asking price for the land.

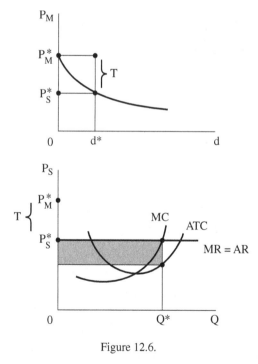

Figure 12.6.

The small shaded area is the profit rectangle, or site rent earned at the d* location, because the average total cost (ATC) is essentially the per unit opportunity cost for each unit of Q*. The closer the location is to the market center, the larger is the site rent. Firms that locate farther away would face a lower site price meaning that the shaded profit rectangle in the second panel of Figure 12.6 would become smaller for them. This makes sense because firms closer to the market center face lower transport costs and, when faced with a fixed market price, obtain a larger site rent.

Note the difference between the perfectly competitive firm, as shown in the lower panel of Figure 12.6, with the one developed in Chapter 7.

The firm in both cases takes the market price as given but in Figure 12.6 economic profit is measured based upon the site price (P_s^*) which is the given market price (P_M^*) less the transport cost (T) applicable to the location at distance (d^*) from the physical market.

The site rent surface is the collection of economic profit or site rent rectangles available at various distances from the market. This is shown in Figure 12.7. Site rent s_1 is the largest profit rectangle possible. Obviously this would occur at zero distance from the market center as the figure shows. At distance d_4 the site rent, s_4, is zero, which indicates that the site price equals the ATC and economic profits are thus zero. Any distance beyond d_4 will not cover ATC but so long as average variable cost is covered losses will be minimized in the short run given the fixed cost of land and any other immobile factors. In the long run those parcels of land beyond d_4 would be retired from use at least as far as production of the good in question is concerned.

The site rent surface is more appropriate than is the site price surface because the attributes of the latter are subsumed into the former and, furthermore, the former allows the firm's cost structure to be considered as well. Location will be based upon the profitability of the site as opposed to just the site price received, because the site price only considers transport costs while site rent considers all fixed, variable, and transport costs. A firm producing two different goods to be supplied to a different market may establish the site rent cones for each and determine the location that equalizes the site rents in a fashion similar to that shown above for site prices.

Anything that would change the profit rectangle's size for any given distance will expand or contract the site rent surface appropriately. If the

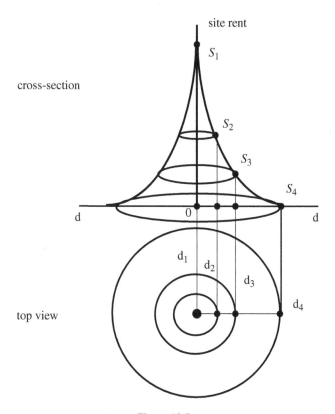

Figure 12.7.

given market price rose (fell), *ceteris paribus*, the site rent surface would expand (contract), and site prices would rise (fall) because transport costs per unit of distance, as well as all other costs, are assumed constant. If the use of the factors of production themselves are subject to transport costs then the cost curves would be higher (lower) for farther (closer) distances from (to) the input market sites which serves to make economic profits lower (higher) and contract (expand) the site rent surface.

It is fairly straightforward to consider the partition of sites for the purpose of producing multiple goods. Consider three classes or qualities of land (A, B, and C) with three goods (1, 2, and 3) as possible production uses of the land classes. For simplicity, two-dimensional, linear site rent functions are drawn in Figure 12.8 but the following results apply in full to a three-dimensional surface.

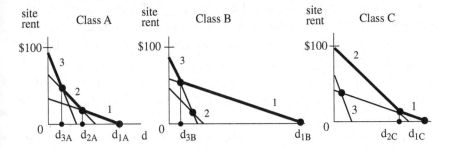

- the bolded portions are the upper envelopes

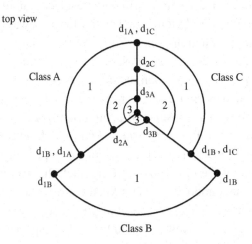

Figure 12.8.

Notice that the site rent functions for each good possess the same slopes in each land class but different site rents (because they possess different vertical intercepts). The same slope assumption indicates that transport per unit of distance from the market is identical which would imply that transport infrastructure and terrain were the same at each site. This assumption is used for simplicity but could be easily relaxed. The different heights for each site rent function shown in the first three panels of Figure 12.8 merely show that the different land qualities lead to different site rents for each good for a given distance from each market center.

Each firm or set of firms operating in each class of land would take the combination of goods which give the maximum in site rents. The upper envelope of the site rent functions for each land class gives the optimal location for the production of each good in the particular land site. Technically, because the site rent functions for good 1 in each land class are identically sloped, d_{1B} represents a farther distance from the market center than the good 1 functions lower down the vertical axis in classes A and C. This is why the top view panel in Figure 12.8 has a contour line extended outward at class B.

A further complication would be to introduce rival physical markets as alternative shipping points for the three goods. The major factor of consideration is land quality in that, for example, logging must take place on forested land and coal mining must take place where there are coal deposits. Site rents are obviously lower the farther away is the physical market from the production point. With alternative physical markets the site rent envelope for the various classes of land would become, in a two-market case, a portion based upon the distances between the two markets. Using the first panel of Figure 12.3 as reference, each market would possess a site rent envelope space instead of a site price space the intersection of which at a point such as E indicates the spacing and the choice of good to be produced. As Figure 12.8 shows, the site rent envelope comprises a multiple of goods. Note that the more goods from which the firm may choose for the land class, the smoother and less kinked would become the site rent envelope. But this can be taken one step further; for example, Figure 12.9 shows how the site rent envelope would look with respect to markets X and Y with class A land surrounding the former and class B land surrounding the latter.

The class A and class B site rent envelopes are taken directly from Figure 12.8. Note that the site rent envelope for class B is read from right-to-left. Care must be taken because, given the land class boundary at d^*, the site rents envelopes experience a structural break. Also, if the distance between markets X and Y are long enough such that the envelopes of one or both sides of the boundary reached the horizontal axis, the space in between on this distance axis would be a "no man's land" as far as production is concerned. In the second panel of Figure 12.9, the production boundaries are drawn as straight lines rather than as concentric ones merely for simplicity.

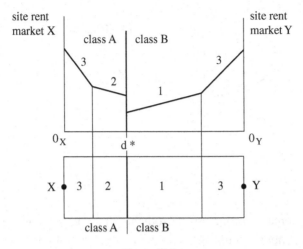

Figure 12.9.

A final point, mentioned but not explored here, is that one need not specify land qualities that are concentric to the market centers. If they were irregular in formation around the market center the site rent boundaries would reflect any abrupt changes in land quality in the market area. It was already mentioned by way of the third panel in Figure 12.2 that even pre-existing infrastructure can make site price contour lines irregular in shape.

Industrial Location

The discussion of site prices and site rents highlighted their importance in the land use decision and production location decision. This section examines at the production location decision. A key assumption made in the analysis of firm size is that all inputs are available at the production location. This is the equivalent of assuming that transportation costs are zero for inputs that have to be transported to the location of the firm. If transportation costs are not zero, the optimal size of the firm needs to be adjusted to reflect the long run average total costs (LRATC) of transportation to the plant location. This is illustrated in Figure 12.10.

In microeconomic theory, the optimal scale of a firm is its minimum point on the production-LRATC as given by the location of Q. This considers plant size with centralized production and no costs for inbound transportation. To this we now add a feeling for the space under which

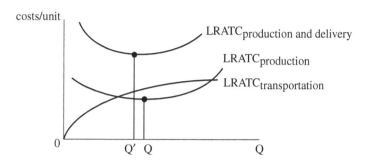

Figure 12.10.

supply and demand for factors of production interact. Suppose that supply of the major input is uniform across this space and that the space itself is topographically consistent. An example could be the optimal plant size for a sawmill located in the middle of a forested area. It follows that as the production scale of the sawmill expands, logs have to be transported ever farther from the edges of the forest to the sawmill. This is where costs in the form of transportation-LRATC come in. As the distance of haul increases, the average transport costs per unit of raw materials consumed is higher; this is why the transport cost curve is rising.

If transport costs were a constant function of distance, the transportation-LRATC would be a straight line. The curvature in the transportation-LRATC reflects the tapering in transportation rates associated with distance of travel. In this way, scale economies in production are tempered somewhat because the full costs facing the firm are given by the vertical sum of the production and transportation curves shown by the delivery-LRATC. Optimal scale is indicated where that curve is minimized as shown by Q'. As long as total transport costs rise with production scale, the optimal plant scale is less than that indicated by production alone.

If the availability of raw materials and transportation costs were the same everywhere then the optimal size of production plants would be identical. The reality is that raw material availability can vary depending on soils, climate, capital and management. The farther that the raw materials have to be transported, *ceteris paribus*, the more the transportation-LRATC would shift up, and the further the optimal size of plant would shift to the left. Figure 12.11 illustrates the cost of collection as it varies in resource

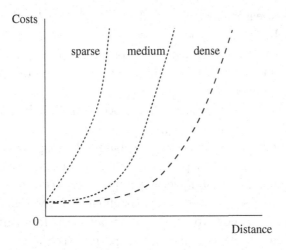

Figure 12.11.

availability. Collection costs increase rapidly with distance for a sparse supply versus a dense resource availability. This helps explain some of the differences observed in production scale.[3]

The previous section discussed location from the point of view of production, but similar decisions must be made on the part of consumers. Producers decide where to locate and produce output while consumers decide where to locate so as to live and work. It is possible to subsume the consumer location choice problem into the producer location choice problem by noting that the locational difference between consumer and producer is roughly that between worker and employer and so this locational difference would be expressed, by competitive markets, in terms of higher labor costs to the firm in compensation for increased travel time to work. Admittedly, the consumer location problem is more difficult because, while the motive for producer location is productivity and site rents, the consumer decision is based upon a sometimes conflicting choice between a location

---

[3]Ethanol plants provide an illustration of the interaction of transportation costs and processing plant size. The optimal scale of a corn ethanol plant can be very large if it is located in the U.S. Midwest where corn yields average in excess of 200 bushels per acre. A wheat-based ethanol plant in western Canada, where the yields of wheat are less than 50 bushels per acre, would not be competitive at the same scale as the corn ethanol plant because it would have to draw its grain input from a much larger area.

that facilitates reasonable access to the work place and one that provides for a reasonable amount of leisure opportunities. The growth of suburban areas is indicative of some of the aspects of the consumer location problem. Nonetheless, the focus of this section is exclusively on the industrial, or producer, location problem.

A complete view of the production process for a firm involves: (1) procurement of the factors needed in the production process; (2) producing output with those factors; and (3) distributing the output to the physical market(s). This process presupposes an optimal production location relative to the physical markets for inputs and outputs. It is in the area of transport costs where a possible trade-off comes about; namely a closer location to the consumer market would lower transport costs for distribution, but if the production process is more land-specific, such as in mining, then procurement and distribution costs face a trade-off.

The location problem is illustrated in Figure 12.12. It is assumed that the transport between the raw materials and the finished goods markets takes place along the most efficient route. The firm can choose where to locate anywhere between the resource and consumer markets. The transport cost curve is the vertical sum of the procurement and distribution cost curves. Note that the procurement cost curve is read from left-to-right while the distribution cost curve is read in the opposite fashion. The least advantageous location is where the total transport costs are the maximum, and the most favored location is where the transport costs are minimized.

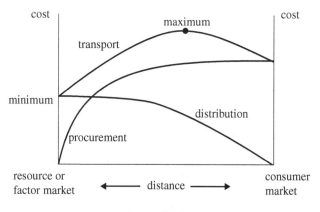

Figure 12.12.

In this example the procurement cost curve rises faster for a given unit of distance than does the distribution cost curve. Consequently, transport cost is higher when located closer to the consumer market than the factor market. The assumption that follows from the curves as drawn is that it is more expensive to transport factors than it is to transport final goods. The transport cost curve is minimized at or near the factor market location, which is thus the optimal location. Had the distribution cost curve risen faster, the consumer market might have been the optimal location. If transportation costs are a significant share of the product's final price, then location can be influenced by whether the production process is weight/volume gaining or losing. Processes that lose weight/volume can save transportation costs by locating close to the source of raw materials. An historic example of production relocation is the cattle slaughterhouses. At one time all cattle were shipped to the cities for slaughter and distribution. With the advent of refrigerated transport, the meat processing industry shifted the location of the slaughterhouses to be near the feedlots. Boxed beef, which is more concentrated, is much less expensive to ship than live cattle.

Processes that add a lot of air or water to the raw materials are usually located near the final market because these inputs are freely available. Soft drink bottling is an example. The syrup is shipped to local bottling plants were it is combined with water. For some raw materials, the process dictates the location. It takes approximately three pounds of raw potatoes to make a pound of frozen French fries. Consequently, these processing plants are located near the potato fields. But, potato chips are bulky and somewhat fragile, so the potatoes are shipped to the locations of concentrated populations for processing and distribution.

Some production processes are neither weight/volume losing, nor gaining. These are called foot-loose industries because the processing facility can be located anywhere. Two examples are honey and oilseed crushers. In both cases, the respective end products (pure honey/beeswax and cooking oil/meal) are roughly the same in weight and volume as the raw materials. Location in this case may depend on the geographical dispersion of the end markets. If the two end products are shipped in different directions, the location near the raw material site might be favored.

A variation in the industrial location problem is a *trans-shipping* point.

Trans-shipping involves the switching of modes of transport during mid-shipping such as, for example, when the cargo of an ocean vessel is loaded onto a truck or rail car at a seaport. A firm may wish to locate at the trans-shipping point in order to engage in further processing to avoid the costs of unloading and reloading of the factors between modes. In particular, if the processing reduces weight, or obtains another economic advantage, the transshipment point can be a preferred location.[4] This reasoning is why cities have historically formed around seaports: industrial production takes place where the cargo congregates. A model of optimal location for processing at the trans-shipping point is presented in Figure 12.13.

The assumptions in Figure 12.13 are the same as in Figure 12.12, except that the trans-shipment point becomes a third alternative for processing in addition to the location at the source of the raw materials, or at the place of

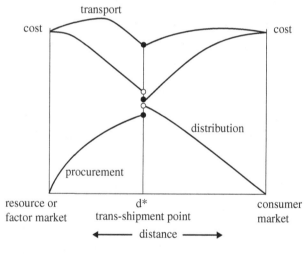

Figure 12.13.

---

[4]A modern example in North America is the transloading of ISO containers at the ports into 53-foot long truck trailers and domestic containers. Three 40-foot containers can be transloaded into two 53-foot long trailers. If the shipper can also do some sorting and mixing of inventories at the transshipment point, then they can also reduce cross-hauling between internal distribution warehouses.

the final consumers. The loading and unloading costs at the trans-shipping point cause a vertical shift in the procurement and distribution cost curves at the distance (d^*) from the two markets.

Note that at d^* the upper portions of the two curves are hollowed out in the sense that distribution and procurement costs rise once the distance is beyond the trans-shipping point because the load/unload charges would have then been included. For this product, the trans-shipment point has the lowest total transportation costs, and is the optimal site for processing. In a simplistic sense, trans-shipping as a phenomenon explains why urbanization and economic growth occurs at *transport gateways* and along trade corridors. Seaports are almost by definition transport gateways, but internal gateways can also be found where geographic features and political barriers cause freight to congregate.

Gateways, Hubs and Trade Corridors

Transportation gateways and trade corridors are a fact of history and an integral part of transportation economics. From earliest harbors like Alexandria and Marseilles, to today's Rotterdam or Shanghai, a port's success is dependent upon its role as an entrepôt to a surrounding hinterland and its location on a trade corridor. Trade routes can change over time because of technological advances and the changing economic fortunes of nations. The ancient Silk Road from China to Rome created wealthy cities all along its route of the camel caravans. The collapse of these political units power and the advent of sailing ships ended the Silk Road. Now efforts are being undertaken to revise this trade corridor based on double-stacked container trains from China to the European Union.

Transport always seeks the easiest, shortest and lowest cost routes, while land settlement patterns determine the location of transportation infrastructure. Transportation gateways and trade corridors exist within broader networks of links and nodes. The network is comprised of competing modes of road, rail, air or water transport that forms the links which converge at hub and gateway cities that are the nodes. A trade corridor is any pathway that facilitates the movement of goods between two or more gateway cities.

Burghardt developed a model of a gateway city that provides a useful framework for the entry points of trade corridors.[5] The Burghardt hypothesis rests on the location and role of cities in a hierarchy of different sizes and functions. Large cities have the economies of scale to provide higher level services like appellate courts and specialized education that smaller cities cannot. At the very pinnacle of the hierarchy are cities that host national and international financial services and entertainment industries. As the largest centers of distribution, these cities dominate commerce and serve as hubs and gateways for transport to the lesser communities in their hinterland.

It is common to hear individuals proclaim their city as a transportation hub or a gateway, but there is a difference. In the simplest sense a transportation hub works as part of a hub-and-spoke network whereby various transport routes or spokes have a common connection for consolidation or distribution of shipments. A diagram of a transportation hub and a gateway city is presented in Figure 12.14. Hub cities may rest on two or more major corridors; flows into and out of the hub city are multidirectional with respect

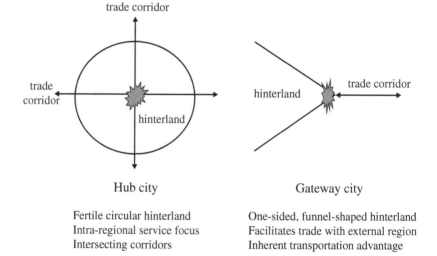

Hub city   Gateway city

Fertile circular hinterland   One-sided, funnel-shaped hinterland
Intra-regional service focus   Facilitates trade with external region
Intersecting corridors   Inherent transportation advantage

Figure 12.14.

[5]Burghardt, A.F. "A Hypothesis about Gateway Cities." *Annals of the Association of American Geographers*, Vol. 61, No. 2 (1971), pp. 269–285.

to its the circular hinterland. Gateway cities have funnel-shaped hinterlands and are located at one end of a major corridor that feeds traffic into and out of its region.

Burghardt observes that gateway cities lie at the geographic extremes of their economic regions and owe their location to a geographical shear zone or some barrier to trade. A Gateway city lies at the transition point with a "fertile" cone-shaped hinterland on the one side, and an "infertile" region on the other. The fertile side has a well-developed multimodal network of transportation infrastructure. The infertile side is served by a narrow trade corridor with long haul transportation services that connect the gateway city to a distant gateway in another market.

Traffic is funneled through a gateway city because it sits at a strategic location where transportation costs can be minimized along a land corridor or a sea route. This could be defined as a "path of least resistance". The inflows and outflows of the gateway city do not proceed in all directions; rather the pre-determined direction depends on the trade corridor that serves the specific economic region. Gateway cities may be distinguished by the geographic and/or economic features that give rise to their location. Ocean ports are obvious gateway cities. Montreal, New York, Vancouver and Los Angeles are gateway cities whose ports link trans-oceanic markets to the interior of North America — a sea-land connection.

It is more difficult to distinguish gateway cities that lie in the center of the continent. Internal gateway cities can emerge where continental features create the right conditions. For example, gateway cities can become located because of mountain ranges, deserts, rivers and inland seas. Calgary, Alberta owes its location and size to the mountain pass that provides a relatively gentle access for the railway through the Rocky Mountains. Calgary emerged as the gateway to distribute goods from British Columbia to the fertile hinterland of the western prairies.

Winnipeg, Manitoba was founded as a transportation gateway to the eastern prairies during the early settlement of Western Canada. With the barren Canadian Shield at its back Winnipeg funneled trade from across the prairies over a long corridor that linked to Montreal and Europe. Agricultural production was consolidated at Winnipeg for shipment to central Canada and a large warehouse distribution center was established for the westward movement of manufactured goods from central Canada to the prairies. The location of Winnipeg at the Red River occurred because traffic had to be trans-shipped at that point. Winnipeg's exact location became solidified when the railway bridge was built across the river and set the route of the trade corridor.

Whebell observes that trade corridor routes in North America became fixed with the construction of rail lines.[6] Although cars and trucks are more flexible, centers that were already served by rail were subsequently more desirable to connect with roads. In North America, the railway infrastructure is oriented with stronger and more direct east/west corridors than north/south corridors. Even in the case of air travel, which is not tied to fixed infrastructure routes, it is generally easier and faster to fly east/west in North America than to travel north/south. This reflects another source of gateway location — political boundaries.

Political boundaries create gateway opportunities because goods and carriers must stop for documentation, inspection and travel approval. Sovereign states also impose regulations that limit foreign competition (cabotage restrictions) and favor the transfer of goods to domestic transportation systems. Like seaports, sovereign borders within a trading bloc stimulate land settlement patterns and employment to serve international trade. It is not clear that either Calgary or Winnipeg would have grown into major cities if the U.S.–Canada border had not limited the reach of cities farther south. Similarly, the cities of Nuevo Laredo, Mexico and Laredo, Texas would barely exist, if clearing Customs were not do difficult at the U.S.-Mexico border crossing.

The size of the region and the range of available transportation services define the hierarchy of gateway cities and trade corridors. Ocean ports continuously compete with each other to attract shipping lines. Airport operators try to catch the attention of airline services. Cities work to provide road infrastructure that serves their ports, railway yards and intermodal facilities.

Once established, gateways and corridors may merge to create networks within which routing and development options multiply. As trade flows grow along any corridor, either infrastructure must adapt to accommodate

---

[6]Whebell, C.F.G. "Corridors: A Theory of Urban Systems." *Annals of the Association of American Geographers*, Vol. 59 (March 1969), 1–26.

the increased movement or the market will use alternative gateway-corridor combinations. Within the broader transportation network, this could affect development options, competitive frameworks, and transportation costs. Historically, cities like Cincinnati and St. Louis served as gateways to the Western United States during the period of frontier settlement in the mid-1850s. Once settlement had moved beyond their location and the railways replaced river barges, these cities became hubs.

As was shown earlier, site prices, and for that matter site rents, are influenced by the pre-existing infrastructure patterns. Transportation hubs became common in transport networks due to the economies achieved in using large capacity vehicles for hub-to-hub transport at larger population centers. Smaller cities are served as the spokes. The hub cities possess the infrastructure necessary to support, for example, a hub airport. Gateway and hub status can be reinforced by adding more infrastructure in order to attract the flow of goods and passengers.[7] Such investments may be subject to the criteria discussed in Chapter 11 relating to cost–benefit analysis (CBA). Of course, the discussion of CBA is usually removed from the purely political choices that are made. Political viability sometimes overrides economic viability to the detriment of achieving social efficiency.

Keywords

isodapane	site price	transport gateway
isotim	site rent	trans-shipping

Exercises

1. The construction of rapid transit systems (e.g., subways, LRT) can attract new investment in offices and apartment building around their stations. This increased demand can elevate land prices within a kilometer around their location.

---

[7]Additional reading:

Levinson, M. *The Box: How the Shipping Container Made the World Smaller and the World Economy Bigger.* Princeton, NJ: Princeton University Press, 2006.
Rodgrigue, J.P. "Transportation Corridors in Pacific Asian Urban Regions," in Hensher, D.A. and King, J. (eds.), *Proceedings of the 7th World Conference on Transport Research.* Sydney: Pergamon, 1996.

Draw an appropriate model(s) to illustrate and explain the impact of a new rapid transit location on nearby land prices.

Why do some rapid transit stations generate more economic activity and ridership than others?

2. Gateway cities are created at geographical shear zones where goods can be easily trans-shipped between different modes of transport, such as from ships to trucks.

Draw and explain an appropriate model or models that explain the characteristics that define a gateway city and illustrate the benefit of locating at a trans-shipment gateway.

Containerization has lowered the costs of transshipping goods at seaports to only 5% of pre-container shipping. Explain how falling transshipment costs affects the advantages and disadvantages of locating of manufacturing and processing at marine port locations.

3. Amongst other things, the price of farmland depends on its distance, and corresponding transportation costs, to reach available markets.

Draw and explain an appropriate model(s) that illustrates the linkage between location, the price of land and the cost of transportation in a perfectly competitive market.

Explain how the benefits of location end up determining the price of farmland.

4. Ethanol plants are being built in the U.S. Midwest and in Western Canada. U.S. ethanol plants use corn that yields ∼13.5 tons per hectare, while Canadian ethanol plants use barley or wheat that yields ∼3.5 tons per hectare.

Present and label an appropriate model(s) to explain how transportation costs dictate that the optimal size of ethanol plants in the U.S. would be larger than ethanol plants in Canada.

Show what would happen to the optimal size of the ethanol plants in the U.S. if climate change were to cut corn yields by half.

5. Politicians look for opportunities to create investments and employment. Some cities have seen significant economic activity result from inland port developments, but in many cases inland ports have been dismal failures.

Use an appropriate economic model, or models, to explain the economic benefits of creating an inland port to facilitate the transfer of cargo from one mode of transport to another.

Failed inland ports are more common than successes. Describe the process you would use to analyze the cost–benefit of a government investment in this form of economic development.

6. Corn ethanol plants produce two products — ethanol and dry distiller's grains (DDG) — that weigh about as much as the corn that is being processed. Corn is shipped in unit trains of hopper cars. Ethanol is also shipped in unit trains of tanker cars because it is too corrosive for pipelines. The majority of the by-product (DDG) is consumed in feedlots in the Midwest, but it is also dried for export overseas.

Draw appropriate model(s) to illustrate the arguments for locating ethanol plants near the source of corn production (U.S. Midwest), versus near the population centers (east and west coasts).

Would your answer change if the majority of the DDGs were exported?

Chapter 13

Transportation and Government Policy

Taxation, subsidization, public ownership, and regulation are ways in which the government can control the price and quantity outcomes of the marketplace. We have seen in previous chapters that markets can, in specific circumstances, fail in terms of not being able to achieve social efficiency when the only interests allowed to operate are those of the firms and its consumers.[1] The government under the mantle of "protecting the public interest" or "for the good of society" may intervene and attempt to correct a market failure or to encourage economic development. The first section examines the case to be made for government regulation and for deregulation.

Regulation and Deregulation

Over the past 30 years or so, the prevailing view of governments in North America has changed from one of regulation of transport markets, to one of deregulation and privatization. In this sense, transport services are now seen as not so sacred as to be shielded from the turbulence of the market. This turbulence is a small price to pay, advocates would say, for the benefits the market provides in terms of quickly achieving economic efficiency. In deregulated markets, prices replace the role of legislation and of governmental bureaucracy to manage the allocation of resources.

Deregulation does not imply a complete removal of all regulations. Government regulation is always necessary to prevent market failure (e.g., monopolization and cartelization) and to provide public goods, like public

---

[1]The market failures are monopolies/cartels, externalities, free-riders and destructive competition.

health and safety. Regulations ensure that safety standards remain in place so that "fly-by-night" operations are outlawed. But note, however, that some extreme free market economists have disputed the merits of this last point. They would argue that the government need not even legislate safety standards for firms. Why? Because the market will work, they claim. Consumers will be able to detect "fly-by-nighters" because of the shoddiness of their services and through word of mouth. These operators will be driven out of business by the lack of customers or they will be forced to lower the price of their services so that the only consumers using those services are the ones willing to accept the risks.

This is all fine, but how many consumers have to be taken advantage of by these firms and how many citizens must be hurt or killed by their use of dangerous equipment on the road, sea, or air before this word of mouth spreads? The problem with the extreme free market view is that it assumes consumers and other citizens are able to quickly acquire and process information and thus be able to sort out the bad from the good. It is by no means clear that this assumption is valid, especially given that information is acquired subject to a time and perhaps monetary cost.

Free trade agreements are essentially a case of deregulation between two sovereign areas in the sense that non-free trade is regulation through tariffs and quotas. While provincial, state, and national governments are currently in the process of deregulation within their respective jurisdictions, international deregulation is a slower process because countries are reluctant to forego what was once their "national interests". Recall that the arguments for free trade were made in Chapter 3.

Although economic regulation in transport has largely ended on freight movements, some passenger services remain under price and entry controls. This is largely a function of jurisdictional control. The federal and state/provincial oversight has been lifted, but regulation of urban transport remains in place. Taxi services are operated as regulated cartels, while mass transit systems are publically-owned and operated as monopolies.

Many cities in North America have regulatory boards that restrict taxi licenses and regulate the rates that can be charged. The rationale for taxi regulation is seldom discussed. Ostensibly, governments that regulate taxis are aware that jurisdictions where taxis are not regulated operate without problems. Regulatory change can have great inertia, especially if a small focused group has a lot to lose by change. In this case the direct, if not the only beneficiaries of taxi regulations are the holders of taxi licenses.[2]

Taxi license regulations were instituted by a previous generation and have now become entrenched. The taxis that received the licenses free of charge benefited economically. As these "regulated rights" have been exchanged over time, the benefits of the regulation (higher fares) has become capitalized into a market value for these licenses. Consequently, those who have to buy a license from an existing operator to enter the business have a higher cost base and after paying for the license may be no better off in terms of income than the original drivers were prior to the regulatory system. The process of asset capitalization is explained after formally presenting a model of the industry.

A stylized view of a regulatory regime in the taxi industry is considered Figure 13.1. A competitive taxi industry in the absence of regulation could be characterized by a long-run equilibrium at point C where the average total cost equals average revenue and economic profits are zero. For simplicity, a horizontal supply function is used that indicates that the industry faces constant costs. The government decides to regulate the taxi industry by restricting entry and/or arbitrating the price.

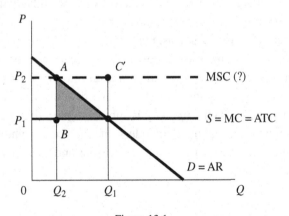

Figure 13.1.

---

[2]Not all taxi license holders operate taxis. In some jurisdictions, the license holder "rents" the license to another person who wants to operate a taxi.

Suppose that regulation restricts entry such that point A is the new equilibrium. Instead of zero economic profits with a Q_1 amount of output, the now smaller taxi industry will supply a Q_2 amount of output and the licensed firms will make an economic profit equal to P_2ABP_1, which is a transfer of wealth from consumers to producers. If a taxi license owner now retires or leaves the industry, they can sell their license to the new entrant. The value of the license will depend on the size of P_2ABP_1, the discount rates of new entrants and their expectations of change in the regulatory system. Assuming that they believe the extra benefits of regulation will be available for long as the new entrant continues to operate, they will be willing to offer the net present value of the extra benefits P_2ABP_1 earned over the future period of years.[3]

The regulation of taxis creates inefficiency because the consumer surplus lost due to the regulation (P_2ACP_1), leaves a welfare loss equal to ABC. Note that the government did not institute this regulation in order to achieve social efficiency. If that were the case, it would have to be shown that P_2 represents the marginal social cost (MSC) within the industry. The government would be required to outline the negative externality that had forced social costs higher than private costs. Only then could ABC be taken to be a net social gain. In Figure 13.1, MSC (?) shows that if such a view were really applicable, the net social gain of AC'C would equal ABC.

The government may believe that the industry needs to be price and entry regulated for reasons such as: (1) the market might monopolize if left unchecked; (2) the competition is destructive in that there are not enough economic profits to encourage research and development (R&D) to help the industry grow and expand into other markets or stave off competition from foreign ones; or (3) the industry is subject to periodic price wars and non-price competition making demanders uncertain as to when to use the service. Again, these are the government's reasons and they are for the most part incorrect.

---

[3]One means of visualizing capitalization is to consider the value of a perpetual government bond (no redemption date or fixed value) that has a fixed coupon rate. Dividing the coupon by the current rate of interest provides the exchange value of the bond. Similarly, if a taxi license were worth \$100,000 and current interest rates are 5%, the imputed economic profit would equal (\$100,000) (0.05), or \$5,000 for every taxi.

Do these arguments make the case for regulation based on the existence of a negative externality? Let us take each of the three points in turn and show why they would not make the case for price and entry regulation. Point (1) is invalid because controlling entry surely will not increase competition. If the market is prone to monopolization due to a firm's control over a critical resource or to a patent protection, the government should not respond to this by simply controlling entry. Point (2) is invalid because the desired normal profit conducive for R&D is built into the firms' cost functions. If not enough R&D is taking place for the government's taste it should offer subsidies or tax breaks to promote it as opposed to tightening the industry in the hopes that a firm that feels less competition would spend more on R&D. The opposite may result. Finally, point (3) is also invalid because a price war in a competitive environment serves to benefit the consumer and forces less efficient firms out of the industry; and non-price competition allows the firm to differentiate its product as a means of attracting customers.

Of course, non-price competition does force firms to operate under excess capacity; but some consumers may consider that aspect a reasonable price to pay in order to have a choice of services. For example, perfect competition in automobile manufacturing would imply one model at a fixed price — an extreme of the parable of Henry Ford's model T choice to be "any color as long as it's black". The for-hire trucking industry offers differentiated services in terms of truckload (TL) and less-than-truckload (LTL) carriage as well as specialization in terms of refrigeration and liquid carriage. While these are all sub-industries, there are crossovers and this merely serves to give more choice to the shipper. As well, the airlines offer different types of services for its users in terms of flight classes and special discounts. If average total cost falls in this regard, economies of scope are present as will be recalled from the discussion in Chapter 5.

The question becomes: why would a government initiate regulations to restrict entry if not to achieve net social gains? The answer is because the firms within the industry may actually wish to be regulated. The *capture theory of regulation* states that a regulator administers regulations that work to the benefit of the regulated. Firms that are already established may benefit from regulation to the extent that entry of other firms, and thus competition, is limited. Two cases in point: the United States "grandfathered" existing routes to established firms in the 1935 Motor Carrier Act; and the Canadian

Transport Commission (CTC) allowed the two major airlines to partition the domestic intercontinental flight market in Canada for years. Examples of regulation for the benefit of the regulated occur in a variety of industries.

The process of "capture" starts with the formation of special interest groups that can synonymously be called pressure groups or lobbyists. These groups indeed have a special interest in the form of: (1) a desire for the profitability of the group of firms they represent; and (2) possession of a high level of understanding of their industry and of the political process. As such, these groups are quite able to influence government when it comes to the formation of pertinent legislation. Indeed, the process of "capture" strengthens as industry leaders are invited by government to sit on regulatory committees and advisory groups so that their special knowledge can be tapped by the government.

Once an industry is regulated for the narrow interests of the industry and not for the achievement of social efficiency there is the inevitable welfare loss as shown in Figure 13.1. However, the firms within the industry capture economic profit, or rent, equal to P_2ABP_1. But there is a simplification being invoked here. The market characterized by Figure 13.1 was a competitive one before regulation was brought in and the firms that existed to produce the output between Q_1 and Q_2 are required to withdraw once regulation takes place. Would they leave freely? The answer is no because they would not sit back and let their competitors achieve positive economic profits at their expense. These firms would have attempted to achieve those profits for themselves. How? They would have, of course, lobbied the government so that they might achieve the regulatory license to remain in production. But their lobbying forces all other firms to lobby as well and in this environment not all firms will bear the fruits of their lobbying expenditure.

The spending of money in order to achieve regulatory protection so that an economic profit is secured is referred to as *rent seeking activity*. This activity, when it occurs, is a further source of welfare loss attributable to regulation. For example, when all of the firms are competing for the rent, its entire amount can be wasted or, in a kinder sense, dissipated meaning that the welfare loss of regulation with rent seeking present is actually, P_2ACP_1 in Figure 13.1.

Think of rent dissipation this way: with total economic profits or rent (R) available, each firm will lobby by offering the government a "bribe"

(*B*) at some amount less than the total rent to be won. The total number of firms lobbying is equal to N. If each firm offered a bribe equal to R/N they would all receive an equal chance of winning and all of the rent would be dissipated. The rent, in other words, is spent by the industry so that a smaller subset of it would receive it. That has to be wasteful! Nonetheless, we notice that the government is the recipient of this rent seeking expenditure through lobbying and may find this process beneficial if one considers the government to act, not out of social welfare, but out of the need to maximize its own revenues and expand its bureaucratic influence. In a sense the rent-seeking model assumes the government to act out of self-interest as would firms and consumers instead of acting in a paternalistic sense.

After regulation has been enacted, there are long-term consequences. The government will always be open to the rent seeking lobbying of other firms that wish to enter. As a consequence, this forces the incumbent firms to further lobby for the purpose of rent maintenance. In this sense the incumbent firms would always see a portion of the rents they have captured dissipated. In the for-hire trucking industry, for example, when the regulatory boards in the United States and Canada heard pleas from new firms wishing to enter, their onus was to rebut the position of the incumbents that most often stated that further competition would be detrimental. The process of making such legal and financial arguments requires rent seeking expenditure by all to continue.

A related problem with regulation that was described earlier for the taxi licenses occurs in the form of *profit capitalization*. This stems from the ability of the owners of the factors of production to capture some or all of the economic profit and sell it as an entitlement to a new entrant. When this occurs the costs of the new entrants in the industry rise such that eventually the private marginal cost of the firms in the industry would rise to, say, P_2 in Figure 13.1 when complete capitalization takes place.[4]

In this theoretical framework the drive to deregulation would come about when the government's priority shifts away from protecting the vested interests of some firms through regulation. Outside interests usually force

---

[4]Another example of the capitalization of benefits occurs in the labor market. Labor union activity in a regulated industry can extract part or all of the economic profits of the protected firms in the form of extra wage payments over and above the workers' opportunity cost.

the government to give up the gains it receives through rent seeking activity. These interests would usually be rival special interest groups such as, in the case of the transport industry, shipper organizations and consumer groups. In the case of profit capitalization, the need to deregulate may occur when the costs facing the firms get out of hand in the sense that the resources used are paid very high premiums above their true economic value and these costs spill over into other industries in their efforts to attract those resources. In the case of a strategic industry such as transportation it is easy to see how excessive costs there can serve to raise the selling price of a lot of goods where most of their value-added comes from transport (i.e., non-manufactured goods). Similarly, the inflation of taxi fares reduces their use and encourages more people to use their private vehicles or rent cars, which increases congestion, pollution and possibly driving after consuming too much alcohol.

Despite the economic theory presented in this section, political choices as well as economic ones drive a lot of the discussions that take place concerning regulation and deregulation. Some may not find an efficiency gains argument with respect to deregulation to be persuasive because, they may counter, the market is subject to cyclical behavior and as such is not suitably stable. Under this counter argument it would be felt that uncertainty with respect to employment, business profits, and prospects for investment would lead to faulty decisions on the part of firms whereby they: (1) over-reach for too much short term profit; (2) build-up over-capacity in their operations through their efforts to compete; and then (3) down-size and out-source when they attempt to correct their errors in judgment. Regulation creates rules which establish certainty; and with certainty comes stability. The choice of stability over efficiency is a value judgment and the desired mix of these two items for an industry and for a society is a decision to be made at the political level. As political moods change so will the desired mix.

Regulation produces units of stability. In this regard, regulation is presented in the form of a typical production function in the first panel of Figure 13.2.

With a low degree of regulation increasing returns occur in the form of establishing the rules for efficient market transactions: property rights, contract enforcement, information, etc. Of course, as regulation increases further, diminishing returns set in due to extra resources being devoted to

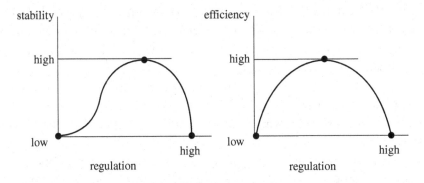

Figure 13.2.

compliance. In this situation, stability is rising because evermore aspects of business are being subject to specific rules or protocols. Each firm, however, is trading off resources used for expansion and research and development and replacing them with lawyers, internal auditors, and safety inspectors all in the name of compliance. Each unit of stability is harder to come by from an extra unit of regulation. Finally, negative returns will set in once regulation goes beyond that level necessary to maximize stability. It is here that bureaucratic red tape in the form of regulation is stifling business activity.

It may also be the case that regulatory fines have become so high that firms respond by scaling back operations out of fear of making a mistake in procedure or facing a court challenge. Stability falls because excessive regulation has replaced *market uncertainty* with *compliance uncertainty*, which is, nonetheless, a form of business uncertainty that is detrimental to the operation of firms.

The second panel shows the relationship between regulation and efficiency. Before the region of negative returns from excessive regulation sets in, it is preceded by a region of diminishing returns. In that region each unit of regulation leads to greater efficiency but does so in decreasing marginal units. Why? Each unit of regulation is less important to the achievement of efficiency than is the previous in that each unit aids less and less in the market's ability to adjust to economic changes; that is, to be efficient. This is akin to the process of diminishing marginal utility for a good or service. When negative returns set in, regulation is hampering the market in its ability to allocate resources to the production of those goods and services desired by consumers as well as to allow firms to produce them using a least-cost combination of resources. In this way, allocative and productive efficiency cannot occur.

It should be noted that the level of regulation that brings about the maximum point on the efficiency curve is likely to be far lower than the level that maximizes stability. This is the heart of the concept of the efficiency-stability trade-off.

In summary, some of the problems of government regulation of industry, abstracting from the presence of market failure, involve three key points. First, there is an inability of the regulator to adjust in marginal terms that reflect the slight changes in the cost and demand structures involved in the market. Markets can easily accomplish this task by the ability of price adjustments to account for these changes and thereby ration output and resource use. Second, freedom of entry cannot be tolerated under regulation because vested interests will rent-seek against it. Furthermore, the regulator must assess the merits of entry within a quasi-judicial setting as opposed to the marketplace, which provides incentives for entry only when a sign of extra profits exists and where the discipline of competition forces all firms to behave in an economically efficient manner. Third, regulation cannot deal with rapid change and, to the extent that the lack of competition stifles the incentive for firms to engage in R&D, technological change itself may be stifled. In this sense an economy that grows quickly does so when bureaucratic red tape is minimized.

A final comment about regulation concerns the risk of change. While regulations can be long-lived, most do not last forever. When change does come, the capitalized value of operating licenses, quota rights or specialized assets can evaporate overnight. Naturally, the regulated parties will fight with every means available to block change, but at best they can only hope to receive some compensation or the ability to write-off their capital losses against other income. A current example is the advent of car-sharing car services, like Uber and Lyft, in competition with regulated taxis. Much as the taxi industry may argue the car-share competition is unfair, consumers who want lower prices and better service represent more votes than the taxi drivers. In the case of economic regulation, "the politicians giveth, and the politicians taketh away.

Taxation and Subsidization

This section examines some of the implications for transportation markets when the government wishes to tax or subsidize certain activities within these markets. The discussion of externalities in Chapter 8 showed that the government may tax (subsidize) a market that produces a negative (positive) externality. Of course, when the conditions of the Coase theorem are satisfied, the market may be able to internalize the externality without the need for government intervention. This section will highlight some of the, perhaps, unintended effects of taxes and subsidies.

Consider the case where a tax is "earmarked" to a particular purpose. Suppose the government devoted the revenue gained from a fuel consumption tax to a trust fund that would be drawn upon only for the purpose of road construction and maintenance. There are some positive and negative attributes to *tax earmarking* schemes and each is discussed below. The positive side of earmarking is that better roads are had with less political interference because the trust fund is inviolable. The taxpayers know exactly how their taxes are being spent and they can easily pinpoint the benefits they receive from paying taxes to the government.

In many cases one pays taxes and feels negative utility from that act because one cannot easily determine the offsetting benefits to which these dollars are contributing. This phenomenon is known as *fiscal illusion* and the trust fund serves to eliminate this problem. The negative side of the trust fund essentially involves the idea that the non-discretionary nature of the spending means that the revenue cannot provide for any negative externalities or spillovers caused by the road. Consider that better roads have more vehicle accidents to the extent that more people will choose to live farther away in the country and commute to their jobs in the city. How will these extra accidents be paid for? Under a system of universal health coverage, such as in Canada or Sweden, the extra medical costs will come out of general tax revenue meaning, furthermore, that some non-users of the road are paying for a negative spillover that they did not cause. Likewise road users will not see their fuel tax payments devoted to the full social cost of the road. This point is made in Figure 13.3.

The marginal private cost (MPC) with the inclusion of the fuel tax (t) falls short of the MSC of the road. The only effect of this earmarked fuel

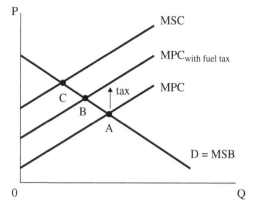

Figure 13.3.

tax on road usage is that it is lower at B as compared to A. In this sense the users are at least contributing less to the congestion problem and to the wear-and-tear of the road, which cuts down on the need for further maintenance work. These two effects fall under the jurisdiction of the trust fund because they are direct costs of road usage that show up on the quality of the road whereas vehicle accidents are indirect costs of road usage. In other words, only the so-called *tragedy of the commons* portion of road usage is efficiently priced by the tax.

A portion of the negative externality involved is essentially a tragedy of the commons type. Basically, each user reasons that his specific contribution to congestion and wear-and-tear is negligible and thus feels justified in using the road. The problem is that every user feels this way meaning that enough congestion and wear-and-tear will take place so that the road (the commons here) requires maintenance. If this point were made to the user the tragedy is that he would say that if the road were going to need maintenance anyway then it would hardly matter what he did. This is the rationale for a tax on congestion and wear-and-tear. It is easy enough to correct that portion of the externality through a non-discretionary trust fund because the congestion and wear-and-tear is relatively easy to estimate based on the area's population, the quality of the road surface, and average weather conditions to name a few. The correction of the portion of the negative externality caused by extra health care costs due to vehicle accidents is much harder to estimate because social and psychological factors come into play when attempting to estimate the probability of accidents on a given road.

A large part of the road tax would have to be discretionary to cover the likelihood of fluctuations in the accident rate. In other words, the trust fund would have to be much larger and its use more discretionary if the goal of the fuel tax is to make road users pay the full social cost of their actions. Of course, one can see another problem if the fuel tax were used to account for vehicle accidents. If the fuel tax rate were raised to account for a higher vehicle accident rate, all users would be paying more in taxes, including drivers with no record of accidents, which is hardly fair. That point speaks to the problem of attempting to design an equitable tax. In the end, to ensure that only the drivers with accident records pay for the social costs of accidents it would be better to raise the price of their driver's licenses or vehicle registrations. As one can see, the design of a tax to perform exactly as intended is not easy.

In the case of subsidies, there are two types: a lump sum and *unit subsidy*. A subsidy may be provided to a city transit authority to be used as it sees appropriate is a *lump sum subsidy*. A unit subsidy is provided in proportion of the amount of usage. For example, a special fare provided for handi-transit that involves a subsidy paid to the operators based on ridership is a unit subsidy. Each type of subsidy is considered below.

A lump sum subsidy paid by the government to the provider of transport services usually has no specification as to how it is used in the provision of services. In the case of a transit operation, the money may be devoted entirely to bus purchases and maintenance, it may be devoted to purchasing more fuel so that the existing buses may operate over longer durations, or perhaps the money may be used to increase the wages of all shop workers and drivers. No incentive accompanies a lump sum subsidy to force the recipient to provide better customer service or be efficient. In fact, the incentives to improve efficiency may be perverse in the case of public transit services. A manager who successfully cuts costs may be rewarded the next year with a lower operating subsidy.

Under a monopoly situation, as characterized by most public transit systems, a subsidy to permit marginal cost pricing would be efficient. The problem is that the subsidy is paid to the firm. Short of direct government control or regulations, there is no guarantee that the subsidy benefits consumers. The lump sum subsidy could be most effective if it were paid to the low income users of the transit system in the form of non-transferable vouchers or block discounts. However, politicians are loath to invoke means tests or any system that stigmatizes of low income riders.[5] If it were a straight income supplement then demand may fall if the average user looked upon transit as what economists call an inferior good. But even the voucher and discount system are not immune to a fall in transit demand. This point is best illustrated in the context of a unit-subsidy.

In order to achieve efficiency, a negative externality may be taxed so that the producers realize the social cost of their actions. For example, the fuel tax raises the cost of vehicular travel; a toll serves to lower congestion on crowded roadways. But the political environment may work against levying these sorts of taxes in accounting for the negative externality. An alternative may be to offer a subsidy to users so that they might switch to the more "socially acceptable" means of transport such as car-pooling, mass transit, or bicycles. The assumption is that the users of alternative transport methods create a positive externality (MSB), in the form of less congestion, pollution, etc.

Consider the market for mass transit as shown in Figure 13.4. At Q_A, MSC<MSB which means that social inefficiency is occurring. When a unit-subsidy equal to the distance AE per unit is paid to lower transit fares, social efficiency at B will be achieved because Q_B riders will be encouraged to use mass transit. But note that the net price of P_{Bnet} is lower at the larger quantity Q_B than the original price P_A. Consequently, the expected total cost of the subsidy would be $P_B BC P_{Bnet}$.

The subsidy serves to increase the usage of mass transit at the expense of car usage. However, there is a slight oversimplification with Figure 13.4 that could make the subsidy more expensive. Consider the cross price-elasticity of demand between cars and mass transit. With a lower net price for transit, the demand for car usage will drop. If the switch to transit lowers street congestion, then one of the costs of using a car falls, too. This fall in car costs would actually shift the demand for mass transit somewhat to the

---

[5]The development of electronic fare systems might be a means of providing low income riders with codes that give them a lower fare without signaling to anyone other than the bus operator what they are paying.

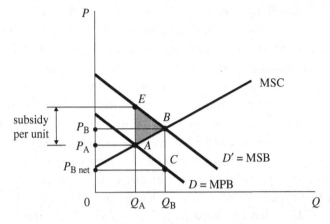

Figure 13.4. Mass transit.

left of D in Figure 13.4. Consequently, the subsidy needed to achieve Q_B, if it were the government's target level of usage, would have to be larger than $P_B BC P_{Bnet}$ as shown in the figure. The larger is the magnitude of the cross price-elasticity of demand, the more substitutable are cars and mass transit, the more significant this effect is.

As Figure 13.4 stands, the net increase in social welfare due to the subsidy is the area AEB. The unit-subsidy may take the form of a discount on the purchase of transit tokens in fixed sets or monthly passes sold at discounts. Every unit of usage comes with a constant discount.

Issues of Economic Development

It was shown in Chapter 1 that transportation services facilitate trade. Does investment in transportation infrastructure also facilitate economic development? There is no clear answer. Certainly the answer is yes, by transitivity, if it is the case that trade facilitates economic development but even that connection is not clear.

Economic development is something that does not possess a widely accepted definition. A great deal of subjectivity is involved in defining the concept because social and political factors are at work here just as much as economic ones. It is true that economically efficient transportation systems serve to keep costs low which also serves to raise productivity. Recall in Chapter 4 where the inverse relationship between cost and productivity was discussed. Productivity is an engine of economic growth, but there is a large difference between growth and development. This section outlines some of the ingredients that go into a workable definition of economic development and then discusses the connection it has with transportation.

It is necessary to first determine the size of the output to discuss economic development within an area. Consider the national level. The total output of a national economy may be measured, in dollars, in terms of gross national product (GNP) or gross domestic product (GDP). For example, the GNP of a country measures the total market value of all final goods and services produced by its citizens with the income they earned during a particular time period, say over the year. There is a subtle part of the GNP definition that must be borne in mind. The country's money income can be invested abroad in order to produce goods on foreign soil the production of which obviously does not add to the country's domestic production but is nonetheless a source of further income for its citizens. If one wishes to only look at the production taking place exclusively in the country, then GDP is the appropriate measure. GDP measures the market value of all final goods and services produced on domestic soil.

The first ingredient in the economic development concept is GDP, but let's consider the GDP definition a bit more closely. Why "final" goods and services? The value of a final good or service is the aggregate of the values of its component parts as well as other services involved in assembly and design. For example, to count the value of a windshield produced as well as the value of the car in which the windshield is placed is to count the value of the windshield twice. The windshield was not a final good but the finished car was; therefore, counting the market value of only the final good avoids double counting.

Why market value? Because the true value of all private goods and services are efficiently determined in the marketplace so as to equal the full opportunity cost of all the factors of production used in it. Certainly this is not so for public goods as well as in markets working under monopolization or where externalities are present. These are all examples of market failure. Thus, GDP is an accurate and useful measure of economic activity so long as markets work such that social efficiency is achieved. Based on the examples of market failure in the text thus far, one can conclude that market failure is not so easy to assume away let alone to correct.

A refinement of GDP is the next step. GDP is subject to a distortion due to price inflation because it measures market values at the particular year in question. Suppose, in a simple case, that GDP doubled in dollar value from one year to the next. Does this mean that production has doubled over that time? Yes, only if prices did not change over that period. If prices doubled then the market value of the same goods and services produced also doubled meaning that the amount of production was unchanged. To account for the distortion that price inflation causes it is necessary to compare GDP over various years to some base year of prices. Doing this achieves what is known as real GDP. One would certainly not be properly tracking economic development in a country if the production figures used grew in dollar terms and not real terms. To the extent that countries experience different rates of price inflation one could not accurately compare growth differences, let alone differences in economic development, across countries for particular years unless real GDP were used.

From real GDP another refinement is necessary. Suppose, in another simple case, that real GDP doubled from one year to the next. In this case the production level has definitely doubled. But there is another distortion to consider in terms of population growth. If production doubled but the population more than doubled then each citizen would have less real output than before if all output were divided evenly. To account for the effect of population changes one should divide real GDP for the year in question by the population of that year. The result is *real GDP per capita.*

Thus real GDP per capita is the closest macroeconomic measure of economic development that can be had from the economy-wide figures known as the National Accounts; but even this measure is misleading. Increases in real GDP per capita do indicate that the pie is growing for each citizen but some further refinements are needed. These refinements require a closer look at the microeconomics of the economy in question. One needs to find out the composition of real GDP per capita. Why? Because there is likely not to be much economic development taking place if the vast majority of the goods produced are, for example, going toward the building of a war machine. So the type of goods and services produced are important and this is where the subjectivity comes in. Perhaps the production of state-of-the-art household appliances, the building of cities, and of railways and roadways are the sorts of production required. On the services side perhaps the provision of health care services and education on a wide scale are necessary.

From the idea of producing the above goods and services on a wide scale the economy needs enough people to be able to afford them. This indicates the emergence of a "middle class" of income earners. Historically, the middle class was comprised of skilled laborers and professionals that lived and worked in urban areas. In order for there to be a middle class, real output shown in the real GDP measure must be distributed so that the bulk of it goes to the middle class with the remainder divided up among the rich and poor classes. Again, the proportion of real output or income that should accrue to the middle class is subjective. Stable non-authoritarian societies occur in the midst of a large middle class. Thus, one must examine the distribution of income among the various income classes so as to determine if the economy is stable enough to sustain the economic development process.

Following the building of the railways in the 19th century, the economic development power of transportation became a widely accepted fact. Of course, this belief was reinforced by the economic development that occurred as more modes of transport were introduced that increased travel speed and lowered the cost of freight service. Governments readily invested in highways, bridges, airports, canals, and ports during the 20th century.

Almost any new infrastructure investment or technical change in transport can have a positive impact on the GDP. But, these investments are also subject to diminishing marginal returns. As the 20th century progressed every jurisdiction clamored for more investment in transportation infrastructure to support their economic growth. With aging infrastructure, however, the demands on the treasury keep increasing to maintain and replace public roads, bridges, airports, etc. Coupled with too many failed projects and "white elephant" structures, belief in the economic development power of transport vanished. In fact, the mocking phrase "build it and they will come" replaced support for infrastructure investment.

The pendulum generally swings too far when policy positions change, however a more realistic view of transportation investment is emerging. The Asia-Pacific Gateway and Corridor initiative[6] is being hailed as a model

---

[6]http://gateway-corridor.com/.

for economic development. The Canadian government made strategic investments to remove bottlenecks and expand the capacity through the Port of Vancouver that is Canada's primary trade route to Southeast Asia. This was well received domestically, and by trading partners, like China, that can see the benefits.

Part of the confusion regarding the power of transportation in economic development may be the impact of transport infrastructure *per se*, and the impact of technological improvement in transportation. The economic development of Southeast Asia since 1980 cannot be separated from the innovation of containerized intermodal shipping. Building container ports and ever larger container ships almost guaranteed economic development and growth. But, this technology is now rapidly maturing and its power for economic development is diminishing. The lesson for policy-makers is that investment in technological improvement has a payoff for economic development, rather than just investment in transportation infrastructure as such.

One final point is that the government must be a proponent of economic development and not an opponent if it is going to take place. The government must foster a middle class by being democratic in nature, clearing up market failures when they exist, and disallowing government corruption and any other crimes that may affect the operation of business. Thus, in summary, economic development occurs when real GDP per capita is growing along with concurrent evidence of the further production of consumer oriented goods and services, a distribution of income conducive for a middle class, and a government that is democratic, market-supportive, and non-corrupt.

How does transportation fit into the economic development process? There is no doubt that the two are related. The tougher problem is to separate out correlation from causation. For example, history has shown that the production of railways in Europe, the United States and Canada was part of — that is, correlated with — the emergence of the Industrial Revolution in these countries. Of course, railways served to lower transport cost relative to alternative modes at the time, which increased productivity in all regions served by rail. As well, the railway hastened settlement expansion in Canada and the United States. Finally, railway production required the presence of a manufacturing base and its development was responsible in part for the growth in urban areas and the lessening of dependence on agricultural production. In this sense, railways have been seen as a cause of economic development and not the other way around.

The other means of transport such as air, water, and non-rail surface modes have developed more so out of the desire to compete with the railways and to more efficiently provide for consumer needs. Notice that consumers are involved to a large measure and that these other modes come into play once the urbanization and middle class developments are well underway. For example, the building of a modern road infrastructure requires the use of a sufficient amount of vehicles to validate it. And because usage is best achieved through cars there must be a sufficient demand for car usage. Of course, car usage has always been seen, especially on an intercity basis, as a middle class activity. In this case, economic development is a causal factor in the growth of car usage and road infrastructure and not the other way around.

A final point to note is that economic development occurs in stages. While much has been written concerning the nature of these stages they may be characterized simply as: (1) the formation of a stable society based on some form of primary or agricultural production; (2) the prospering of international trade and light manufacturing; (3) the economy achieves sustainable economic growth through urbanization and greater reliance on advanced technology; and (4) the stage of mass consumption is reached throughout the economy. Transportation facilitates trade on an intra- and international scale, fosters increased productivity, and becomes a part of the consumption process in terms of leisure travel. In this way transportation becomes a tightly woven part of all of the stages of economic development.

Keywords

capture theory of regulation	lump sum subsidy	tax earmarking
	profit capitalization	tragedy of the commons
fiscal illusion	rent seeking activity	unit subsidy

Exercises

1. Congestion is universally disliked by automobile drivers. Three general solutions to rush-hour street congestion are (1) electronic tolls on

automobiles, (2) construction of dedicated mass transit right of ways and (3) subsidization of mass transit fares. Imagine that you have been employed to brief the Mayor on these alternative strategies.

Use an appropriate model, or models, to illustrate how each of these alternatives would affect congestion. You may assume that the Mayor has a strong background in economics.

Prepare a brief on the pros and cons of each policy solution, who will pay and who will gain, and their likelihood of success in reducing congestion.

2. The number of taxis on the street is strictly limited by licenses by a government agency that also sets taxi fares. Since deregulation, other transportation costs have fallen and their service has improved. In contrast, taxi rates have become more expensive and the number of taxi licenses has not changed in decades. The value of a single taxi license is now worth about $350,000 and taxi service complaints are common, especially on the weekends.

Use an appropriate economic model and analysis to explain why these taxi licenses can take on such high values.

A new internet ride-sharing service called Uber is ready to offer rides through a cellphone app. Where Uber already operates in the U.S., their rates are lower than the regulated taxis fares. Use an appropriate model to explain the likely impact of Uber on the value of the regulated taxi licenses.

3. The bus transit system is owned and operated by the City. Passengers are provided with a service that is coordinated and can be accessed with a common ticket, or fare. Such a system could be operated by the private sector, but public transit bus systems are ubiquitous across Canada and the United States.

Draw and explain an appropriate model(s) that illustrates why private bus systems have not been allowed to operate in the cities.

Explain the benefits and costs of the publicly provided system.

4. The *"build it, and they will come"* role of transportation in economic development is subject to debate. The construction of new transportation infrastructure, or an improvement in transport technology, is viewed as necessary for economic development, but as insufficient to create economic development.

Draw and explain an appropriate model(s) that illustrates the rationale for this more cautious view of transportation as a key to economic development.

Explain how changes in transportation infrastructure or technological advances, could affect product mix demands and the growth of gateways and hubs.

5. Taxes and subsidies are used to modify consumer behavior to obtain a social welfare improvement.

Use an appropriate model, or models, to explain the economic justification for taxes and subsidies used in transportation and provide examples to illustrate your argument.

Sometimes governments provide subsidies or impose regulations on transportation that do not improve social welfare. Identify some examples of this behavior in transportation policy and explain how it is possible for governments to make such bad decisions.

6. A well-operated mass transit system in North America is one that obtains at least half its total revenues through the fare box (passenger fares). The remaining revenues are obtained as subsidies from municipal, provincial and federal governments.

Draw and explain an appropriate economic model that illustrates the rational for subsidizing mass transit.

Subsidies can be given to the transit authority as a lump sum payment (with specific operating rules), or distributed on a per rider basis. Explain the difference in these two methods of payment, and give the advantages and disadvantages of each.

7. Taxi services are regulated in almost every city of North America. Over time, taxi fares have increased, but the number of taxis remains fixed while the value of taxi licenses has increased substantially. The owners of the taxi licenses do not want the system to change, or more taxis licenses to be issued.

Explain how the taxi industry fits the model of a regulated cartel.

The Chair of the government agency that regulates the taxis is a former manager of one of the two large cooperative operated by the regulated taxi license owners. And, the taxi license owners have been active in their support of the politician that the regulatory agency reports to. Explain how the concepts of *rent seeking* behavior and the *capture theory of regulation* operate in the case of taxis.

Chapter 14

Regulatory Enforcement and Compliance

Government uses *fines* as a means of enforcing regulations. Fines serve as an incentive to comply with the law as it is set out, as well as to punish those that do not wish to follow the letter of that law. Unlike taxes that are levied on legal activity that the government would nonetheless like to see limited for the sake of social efficiency, e.g., negative externalities, fines are levied on illegal activity. The legal distinction is important because as we have shown in Chapter 13 taxes will indeed limit the extent of a permitted activity, so long as: (1) demand or supply is not perfectly price-inelastic; and (2) the taxpayers are willing to comply with the tax. Illegal activities require detection, interdiction and enforcement of fines to achieve compliance.

Non-compliance with fine payment may bring about a garnishment of wages as well as further penalties imposed by the government. Despite the enforcement of penalties, non-compliance with regulations occurs in the economy; indeed the "underground economy" represents a rebellion against the system. A person or firm may rationally decide not to comply when the private benefits received by not complying exceed the private costs of paying. Of course the private cost depends on the individual's expectation of getting caught and the size of the fine. Otherwise law abiding car drivers may speed, roll through stop signs and risk parking in handi-cap spots, if enforcement is generally lax and/or the penalties are trivial.

This section examines how those facing taxes or regulations in their transport activities decide upon the optimal choice — to comply or not comply in the midst of fines. The technique of *game theory* is introduced as a way of determining an optimal strategy for the potential offender and the implications for the regulator.

The Role of Fines

Take as an example of the compliance decision, the issue of overloading freight trucks beyond the regulated amount sanctioned for the road surface in question. Compliance even on a voluntary basis is not that easy given the inconsistencies between the regulations of Canadian provinces and the U.S. states. Even adjoining jurisdictions may possess separate regulations with respect to truck weights, trailer dimensions, and axle specifications.

The social cost of road damage caused by overloading freight trucks is a negative externality for non-truck drivers that is expressed in the form of the extra time and money costs. Owners of cars, buses and light delivery trucks experience damage to their vehicles due to pot-holes and the need to travel at slower speeds. Note that while those types of damages also accrue to complying truck drivers, those costs are not a real externality because these drivers are part of the same market.[1] An optimal fine structure should deter overloading, but should the guilty party be required to pay his share of the social cost — a tough calculation in the real world? Without regulations, a private incentive remains for a trucker to overload his truck: the marginal revenue (MR) gained from an extra kilogram added is larger than the marginal private cost (MPC) faced by doing so. With freight rates in trucking being weight-based and operating costs increasing less than proportionally with weight, MR>MPC for an extra kilogram is assured.

If the government feels that overloading will occur no matter what fine structure is instituted, the other recourse is to toughen the weight limits so that, if we assume that the proportion of non-complying truckers does not increase, the majority of now-lighter loads will compensate for the minority of overloads as far as road damage is concerned. Of course, this strategy punishes the compliers instead of the non-compliers. Instead, it may be possible for the trucking firms to get together and engage in self-regulation. Before looking at how the structure of fines specifically affects the overloading decision, let us examine how self-regulation may eliminate the need for fines.

---

[1] Recall the discussion of pecuniary externalities in Chapter 3. For example, if someone buys the last chocolate bar on the shelf at a store another consumer will be inconvenienced and perhaps made worse off but that is not an external affect to the transaction; it is the price to be paid for rationing.

This process of self-regulation is similar to the way the Coase Theorem (discussed in Chapter 8) specifies how, under certain conditions, the parties affected can internalize an externality. Of course, the property rights of road usage extend equally to all trucking firms meaning that Coasian bargaining is not fulfilled when there are a large number of firms. This is not a great problem because of the type of externality involved. Typically, a negative externality exclusively affects third parties and the creator suffers no damage; but in the case of road damage even the overloaders themselves are negatively affected by their own actions as long as they continue to use that same stretch of road. As well, if the trucking industry is formed into an association of firms then "insider" bargaining may take place through its auspices. The firms may come to recognize the value in cooperation. Why? Because the self-punishment occurring here creates a tragedy of the commons situation whereby one firm decides that it might as well overload because its competition is going to do it anyway. Using two firms as representatives of the trucking industry one can cast this situation in terms of a game known as the *Prisoners' Dilemma*. The structure of this game is provided in Figure 14.1.

As seen in the figure there are two firms, A and B, that both face the same two choices: to comply with the weight restrictions or to overload. Each dollar figure in the specific cells represents payoffs to each firm given the choice made by the other. Consider how the equilibrium in this game is achieved. The numbers placed in each cell are part of an assumed scenario and their size is not important; rather their magnitude relative to each other

		firm B	
		comply	overload
firm A	comply	$1, $1	−$2, $2
	overload	$2, −$2	−$1, −$1

ordering of payoffs (A, B)

Figure 14.1.

is what is important. Consider these numbers. The upper right-hand cell indicates that when firm A overloads it receives a payoff of $2 and the complying firm, B, receives −$2 indicating that the overloading firm is reaping a revenue gain, net of the road damage it causes, from being able to transport more than its competitor while firm B faces the cost of road damage net of the revenue earned by staying within the weight restriction. The lower left-hand cell tells the same story with the firms exchanging places. When both firms overload, as seen in the lower right-hand cell, the damage is such that both firms receive net losses of $1 even though they can transport more weight. Of course, if both firms overload competition forces down freight rates. Any extra revenues from overloading are spread out more evenly thus removing any comparative advantage to overloading.

The total cost across both firms from overloading, net of revenues earned, is $2. This was equal to the amount borne by the complying firm when the other overloaded because that firm faces both damage and a loss of revenue due to not competitively overloading. When both firms agree to comply with the weight restrictions, as seen in the upper left-hand cell, they both receive a net gain of $1 because the cost of road damage is minimized and this is assumed, along with the revenues earned, to outweigh the cost of having to make more trips because less can be carried per trip.

Now consider how the two firms in Figure 14.1 will set their strategies in playing this game. Firm A, for example, will look at the payoffs it would receive under its two choices given that B has already made its choice. If B is assumed by A to comply, A sees that it is better to overload because its payoff of $2 would exceed the $1 gained through compliance. Of course, if A assumes B will overload then A sees that, again, it is still better to overload because a loss of $1 is better than a loss of $2 through compliance. Thus, A's strategy would be to always overload. Of course, B can use this same reasoning when assuming that A had already made its own choice. So the equilibrium for the game occurs in the lower right-hand cell with both firms receiving net losses of $1. This result is specifically known as a *Nash equilibrium* in game theory, meaning that there is no incentive for one player to change his decision given that the other player does not change his own. For example, from the lower right-hand cell, assuming that B does not change its decision and continues to overload, there is no incentive for A to stop overloading because that would mean trading a $1 loss for a $2 loss.

Again, the relative sizes of the numbers are important. Suppose that the cost of mutual overloading in that same cell were greater than a $2 loss for each instead of the $1 loss. In this case there would be no Nash equilibrium for the game.

Staying within the confines of the numbers given in Figure 14.1 it is possible that both firms will self-regulate and move to the upper left-hand cell and both receive payoffs of $1 each. How? And for that matter: why? Notice that if both firms agreed to comply with the weight restrictions each would receive a payoff of $1, which is certainly better than the loss of $1 they face. Both firms would be made better off through cooperation. Of course, this agreement may not be stable in this game because, for example, if firm A promised B that it would comply, A would overload once B, in the spirit of cooperation, complied thus moving the result to the upper right-hand cell with A receiving $2 instead of the $1 for complying. In other words, self-regulation is difficult because there is an incentive to cheat in this game. The problem with this conclusion is that it is an over-simplification because it assumes that the game is played only once and that these firms will never meet and play the game ever again. Games played only once are referred to as *one-shot games* while those that are played more than once are referred to as *repeated games*.

If the game in Figure 14.1 were played by these two firms a multiple of time periods without end they would eventually realize that their strategies are condemning them each to a loss of $1 whereas cooperation would allow them each to achieve a gain of $1. In this way, the two firms "learn" to cooperate. One might ask how the incentive to cheat is removed. Cheating will always be possible but the question now becomes one concerning how the other firm will deal with it. It turns out that the optimal strategy for both firms in this repeated Prisoners' Dilemma game, in which both players make their choice at the same time, is one called the *Tit-for-Tat strategy*. One firm will make it known to the other that it will always duplicate the previous move of the other in the next time period of play in order to either maintain cooperation or punish cheating. This means that if B complies at one time period A will respond in the same way in the next time period; but if B overloads during one time period while A has complied, A will "punish" B for cheating by overloading during the next time period no matter what B does in that time period. Note that this punishment lasts one

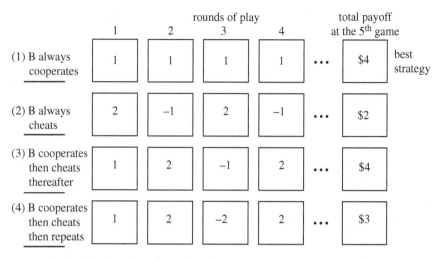

Figure 14.2. Payoff stream to firm B when firm A uses the tit-for-tat strategy.

time period and A will go back to complying next period even if B did not learn its lesson and cheats again. Is firm A, to put it bluntly, being a sucker? No! This strategy will make B cooperate because it is still better to always comply along with A than to cheat and be punished in a cycle. To prove this, consider the stream of payoffs to firm B in Figure 14.2.

At the 5th game the stream of payoffs is largest when B chooses stream (1), the always-cooperate strategy. Stream (3), though tied with (1), is inferior as will be outlined below. Stream (2), the always-cheat strategy, starts out with B cheating and reaping a $2 gain because A starts out by cooperating; but this brings about punishment from A in the next round thus giving B a $1 loss. Because B will always thereafter cheat under stream (2), all subsequent payoffs are a $2 gain, when A goes back to cooperation, followed by a $1 loss due to punishment. Stream (3), the cooperate first then cheat thereafter strategy, gets B an initial $1 gain for cooperating followed by a $2 gain from cheating but thereafter the stream is a duplicate of (2) in that it alternates between a $1 loss and $2 gain. Finally stream (4), the cooperate-cheat-and-repeat strategy, gives B a $1 gain for cooperation, a $2 gain for cheating, a $2 loss for cooperating again but being subject to punishment from A for the previous cheating, then a $2 gain from cheating while A returns to cooperating.

Notice, again, that stream (3) ties stream (1) in the figure. The first point to note is that a tie does not make stream (3) superior to stream (1). The second point is that if we proceeded through the 5th game the payoff in stream (3) would fall to $3 while stream (1)'s payoff would rise to $5. If the series of games had a definite end after the 4th game one might think that B could choose stream (3) by making sure that the ordering would allow for the $2 gain at the last round. After all, the payoff would be the same as in stream (1). But such a strategy is likely doomed to failure. Why? Because as long as A and B have equal information A would recognize the constant cheating after B's initial cooperation and deny B the $2 gain on its last move by cheating as well. B would ultimately get $1 on its last move thus making it inferior to stream (1).

Now consider the overloading decision in terms of specifying a fine for non-compliance and having the government institute random inspections. Admittedly this section is technical in its analysis but it does serve to highlight the problem the government faces in overseeing compliance efforts on the parts of firms. Random inspections mean that a firm using a fleet of trucks has to figure out the probability of: (1) being pulled over and inspected; and (2) being overloaded while being inspected so as to incur a fine. Of course, the probability of being subject to a fine rises to 100% if the route traveled possesses a permanent weigh station under 24-hour operation. The decision of the firm takes the form of the equation as given in Figure 14.3.

In words, Figure 14.3 is saying that the firm wishes to maximize profits (P). Profits can be gained by overloading when not caught but can also be lost if caught with an overload and the fine is large enough. The firm would increase the proportion of trucks in its fleet that run overweight (B) up to the point where the increase in expected profits equals the increase in expected fines. The word "expected" is used because the fines the firm faces, and thus the profits realized, is subject to a probability (p) of getting caught with an overloaded truck when one is pulled over and inspected. This probability is based on the firm's beliefs as to its value. So the decision to overload is conditioned by the government-controlled fine level (f) and also by the firm's own belief as to how likely it is to be caught.

The probability function defined in Figure 14.3, however, is precise in its formation of subjective beliefs. It is assumed that the probability of the

$$P = (1-B)(R_c - C_c) + B(R_o - C_o) - \text{Bpf}$$

with: $0 \le B \le 1$

and $p = p\,(\Sigma_i\, B_i\, s_i)$

expected profit   total revenue   expected total cost

where: B = proportion of fleet subject to a fine (f) at probability (p);

R_c, C_c = revenue and cost due to compliance of trucks;

R_o, C_o = revenue and cost due to overweighting of trucks;

$R_c < R_o$; $C_c < C_o$; $(R_c - C_c) < (R_o - C_o)$.

N.B. $p = p\,(\Sigma_i\, B_i\, s_i)$ implies that the probability of inspection is a function of the mean weighted proportion of overweight tructs such that:

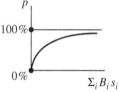

e.g., with two firms each possessing 50% market share and 50% of each firms' fleet being overweight, the mean weighted proportion is: $B_1\, s_1 + B_2\, s_2$ or 0.5(0.5) + 0.5(0.5) = 0.5. If firm 2's overweight ratio where 10% then we would have 0.5(0.5) + 0.1(0.5) = 0.3.

Figure 14.3.

firm getting caught is conditioned upon how much overloading is going on over all of the firms. In other words, the policing effort increases when the propensity of the industry to overload increases and, in this way, one firm's expected profits are dependent upon the compliance efforts of the other firms thus creating an interdependency of expected profits. A prevalence of trucking industry compliance lowers policing and increases the expected profits of the non-compliers while a prevalence of non-compliance increases policing and reduces the expected profits of the non-compliers.

In terms of enforcement, suppose the government sets the fine to be "monstrously" high. Will the effect be to fully deter overloading? Will the result be socially optimal? No on the first count and not likely on the second. In terms of deterring overloading the fine is only fully effective when: (1) the firms feel that the chance of getting caught is 100%; or (2) if the expected value of the loss, given the probability of getting caught, is greater than the expected value of increased revenue due to overloading. Point (1) requires perfect policing which is impossible, and point (2) is not as easy to fulfill as it sounds because with a high fine some firms will be deterred thus causing policing to fall and the probability of getting caught (p) to fall which thus increases the profitability of overloading for perhaps some firms. In terms of social optimality a monstrous fine would only be effective when road usage were such that the marginal social benefit of usage equaled the marginal social cost. The probability of being caught combined with the fine must lead to an increase in expected private cost exactly equal to the actual social costs of overloading. With p out of the government's direct control and subject to the actions of the trucking industry, the task of setting the socially optimal fine would not be easy. The government's policing effort is assumed to merely react to the amount of overloading that it perceives; it does not directly affect the actual amount of overloading.

It is obvious that a "game" is also being played in terms of the government's strategy versus that of the firms. In this sense, another game may be set up between the government (G) and the industry which is assumed to act in the way as given by a representative firm (A). This game is shown in Figure 14.4.

The government can choose whether or not to operate a weigh-scale along a road and the firm can decide whether or not to overload. Unlike the game in Figure 14.1 no specific values to the payoffs are given so that only general results may be determined here. In fact, without specific values one

		G	
		scale closed $(1-y)$	scale opened y
A	comply $(1-x)$	$-C, 0$	$-C, -L$
	overload x	$G, -D$	$(G-F), (F-L-D)$

ordering of cell payoffs: (A, G)

where:
x = probability of overloading; $0 \leq x \leq 1$
y = probability of operating the scale; $0 \leq y \leq 1$
C = compliance cost; $C < 0$ (negative to highlight cost)
G = extra revenue from overloading
D = road damage from overloading
L = cost of scale operation; $L < 0$ (negative to indicate cost)
F = fine

Figure 14.4.

B

	cooperate	defect
cooperate	R, R	S, T
defect	T, S	P, P

A (cooperate / defect)

ordering of cell payoffs: (A, B)

where:

R = reward for mutual cooperation;
T = temptation payoff;
S = sucker's payoff;
P = punishment payoff

N.B. A Prisoners' Dilemma requires $T > R > P > S$ and $R > \dfrac{(T + S)}{2}$.

In this way (P, P) is the Nash Equilibrium. Of course, a move to (R, R) is a gain in efficiency. R, S, T, and P need not be the same for both players.

Figure 14.5.

may ask whether or not this game is a Prisoners' Dilemma type. For this game, there are enough inferences that can be made to conclude that it is not a Prisoners' Dilemma. If it were, the payoffs would have to be of the relative values shown in Figure 14.5.

With part of the requirements for a Prisoners' Dilemma being $T > R > P > S$ we see that for the game in Figure 14.4 this would imply for player G: $-L > 0 > (F - L - D) > -D$. What is not realistic would be to require $-L > 0$, or equivalently, $L < 0$ because the implication is that there is no real cost for the government to operate the weigh-scale; in fact, with a negative cost the mere operation actually pays the government! Also, $0 > (F - L - D)$ means that the government would not recover enough money from the fine to cover operating costs and road damage. Thus, Figure 14.4 has payoffs that cannot constitute a Prisoners' Dilemma game and this means the situation whereby both players punish each other — the government must keep the scale open and the firm must pay a fine for overloading — as given by the lower right-hand cell is not the Nash equilibrium. Of course, if $G > -C$, which must be the case because C is negative, and if $(G - F) > C$ then firm A's *dominant strategy* would be to always overload. And as long as the fine (F) does not exceed the extra revenue from overloading (G) it seems that the firm should always overload. Of course, it would be easy for the government to set F so high that G is overwhelmed and firm A would always comply given $(G - F) < -C$; but the government must always keep the scale open for this fine to be levied. Keeping the scale always open would force firm A to consider only the upper and lower right-hand cells. Notice the result is a fine high enough so that $(G - F) < -C$ occurs in this game along with the scale always staying open. With the firm now always in compliance, the government would save a cost of (L) by closing the scale but by closing the scale the firm could receive G by overloading instead of paying C by complying. Thus, the government would be forced to pay L to keep the scale going but, paradoxically, the scale is not necessary because the firm is always complying. The game would end up in the upper right-hand cell.

This situation is reasonable so long as the cost of scale operation (L) does not exceed the road damages (D) that the operation is meant to avoid. If that were not the case, then it would be better for society if the damage occurred and the firm overloaded. In this case the game would end up in the lower left-hand cell. Note that both cells have their flaws from a societal point of view: either the government pays for a scale as a deterrent but no fines will ever have to be paid or the scale closes and the damage is not paid for by the firm because the opportunity cost of levying the fine is too high (i.e., $L > D$). Sometimes regulation serves as a deterrent whereby fines would never have to be collected because their mere existence is enough to provoke compliance. Thus, the game in Figure 14.4 would possess two possible equilibria (i.e., the upper right-hand cell or lower left-hand cell) depending upon which choice the government sticks with.

Another way to specify the game in Figure 14.4 is to include probabilities of actions. In the game the combined probability of the firm overloading a truck and getting caught by an open scale is xy. In this way the expected payoff to the firm is $(G - F)xy$ and the government's gain is $(F - L - D)xy$. Thus each move in the game is subject to uncertainty. Given that a player will employ any of the two choices at any one time, the player faces four possible outcomes. The sum of these expected payoffs for the moves gives the expected payoff of the entire game (V_A and V_G, respectively). Because no one move is ever certain the players are said to be employing mixed strategies.

$$V_A = (1 - x)(1 - y)(-C) + (1 - x)y(-C) + x(1 - y)G + xy(G - F),$$

which after simplification gives

$$V_A = x(G - yF) - C(1 - x), \tag{14.1}$$

$$V_G = (1 - x)y(-L) + x(1 - y)(-D) + xy(F - L - D),$$

which after simplification gives

$$V_G = y(xF - L) - xD. \tag{14.2}$$

Now the question becomes: what respective level of x and y should A and G choose? Each will choose a probability of action such that the other cannot increase its payoff by altering its given action. So for the equilibrium value of x, firm A assumes G has a fixed choice made (meaning that y is in effect equal to 1). Take the expected payoff to G with and without open scales, but under A's choice of action, and set them equal meaning that G would be indifferent in its choice of action. Thus we have:

$$(1 - x)0 + x(-D) = (1 - x)(-L) + x(F - L - D),$$

which after simplification gives

$$x = (L/F). \tag{14.3}$$

Similarly for y:

$$(1 - y)(-C) + y(-C) = (1 - y)G + y(G - F),$$

which after simplification gives

$$y = \frac{(C + G)}{F}. \tag{14.4}$$

Equation (14.3) shows the firm's choice to overload is determined by the ratio of the government's enforcement costs to the overloading fine; that is, it is the ratio of the government's potential cost to its potential gain. Equation (14.4) shows the government's choice to open the scale is determined by the ratio of the firm's net gain from overloading to the overloading fine; that is, it is the ratio of the firm's potential gain to its potential loss. Notice that the cost of road damage (D) does not appear in either of the above decision parameters. Why? Because the game has been structured such that an overweight truck would be assessed a fine if caught and then be allowed to continue without off-loading. In this way, road damage will occur whether or not an overweight truck is caught and thus its cost should not enter the structure of the choice parameters.[2] But, as seen below, this cost does enter the government's expected payoff based on x and y.

Plugging Equations (14.3) and (14.4) into Equations (14.1) and (14.2) gives:

$$V_A = (L/F)\{G - [(C + G)/F]F\} - C[1 - (L/F)],$$

which after simplification gives

$$V_A = -C \tag{14.5}$$

and

$$V_G = [(C + G)/F][(L/F)F - L] - (L/F)D,$$

which after simplification gives

$$V_G = -\frac{LD}{F}. \tag{14.6}$$

Notice that the expected payoffs in equilibrium are negative for both firm A and for the government. In this way each player's *mixed strategy* is mutually punishing. The only way for gains to accrue to both would be under collusion where, unrealistically, the firm would have to be allowed to not pay a fine at times for the promise of not overloading every truck when the scale is closed down for a while to save on costs.[3] Both firm A and the government are in adversarial positions in this game and the maximum expected payoffs to each are negative.

---

[2]If the game were restructured such that off-loading did occur then the cost of damage would in fact enter x. What is required is to introduce a variable for the cost of off-loading assessed to the firm and a variable for the reduced cost of road damage due to off-loading. Such a model is explored in: Prentice, B.E. and Hildebrand, M.D. "An Economic Approach to Truck Weight Regulation Enforcement." University of Manitoba Transport Institute: Research Bulletin No. 4 (1988).

[3]In this vein, some economists have argued that the crime rate would fall if all criminals formed a union and negotiated with the police as to days when police patrols would, and would not, take place.

Equation (14.5) indicates that the firm is expected to incur the cost of compliance (C) when employing the mixed strategy while Equation (14.6) indicates that the government will incur the cost of road damage (D) as a proportion to the ratio of operating cost to fines (L/F). Also, Equation (14.6) indicates that as long as there is to be some level of road damage it is not possible for the government to set a level of fines so as to recover all of the costs of operation for the scale. That is, no matter how large F is made, D/F will never equal zero so as to wipe out the cost the government incurs from L. Indeed, Equation (14.3) indicates that no matter how large F becomes, (L/F) will never equal zero under a mixed strategy meaning that there will always be a non-zero probability of the firm overloading.

Of course, it should be understood that results will vary based upon the actual numbers specified in the cells of Figure 14.4. If the numbers indicated a dominant strategy then the mixed strategy for both players established above would be discarded. One column (or row) would dominate the other so that there would be no need to calculate x and y. Inspecting Figure 14.4 reveals the overload row could dominate the comply row if $(G - F) > -C$. In this case the firm would overload 100% of the time. Likewise, the scale-closed column could dominate the scale-open column if $-D > (F - L - D)$ or $D < -(F - L - D)$. In this case the scale would remain closed 100% of the time. What is worth noting is that this game is structured so that the "comply row" could never dominate the overload row which means that either there is a dominant overload row (with $x = 1$) or the firm will play a mixed strategy. In this way, the government could never set a fine that would force 100% compliance and thus eliminate all road damage. In fact, because the cell numbers are crucial to the strategy played it is not possible to set an optimal fine in this context.

A final point is to note that the cost of compliance (C) is indeed a real cost to the firm. The trucking firm must spend time and money to train its drivers; it may scale its own suspect loads before they are sent on; and may even turn down customers that require the shipment of loads that are too heavy to comply with the regulations. It is possible that such customers may transfer business to those firms that are more willing to take their chances.

This section has shown that as long as an adversarial situation exists, cooperation of a self-regulatory nature may come about in repeated games of a Prisoners' Dilemma type. When the games are in an alternative structure, cooperation may not be feasible. The government has to maintain regulation along with a fine structure to act as a deterrent to the incentive a firm faces in securing extra profit from illegal activity.

Ironically, the real beneficiaries of the weigh scale fines are members of the trucking industry that are protected from a tragedy of the commons market failure.

In summary, it should be noted that game theory does not easily apply when the number of players becomes large. By this we mean that each side may not possess a uniform strategy because the set of players are, by nature, non-homogenous. In industries with monopolistic or duopolistic tendencies, such as airlines and railways, the strategy of the providers is relatively easy to establish. However, the same cannot be said of trucking firms and ship owners due to the wider range of operational options for their respective industries. The two-player game is applicable, however, in a game that consists of the government and a representative firm, even when the number of actual firms is large. The trick is to establish reasonable attributes for this representative firm.

Adverse Selection and Moral Hazard

This section is concerned with the relationship between two groups that economists refer to as principals and agents. The principal wishes to induce the agent to undertake an action that incurs a cost to the latter. The *principal–agent problem* involves the idea that the principal may not be able to observe the agent's behavior but can, however, observe the final result of the agent's actions. But was this output totally the result of the actions the principal wished to induce? Therein lays the problem. An employer would like an employee to give maximum effort to his work and would pay in order to induce this. The result is a certain amount of employee output but the employer will never know if maximum effort was in fact given.

The incentive structure set up by the principal is an attempt to influence the agent's behavior. It does not really coerce, even though that may be the intent of the principal. The agent is free to choose the action he wishes to take, given the incentive the principal provides. A lot of his actions are unobservable and this leads to what is known as the *incentive-compatibility problem*. The principal's task is to devise a method of payments or other such incentives that induce the agent to perform the way the principal wishes.

The task is not always easy, but technology has helped. At one time, truck drivers were one of the least supervised employees in society. From the time drivers left the yard, until they returned, they were unobserved "Kings of the Road". Now with computers and wireless communications, truck drivers (the agents) have become one of the most supervised workers in the economy. Consider the incentive compatibility problem from the social point of view. In the use of seat belts in automobiles, the principal (government) wishes to cut down on road deaths by persuading (or coercing, depending upon one's point of view) the agents (drivers) to wear their seat belts. The principal wishes the agents to drive (i.e., perform an action) in a manner less conducive to road deaths. The fear of a fine provides the incentive. Or does it? The problem is that while the seat belt usage is an incentive, from the government's point of view, to make for safer roads the drivers, while feeling safer in their own cars, may take this as an incentive to drive faster because being belted-in will lead to less personal damage in case of a collision. If enough drivers take the incentive to drive faster, the roadways may actually face an increase in accidents. The collisions that now occur may be severe enough to render seat belts irrelevant to the life of the driver.

What is the solution? Consider that incentives must be made compatible; that is, if travel speed on the road is the cause of road deaths then road speed must be diminished. Let's take an extreme example. Suppose the government made it mandatory that steering wheels had to have a retractable spike that extended to about two inches from the driver's heart, if they exceed the speed limit. Does this provide the incentive for the driver to slow down? Certainly if excessive speed is to be avoided such a device provides a better incentive than does being belted-in because the spike drives home — pardon the pun — the effect of excessive speed. In other words positive actions require incentives and negative actions require disincentives.

Road safety regulation all boils down to government intervention in the marketplace in an attempt to reduce the negative effects of accidents. Drivers and the public at large would likely welcome any reasonably priced plan on the government's part that would lower the probability of a road accident occurring. But a trade-off exists which goes beyond any such plan. The problem is that drivers also face higher costs when they exercise extra care in their driving: more concentration on the road and slower travel times due to more defensive driving. The temptation for a driver to forego some of that care should be less than the probable value of the fine. Certainly, the disincentive does not need to be as draconian as the steering wheel spike. The fine only needs to be sufficient to alter drivers' behavior to an accepted norm.

Consider the incentive-compatibility problem associated with managing congestion. Suppose a government wishes to reduce the number of vehicles on the road by placing a hefty charge on car ownership, as does the city-state of Singapore. Such a charge may serve to counteract other congestion charges such as tolls. Why? The ownership charge serves to raise the fixed cost of driving a car relative to the marginal cost (which includes the toll charge). In this way, the government is laying the ground for a taper effect. Taxis, delivery vehicles, and private motorists have an incentive to drive more with their vehicles in order to take advantage of the fall in average total costs. Having paid so much up-front for a vehicle, one may feel the need to make the most out of using it. In this way, congestion may worsen. Because congestion is related to the physical movement of traffic, and not the number of vehicles themselves, congestion costs are best felt on drivers in terms of their marginal cost of driving (i.e., fuel, parking, and toll charges).

Consider the principal-agent problem in the provision of insurance. Regarding transportation services, insurance plays an important role in terms of insuring the value of cargo against damage; insuring drivers against damage caused by their vehicles; and insuring passengers against death in airplane crashes. In general, insurance pools risks and charges each customer an amount called a premium based on the average risk of the pool. The premium that the principal (the insurer) charges the agent (the policy holder) must be considered in the light of two problems that arise between principals and agents in this context: one is the *adverse selection problem* and the other is the *moral hazard problem*. Both are discussed in turn.

The greatest incentive to buy insurance lies with those agents most likely to file and collect claims, which, of course, are the least desirable buyers from the point of view of the insurer. The adverse selection problem faced by the insurer involves not perfectly knowing the nature of the candidate he wishes to insure. Some things such as health (physical or financial) are easy to determine but how about future health, or proneness to accidents, or even clumsiness? The implication is, for example, that careless freight transporters will apply for insurance along with the more careful ones. Because the careless ones will be putting in for more claims, to the extent that their claims are successful, they will drive up premiums for both themselves and for the careful transporters as well because it is not possible to separate these two groups based upon subjective observations of carelessness. For health insurance it is easy enough to lower the premiums for the young, the non-smokers, or those not in earthquake zones; but how would a freight insurer or passenger flight insurer accomplish this? Note that the current level of society's love for risky behavior or incentive for carelessness is not affected by the adverse selection problem. The societal level is given, but the insurer would wish to separate the high risk takers from the low ones.

The moral hazard problem will, in fact, affect society's risk-taking or carelessness attitudes with respect to actions. In terms of insurance, the policy-holder's knowledge that a payoff will come in the case of a mishap may bring about the very behavior the insurer does not want to occur. The example of mandatory seat belt usage discussed above created a moral hazard problem for the government because driver behavior was affected in a way the government did not intend. Consider automobile insurance. The insurer compensates the victim(s) and perpetrator(s) of accidents for damages assessed. In the case of civil proceedings a judge may determine the necessary compensations and the liable party pays through his insurance company. In this way one might argue that the party would refrain from risky behavior in order to not face a premium increase if found liable. But also consider a counterpoint whereby, if an accident were to occur, the guilty party has an incentive to perhaps reduce the odds of an accident but may do it in such a way as to increase the size of the potential loss. The higher loss serves to validate the premiums that have been paid to date. Consider "no-fault" insurance as practiced in some jurisdictions. The insurer assesses damages and victims must accept the decision without recourse to the courts. To the extent that damages may be underestimated as far as liable drivers are concerned the cost of driving falls and a moral hazard problem arises. In either case, behavior is not occurring the way the insurer would like it.

The way the moral hazard problem can be dealt with in terms of increased "bad" behavior within the case of insurance is to not offer full insurance and instead force the liable party to pay a "*deductible*". In this way the insured party pays a portion of all claims. The effect is that, to some extent, the driver will drive more safely and administrative costs will be lower because the driver has no incentive to file claims below the deductible. But how might moral hazard in terms of avoiding accidents by filing larger claims be dealt with? A device known as "*co-payments*" may provide the answer. Whereas a deductible is a flat amount to be paid no matter what the total settlement is, a co-payment represents a proportion of the total settlement that must be paid. With bigger losses come bigger co-payments, which acts as an incentive to keep losses low.

The moral hazard problem can thus be handled by deductibles to discourage the prevalence of carelessness and co-payments to discourage claims for large losses. A problem occurs when the insurer tries to combine these tools to combat the two variants of moral hazard. A typical response is to institute a deductible and a small co-payment for losses above the deductible. But consider the problem from the insurer's point of view. Suppose a car manufacturer discovers a possible defect in this year's output of cars and that they have by now all been sold to their customers. The defect may very well lead to a lot of road accidents. The manufacturer could: (1) recall and repair the cars at a cost of, say, $50 million; or (2) do nothing and risk the liability of guilt through court action. Point (1) brings about a definite cost whereas point (2) brings about an uncertain cost that could be either above or below $50 million. The insurance company that covers the car manufacturer has already thought of the possibility of defects occurring and that the choice to recall or not could one day be faced by its car manufacturer client. What does the insurance company think about before covering the car manufacturer? Two thoughts should occur: (1) if it insures the manufacturer against the costs incurred in recalls, the manufacturer has an incentive to have a lot of recalls and not worry about avoiding shoddy production techniques that lead to defects; and (2) if it only insures large losses owing to major recalls the manufacturer would avoid, for the most part, having any recalls.

Where do large deductibles combined with relatively smaller co-payments fit into this problem? The large deductible discourages a recall while the small co-payment encourages it meaning that there is a trade-off occurring and if the manufacturer dislikes having to pay the deductible, it is likely that no recall will occur and the insurance company may be paying out liability settlements rather than recall costs. Are the solutions then large deductibles and large co-payments? In this case, the manufacturer is less likely to buy insurance or, instead, will insure for a smaller amount. One possible solution is for the insurer to consider that, in manufacturing, production problems are best handled early because if they continue unchecked the overall cost of correction rises. In that spirit, the insurer may provide recall insurance with no deductible levied but with a large co-payment required. Because all small claims would be paid in full, small problems would stay small and the overall payout by the insurer would be a set of small payments that, in total, would be less than either a large payout due to prolonging the recall decision or due to the manufacturer's liability building up through letting the customers bring in a large class action suit. The large co-payment will deter large claims or deter letting the matter go before the courts.

The heart of the adverse selection and moral hazard problems come from the fact that the agent has more information than the principal. In this way, it is nearly impossible for a principal to know whether agents, because of insurance protection, will: (1) take on extra risk or adapt more careless behavior leading to consistently more insurance claims, more damaged freight, or reduced effort; or (2) just file larger insurance claims covering damage to more expensive, fragile or volatile freight, or experience bouts of slackened work effort. Of course, if moral hazard were not problem enough the principal must face the adverse selection problem in terms of knowing beforehand who is, in fact, possessive of action that is too risky or too careless.

Keywords

adverse selection problem	incentive-compatibility problem	principal–agent problem
co-payment	mixed strategy	Prisoners' Dilemma
deductible	moral hazard problem	repeated game
dominant strategy	Nash equilibrium	self-regulation
fines	no-fault insurance	tit-for-tat strategy
game theory	one-shot game	

Exercises

1. The city police commission was disappointed with the revenues they earned from the new speed cameras that they installed at many traffic light intersections. Fine revenues were less than half of what they had anticipated based on the number of speeders observed before the cameras.

   Design and explain an appropriate game theory model that illustrates the strategy of speeding and law enforcement.

   Use the game theory model to explain how it could have been used to predict why driver compliance and police enforcement strategy yielded such a result.

2. Mapleflot and EastJet operate national airline networks. During low traffic periods, both airlines offer greatly discounted air ticket prices and generally match each other's prices. These "price wars" do not increase their market share or attract many new customers. It seems the only winners are consumers who get to travel at less than full cost during low traffic periods.

   Draw an appropriate model(s) to illustrate this competitive behavior and explain why the two airlines never seem to learn the futility of their actions.

   How would you advise an airline to respond to this repeated situation?

Glossary

Absolute advantage: it occurs with respect to any good or service produced in a region or country that has a lower cost of production relative to its cost of production in another region or country. While a region or country may have an absolute advantage in many goods and services, its comparative advantage will only exist with respect to one good or service. It may also be the case that no absolute advantage exists. See comparative advantage.

Adverse selection: a principal–agent problem whereby the principal sees the world as made up of two sorts of agents: those that act appropriately and those that do not. A freight insurer will accept accident claims from carriers but cannot easily know whether the claim was due to a truly accidental event or to the carrier's predisposition to be careless. Until this is known, the insurer will be covering a carrier that he otherwise would not. See moral hazard.

Allocative efficiency: see efficiency.

Average cost pricing: the setting of the price of output at the point where average cost equals marginal benefit, as represented by the demand curve. Like marginal cost pricing, this occurs naturally under perfect competition in the long run because zero economic profit must be the result. However, there is no incentive for a monopoly firm to operate that way. If the monopoly possesses economies of scale, average cost pricing would also bring about zero economic profit. But, unlike for marginal cost pricing, governments need not subsidize the firm if it requires the firm to operate using this scheme.

Backhaul: one of the two components of the round trip of freight or passenger transport; the other being the fronthaul. Because the fronthaul leads to one, and only one, backhaul they are both in joint production and represent joint costs of round trip production.

Barriers to entry: see monopoly.

Blanket Rates: Blanket rate structures are single rates that cover a wide area. They can be found as common rates for groups of commodities hauled long distances, e.g., grain. Blanket rates also occur where competition along a route forces rates to be reduced to below the predicted rate structure and cost profile.

Cabotage: literally "coasting" or "to coast". In terms of transportation law, it involves the activity of a foreign vehicle and/or operator on: domestic soil, within domestic waters, or in domestic skies. These activities are often highly regulated as a form of employment protection for domestic labor. To the extent that cabotage restrictions impede the operations of foreign carriers — especially in backhaul markets — they may be looked upon as a source of inefficiency in transport provision. As such, cabotage is a non-tariff barrier to international trade.

Captive shipper: A shipper who has no practicable alternative carrier for shipping its goods. This is due to the shipper needing a particular mode of transport in a market where the carrier faces no competition. Even if it is not mode-dependent a shipper could also become captive if it requires a particular route or a particular time of service.

Capture theory of regulation: a theory asserting that regulations are created for the sole benefit of the firms being regulated. Firms, using their collective power to lobby, "capture" the agenda of the regulator in order to bias forthcoming regulations in their favor.

Ceteris paribus: a Latin phrase meaning "all other things remaining constant". It is a device that allows one to capture the effect of one moving part in a system by holding the effects of all other moving parts constant. For example, one could specify an inverse relationship between the freight rate and the quantity of a freight carrier's services to be demanded. But this holds only so long as all other determinants of this demand (such as the level of freight produced by shippers as well as the sale price of the freight upon delivery) are held constant.

Coase Theorem: after Ronald Coase. The theorem provides a private market solution to the externality problem under certain specific conditions. These are: property rights exist and are well defined; transaction costs are zero in terms of negotiation; and the number of negotiators is small. When these conditions are satisfied there is an incentive for the affected-party to negotiate (or bargain) with the producer of the externality and the payments process will be defined in terms of which of the two initially possesses the property right. In this way, property rights are bought and sold and the result of the negotiation will be independent of the initial allocation of those rights.

Common costs: are the non-traceable costs of a production process. The factors leading to these costs need not be used in fixed proportions, as they must be under joint costs. With costs occurring that are common to two or more sub-components of production it is not possible to define a clear way to allocate these costs. There is no definite rule allowing for how the costs of a flight crew, for example, are to be allocated between the freight and passengers that might be carried on their common airplane.

Comparative advantage: occurs with respect to the good or service produced in a region or country that has the lowest relative cost of production over the other trade partner(s). Gains from trade lie in specialization of production as indicated by the good or service that possesses the comparative advantage. Even regions or countries without an absolute advantage in any good or service will always possess a comparative advantage in at least one of them.

Congestion costs: the cost incurred in a system due to a crowding effect, which leads to a strain on the capacity of the system. On roadways, congestion costs occur in the form of time delays, the idling of vehicle engines, and external effects on the environment. After a certain point, an increase in traffic flow comes about with a decrease in the average speed of the vehicles within that flow. The slower speed raises the cost of the trip.

There is thus a negative relationship between speed and flow on the one hand and speed and cost on the other.

Constant costs: the cost of each extra unit of a good or service being the same over a significant range of production. In this way, marginal costs are constant. Over this range there can be no forces that serve to raise per unit costs such as congestion or diminishing returns. When these costs are common to more than one sub-component of production the traceability problem prevents them from being properly allocated among the sub-components.

Constant returns to scale: indicates a constant long run average total cost of production. There are no economies or diseconomies present in the expansion of the firm's operations. If a transport firm operates such that each previous vehicle employed must be at capacity usage before another is brought into service, the expanded fleet cannot take advantage of coordination techniques such as interlining among its vehicles. In a sense, each vehicle operates within an independent route. Ocean vessels provide the best example of this phenomenon for that reason.

Consumer sovereignty: see efficiency.

Consumer surplus: the net total benefits the consumer derives from paying a uniform price for a good or service. The uniform price paid for all units bought is equal only to the benefit derived from the last unit bought. All of the previous units have a benefit higher than the price paid as indicated by any downward sloping demand curve.

Co-payment: a percentage of the total value of the insurance claim that the claimant must pay. This scheme serves to lessen moral hazard in terms of the filing of large claims and, as such, lowers settlement payments. See deductible.

Cost–benefit analysis (CBA): a technique used to evaluate the favorability of a project in terms of the costs and benefits it generates over its life. All appropriate costs and benefits must be accounted for, monetized, and discounted to present value using an appropriate rate of discount. This allows the present discounted value of the net benefits flow to be compared to up-front costs. A firm that does not consider any externalities arising from the project is said to undertake private CBA. If these were considered, social CBA would be the proper term.

Cross-price elasticity of demand: the ratio of the percentage change in the quantity demanded of a good or service to the percentage change in the price of another good or service that brought it about. It measures the price-sensitivity of demand for a good or service in terms of another good or service.

Deadweight welfare loss: a measure of value of consumers' surplus and/or producers' surplus lost because of inefficient allocation of resources.

Deductible: a lump-sum portion of an insurance claim that the claimant must pay. In this way, the claimant does not receive full insurance. The claimant has no incentive to file a claim less than the size of the deductible. This scheme eliminates moral hazard in terms of the filing of many, possibly frivolous, claims.

Derived demand: a demand that exists for a factor of production. The demand for freight transport is a demand derived on the part of the shipper arising from the consumer demand for the freight itself in the marketplace to which it is being delivered.

Destructive competition: a form of competition that leads to a market price and/or quantity which is unsustainable for all suppliers. This is in contrast to a natural monopoly where the market result is sustainable for one firm. Informally, the firms are engaged in cut-throat competition. Firms will either leave the market or remain but sustain negative economic profits. Destructive competition indicates that no stable equilibrium exists in the industry.

Diminishing marginal utility: a fundamental assumption of the preference structure of a consumer. With a constant income, a consumer's value (or utility) derived from each extra unit of a good or service consumed will diminish because he is moving closer to satiation. It is one of the explanations for a downward sloping demand curve.

Direct costs: the payments to the factors of production directly employed in the production process. They are divided into fixed costs and variable costs in the short run. Typically these costs are: wages for labor; interest for capital; rent for land; and normal profit for the entrepreneur. A transport firm's costs in the form of fuel and vehicles may be included in the capital component.

Division of labor: the splitting up of the labor component of a production process into specialized sub-components. In this way a worker may concentrate his efforts in an area best suited to his talents. The assembly line, which involves specific workstations, is the most obvious example of the division of labor.

Dominant strategy: is a player's unique and best response to every possible choice of responses that could be taken by another player. A Nash equilibrium is a narrow version of this definition in that a player is making his unique and best response to a player that is assumed to be making his best response as well. In other words, all Nash equilibria result out of the playing of dominant strategies but the reverse need not hold because dominant strategies may exist in games that do not have any Nash equilibria. See Nash equilibrium.

Earmarking: occurs when a tax or subsidy is provided on condition that the money is used for a clearly defined purpose. A fuel tax may be earmarked such that all revenue earned is put into road construction and maintenance. A transit subsidy is earmarked when it takes the form of a voucher provided to users as opposed to simply giving the money to the transit provider.

Economic development: the increase in a region or country's overall well-being. This may be production-based, employment-based, as well as socially based. Transportation infrastructure plays both a cause and an effect in this process of economic development.

Economic profit: the total revenue above total cost. Normal profit in economics is distinct from simple accounting profit. Normal profit obtains when all factors of production (including the entrepreneur) have been paid their market value or opportunity cost. Economic profit is also referred to as "economic rent" or the payment for bearing risk.

Economic Rent: the payment to a factor of production in excess of that which is needed to keep it employed in its current use.

Economies: a term used to indicate a lowering of long run average total costs over some range of a particular variable. For example, economies of scale indicate a fall in the long run average total costs of production for a firm as its size (i.e., scale) increases. Note that transportation firms may achieve an increase in "scale" through: vehicle size, fleet size, distance and weight, infrastructure, density, and scope. When the sources are internal to the firm they are known as internal economies; when they are due to sources beyond the firm they are known as external economies. External economies are equivalently referred to as production externalities.

Efficiency: is a term possessing a precise definition in economics. Its two sub-components are allocative efficiency and productive efficiency. Allocative efficiency involves the allocation of factors of production for the purpose of producing only those goods and services that are in demand. Supply responding to demand highlights the idea of consumer sovereignty in the allocation process. Productive efficiency involves the production of said goods and services using the least-cost combination of factors. Thus, efficient production involves firms supplying goods and services at the lowest cost such that markets for this production will clear.

Excess capacity: occurs when a firm is operating at a break-even level of output that is not at the minimum point of average total cost. In this way, the output produced is less than the level that would occur under perfect competition. Excess capacity is a characteristic of monopolistic competition.

Externality: is a term used to indicate an effect on a third party due to a production or consumption process of two other parties as part of their own market transaction. The two parties create these external effects because the costs or benefits, as the case may be, to the third party are not valued in the market transaction. While this represents a so-called "real" externality, pecuniary externalities do not involve the presence of unpriced costs or benefits. They involve the transfer of real income among the set of market players. For example, road congestion caused by private motorists might be considered a real externality to the delivery activities of truck drivers if one considered the latter as third parties to the market for overall transport. Clearly they are not. Because the road defines the marketplace, the value of road usage to the extra motorists comes at the expense of the delayed truck drivers. Only if one wishes to distinguish between passenger transport and freight transport, and ignore the road as common to both, could a case for a real externality be made.

Factor price equalization theorem: under specific assumptions, such as a zero cost of transportation, will free trade serve to equalize factor prices across trade areas making trade a substitute for factor mobility. As free trade narrows the differential in the price of a good traded across regions or countries so too must the prices of the factors involved in producing the good be narrowed.

Factors of production: these are the resources needed in order to begin the production process. They comprise four types: land, labor, capital and entrepreneurial ability. Land is used to mean all of the earth's natural resources, which is inclusive of water and the atmosphere. Labor covers all of the physical and mental abilities of workers. Capital involves machinery, tools, plants and warehouses. Entrepreneurial ability involves the managerial and innovative qualities of the entrepreneur who brings together the other factors so that the production process may begin. Of course, transportation services are a factor of production when physical distances thus requiring transport separate the other stages of production.

Fines: represent the cost of noncompliance with laws or regulations. Unlike taxes which are levied on legal activities, fines are charges on illegal activity.

First degree of price discrimination: each buyer pays his marginal willingness to pay (i.e., the price-point on his demand curve is paid to the firm). When all buyers do this the firm captures the entire consumer surplus from the market demand curve. Negotiated prices, scalping, and auctions are examples of this. See price discrimination.

Fiscal illusion: a feeling on the taxpayer's part whereby he easily notices the taxes he pays but cannot easily see the benefits (if any) that come back to him in the form of government expenditure. Devoting tax revenue to specific purposes instead of putting it into general revenue is a way to eliminate this problem. Using tolls or fuel tax revenue to finance roads would overcome fiscal illusion. See earmarking.

Form utility: The value added to basic raw materials in the supply chain when they are converted into finished products.

Free rider: a person or firm that uses a good for free while it has been provided to others at a cost. In this way, the other users have the incentive to act likewise and thus not pay. Free riders take advantage of the non-excludability of public goods making it inefficient for a private supplier to make them available. In this way, public goods are a cause of market failure directly because of free-riders.

Free-on-board (FOB): a stage of freight transport, from the shipper's viewpoint, which indicates the location where the freight's price is set. The buyer would take possession at this FOB point; for example, FOB the airport, or FOB the plant.

Fronthaul: the primary leg of a round trip; the secondary one being the backhaul that results from having to return to the point of origin. By convention the direction of haulage with the greater volume is taken to be the fronthaul direction.

Gains from trade: occur when a region or country benefits from trade in terms of an increase in output that could not occur in the absence of trade. Impediments to gains from trade occur in the form of tariffs and quotas as well as the cost of transportation.

Game theory: is concerned with devising strategies for players of a game (i.e., consumers, firms and government) that are in conflict or competition with one another. Each player faces one or more choices (i.e., moves) that, in combination with those of the other's, bring about a payoff. A truck driver's decision to overload his truck given the chance of passing an open weigh scale; a frequent flier's decision to purchase a ticket at the last minute in the hope of receiving a discount from the airline; or a car driver's choosing between two congested roadways from day-to-day are all examples of an economic game.

Gateway: a connection of transport routes to a common point (i.e., the gateway) that proceed into a specific geographic region. This contrasts with a hub that allows for inward (outward) movements from (in) all directions with no distinct region in mind.

Generalized cost: the full cost of using transport as seen by the user. A firm may charge its cost of transport provision to the user but the user may augment that cost with personal costs such as time, flexibility, comfort, safety, etc.

Heckscher–Ohlin theorem: an advancement of the gains from trade argument beyond simple comparative advantage. A country or region will only produce and export those goods and services that are the most intensive with respect to the factor of production that it has in the most abundance.

Hub-and-spoke network: the filtering of transport from secondary routes (i.e., spokes) to a common connecting point (i.e., a hub). Smaller vehicles are used along the spokes in comparison to those used on the hub-to-hub routes. Such a configuration takes advantage of economies of network density.

Incentive-compatibility problem: arises as part of the principal–agent problem in that the agent sees the incentive provided by the principal in a different context. For example, the government (i.e., the principal) may institute mandatory seatbelt usage so that the drivers (i.e., the agents) will feel safer behind the wheel. However, the action this incentive induces may be such that the driver drives faster because of the extra safety now felt. In this way, safety may be jeopardized.

Income elasticity of demand: the ratio of the percentage change in the quantity demanded of a good or service to the percentage change in the income of the consumer that brought it about. It measures the income-sensitivity of demand for a good or service.

Infant industry argument: a justification for protection from cheaper imports on the grounds that such imports prevent the establishment of a domestic manufacturing base. Less-developed countries often use it as a rationale for trade protection so that heavy industry may be developed for the purposes of economic development and/or self-sufficiency.

Inferior good: a good that has a negative income elasticity of demand. In this way, as the income of the user rises, *ceteris paribus*, the amount of the good or service demanded will drop. Urban public transport is a prime example of an inferior good.

Infrastructure: the capital of transportation provision which facilitates the use of transport vehicles. Examples include: roads, bridges, canals, rail yards, electric power generators, etc. A good way to distinguish infrastructure from the capital provided by the carriers themselves is to label the former as social overhead capital.

Interline: to switch freight from a vehicle that is deviating off of the given route and onto a vehicle set to complete the delivery. This move allows for a more efficient use of a fleet when its vehicles come into contact over a transportation network. Sometimes interlining is necessary to complete delivery such as in situations when the original vehicle is prohibited from entering the jurisdiction of destination.

Intermodal competition: competition among the sub-industries within the transportation industry itself. These are the competing modes of transport of which rail, automobiles, trucks, buses, airplanes, pipelines, and even telecommunications are a part.

Isodapane: the collection of all points where two or more isotims intersect. In this way, a firm that wishes to locate so as to serve two or more consumer markets may choose a location that provides equal site prices in serving these markets. With equal transport costs to, and equal market prices in, two consumer markets, the isodapane would be a straight line bisecting a line drawn between the two markets.

Isotim: the collection of all possible location points away from a given consumer market that would provide a firm with equal site prices if it served that market. With a uniform terrain and transportation infrastructure an isotim would be circular in shape.

Joint costs: are the non-traceable costs of a production process. The factors leading to these costs must, however, be used in fixed proportions. The production of a round trip of freight transport involves a fronthaul and one, and only one, backhaul. The traceability problem prevents the total costs of the round trip to be broken down into distinct fronthaul and backhaul costs.

Joint production: the production of two or more goods or services that always occur in a fixed proportion. For example, in a round trip of freight transport there is one, and only one, backhaul for every fronthaul produced. Soy meal and soy oil are jointly supplied in terms of soybeans. Mutton and wool are jointly supplied in terms of sheep.

Line haul costs: the variable costs of transport. These are incurred as part of the physical transport of freight or passengers. Costs for fuel, drivers, vehicle maintenance and depreciation arise as travel-specific costs as opposed to being part of the fixed costs of transportation provision.

Logistics: involves the control of the supply chain whereby the right goods are delivered at the right place, at the right time, in the proper quality and at the lowest total cost. Transportation is only a sub-component of the logistics process. Others are: marketing, location, material handling, storage, and inventory control.

Long run: in contrast to the short run, a time period when all factors of production are variable in their quantity used by a firm. In a transport context it may be considered as the time frame in which the fleet size may be expanded by way of, say, bringing new ocean vessels on line. Alternatively, it may be the time over which a new roadway of airport is made available.

Lumpy costs: indicate costs that exist in discrete amounts as opposed to existing continuously over all possible amounts of output production. In the long run a transport firm might wish to expand the size of its fleet. The smallest increment is determined by the carrying capacity of the smallest vehicle, which defines the discrete amounts by which production may expand. Similarly, a given length of roadway is expanded lane-by-lane and not in minute amounts.

Marginal, or at the margin: the incremental effect on something produced from an extra unit of something else. For example, marginal cost defines the cost incurred from the last unit of output produced, while marginal product defines the amount of output that is produced by employment of the last unit of a factor of production. The term "at the margin" thus refers to the final effect of the last unit out of a series of previous units.

Marginal cost pricing: the setting of the price of output at the point where marginal cost equals marginal benefit, as represented by the demand curve. This occurs naturally under perfect competition but in a monopoly there is no incentive for the firm to operate that way. If the monopoly possesses economies of scale, marginal cost pricing would bring about a loss. However, governments may subsidize the firm or simply take it over in order to achieve a maximization of total social welfare that the marginal cost price would bring about.

Market failure: occurs when a market, under the forces of unfettered supply and demand, fails to achieve a socially optimal result. In this way the equilibrium achieved would not be efficient. Causes of market failure include: monopoly, externalities, and public goods. When a market operates with a welfare loss existing due to the market power of one of the players, or there are third parties that are affected in some way by the results of this market, a market failure will result.

Mixed strategy: is the result of an economic game where there is uncertainty as to what the players will do in a given move. Each move is subject to a specific probability for that move to take place, which is thus the source of uncertainty. Each player knows only his own probability distribution across all possible moves.

Monopolistic competition: occurs when a firm has market power but barriers to entry are imperfect. Firms will differentiate their product from the competition through such things as advertising and warranties. In this way, competing firms produce output that is not perfectly substitutable.

Monopoly: a market structure defined by the presence of only one seller. This one firm is in effect the entire industry. The lack of competition faced by the monopolist may allow the firm to make positive economic profits in the long run due to an inability of other firms to enter the industry and challenge it. Monopolies can arise due to natural barriers to entry such as a limited availability of a critical factor of production or they may arise artificially due to patent protection or government licensing. Railways and pipelines are the transport modes that are most approximated by this model.

Moral hazard: is a problem that often occurs in the relationship between principals and agents. The principal sets up a policy or program that is to bring about an action by the agent but the latter ends up taking an action unexpected by the principal. From mandatory seatbelt usage to car insurance, the extent to which a driver feels safer as a result of these policies may lead him to drive in a less safe fashion and end up causing more even accidents. In other words, these policies may put a cap on the amount of precautions the agent might normally take. While the adverse selection problem involves the principal ferreting out those agents with the "wrong" predispositions, the moral hazard problem involves agents changing those predispositions in the face of the incentives the principal provides.

Nash equilibrium: after John Nash. It is an equilibrium that occurs in an economic game and is characterized as a situation where one player will not change his selected position given that the other player does not change his. In other words, given the opponent player's fixed choice, the player in question will have made a profit maximizing choice. If both players can say that, the Nash equilibrium of the game will have been found. In the Prisoners' Dilemma game, each player choosing to defect represents the Nash equilibrium.

No-fault insurance: a system of automobile insurance whereby the insurer determines the value of the damages assessed and to be paid on behalf of the perpetrator. The victim normally has no recourse to the courts for a judge or jury finding of damages. While this eliminates litigation it also lowers the cost of driving to the extent that damages might be underestimated. A lower cost of driving could bring about moral hazard on the part of drivers if they perceive the cost of their potential liability to have fallen.

One-shot game: an economic game that is played only once. In this way, the players are not allowed to interact several times so that a better strategy may be developed over that time. Self-regulation is always more likely with firms that often interact. Under the Prisoners' Dilemma conditions, mutual defection of each player would the equilibrium in a one-shot game. See Nash equilibrium.

Opportunity cost: the value of the next best alternative foregone in order to undertake the present activity. For example, in passenger travel the opportunity cost is the value of the next best activity that could have been undertaken if one were not in transit. In this way, no human activity is without some cost that must be weighed against the value of the chosen activity.

Peak load pricing: the setting of prices to demand classes that vary with time over a fixed infrastructure. Rush hour traffic, Christmas airline flights, and grain transport at harvest time are examples of peak demand for transport.

Pecuniary externalities: the activities of participants in a market may create positive or negative impacts on each other. If these impacts result in rising prices or increased time (congestion) then the externality is already internalized, and the effect is pecuniary, rather than one that has real resource effects.

Perfect competition: the simplest, and therefore most unrealistic, form of industrial structure. There are many firms that produce a homogenous product, which is sold to many buyers. Because each firm is a small player relative to the total, each will accept the market price as given. In the long run, there is complete freedom of entry and exit on the part of firms, which serves to drive all economic profits to zero. Finally, all firms and buyers have perfect information in that they are aware of all the prices being asked and offered by others across the market. In transportation, a deregulated trucking industry dominated by many owner-operators working over a large area is the mode that comes closest to this model.

Place utility: the value added to products by moving them in space, usually be transportation and materials handling, that makes them more valuable to users. This is also referred to as spatial utility.

Possession utility: the value added to products when ownership transfers between buyers and sellers in the supply chain. This is also referred to as ownership utility.

Price discrimination: the practice of a firm charging different prices for the same good or service to different classes of demanders. The firm's requirements for this are: (1) monopoly power or some control over the price; (2) the ability to separate out the demanders based on their intensities of demand; (3) the transaction costs involved; (4) the low-price buyers must face barriers preventing them from re-selling their purchases to high-price buyers. Point (4) holds for services but it also holds for physical goods sold in markets characterized by distance or asymmetric information. See first, second, and third degree price discrimination.

Price elasticity of demand: the ratio of the percentage change in the quantity demanded of a good or service to the percentage change in the price of that good or service that brought it about. It measures the price-sensitivity of demand for a good or service. Its determinants are: the existence or closeness of substitutes; the importance of the good or service in the consumers' budget; the proportion of total cost accounted for by the factor (in the case of derived demand); and the length of time allowed for adjustment.

Price elasticity of supply: the ratio of the percentage change in the quantity supplied of a good or service to the percentage change in the price of that good or service that brought it about. It measures the price-sensitivity of supply for a good or service. Its prime determinant is the length of time allowed for adjustment.

Primary demand: the demand that exists for a final good or service. The demand for a pleasure cruise is a primary demand for transportation because the cruise is an end unto itself.

Principal–agent problem: the principal is a person or firm that wishes an action to be undertaken by another person or firm, called the agent. The principal has to figure out the proper incentive for the agent so as to undertake this specific action because such action will impose a cost upon the agent. The problem is that, under asymmetric information, the principal will never know if the action of the agent was a result of the latter's best efforts. Furthermore, the principal will never know beforehand if his desired actions will actually occur given the incentive he provides to the agent. See incentive-compatibility problem.

Prisoners' Dilemma: a specific type of economic game. In its simplest form, two players have the choice of cooperating with each other or "defecting" in an attempt to reap a higher personal payoff. The problem for each player is that "defecting" only brings this higher payoff when the other tries to cooperate. Because the other player may try to defect as well, both may be stuck with a payoff less than that which would have been achieved by mutual cooperation. The game leads to an inferior "equilibrium" of both players defecting while gains from mutual cooperation would still exist. This game applies to industry self-regulation. See game theory.

Producer surplus: the net benefit to the firm arising from a uniform price received over and above the cost of provision. Price will equal benefit at the last unit supplied but all previous units supplied will generate a net benefit for the firm.

Production function: the relationship that defines how factors of production, as inputs, are transformed into a firm's output. The precise form of this relationship is defined by the state of technology.

Productive efficiency: see efficiency.

Profit capitalization: occurs when the owners of factors of production are able to capture some or all of the economic profits earned by a firm.

In this way, the firm's costs of production rise and profits are transferred appropriately. An example of this occurs when labor unions are able to negotiate wage settlements over an above their opportunity cost. Firms may give in to these demands especially when they face little competition in their market due to monopolization or regulatory protection.

Property rights: the establishment of legal ownership. Without property rights markets would not adequately function because the ownership of goods and services as well as resources could be in dispute. In this way, trade would not be possible.

Public goods: a good that cannot be expected to be produced by private firms because of the incentive to free ride. A government must supply the good because it has the power, through taxation, to charge all users for its provision. This type of good has the twin characteristics of being non-rival and non-excludable. Non-rival means that one's consumption of the good in no way affects another's. Non-excludability means that the marginal cost of provision of the good is zero because once one person has it, it is not possible to prevent another from possessing it.

Ramsey pricing: a policy rule proposed by the English economist Frank Ramsey (1903–1960) for natural monopolies that avoids a welfare loss by transferring the consumer surplus to the monopoly such that its output can be set where demand equals long run marginal cost.

Reaction function: the supply response of a firm in reaction to the supply decision of another firm. Such interdependence of firm decisions precludes the existence of an individual supply curve for each of these firms. Reaction functions are used in markets that have limited competition or ones that indicate collusive behavior within the industry. Railways and airlines are likely to possess reaction functions due to the relatively limited amount of competition felt in those transport modes.

Rent seeking: the spending of money or allocation of resources so as to secure an economic profit or rent. A government or other entity accepts non-refundable bids from, or allows itself to be lobbied by, competing agents for the right to obtain a rent. The agents that lose out in this process have wasted money and resources. Under governmental regulation of transportation, operational licenses would be a target for rent seeking activity.

Repeated game: an economic game that is repeated under the same conditions with the same players over several time periods. In this way, the players may alter their strategies beyond those acceptable in a one-shot game. In a repeated Prisoners' Dilemma game, a Nash equilibrium of mutual punishment may be discarded in favor of the superior result of mutual cooperation as is needed by firms that wish to successfully self-regulate. See one-shot game.

S-curve: indicates a non-linear relationship between an airline's amount of service provision and the resulting market share it can capture. Beyond (below) some critical amount of flight share, an airline would receive a disproportionately higher (lower) market share. This theory leads to the conclusion that airport hubs tend to be dominated by one airline.

Say's Law of the Markets: a proposition that, over all markets, the sum of the values of all goods and services produced is equal to the sum of the values of all goods and services bought. It has given rise to the colloquialism: supply creates its own demand. However, this Law is best interpreted as a condition for achieving the general equilibrium.

Second degree price discrimination: the charging of different prices based on the quantity purchased. A discount on bulk-quantity transport relative to single-unit transport of the same good is an example of this. In other words, the firm sets two or more prices over the same market demand curve. See price discrimination.

Self-regulation: a state where a group of firms agree to impose regulations on themselves rather than the government doing it for them and thus having to receive government fines for non-compliance. The problem with self-regulation is that there may be an incentive to "defect" from the self-imposed regulation if a gain could be had at the expense of the other firms. See Prisoners' Dilemma.

Separability: see traceability problem.

Shadow price: an augmented market price of a good or service that will achieve a social price for it; that is, a price that indicates society's valuation rather than just the firm's. A monopoly firm sells at a price higher than the marginal social cost of provision meaning that the shadow price is less than the market price. On the other hand, the shadow price of a river would exceed its market price (of zero) if a firm were free to dump pollution into it.

Shipping conferences: a shipping conference is a group of shipping lines that have formed a cartel for the joint setting of rates and service conditions for transporting containerized exports and imports.

Short run: a time period of production whereby at least one factor of production is fixed in its quantity used by the firm. The variable factor(s) employed as the firm expands production will eventually lead to diminishing returns as the fixed factor faces congestion. While no specific time frame is specified, the short run may be defined as the time over which a firm is not able to expand or contract its plant size or vehicle fleet size.

Site price: the value of the good at the plant location before transportation to the consumer market occurs. If a firm uses for-hire transport, the site price is its source of revenue to the extent that the higher price in the consumer market reflects transport costs.

Site rent: the return to a firm for its output minus the total costs for all mobile factors of production used at a given site. This difference is the total cost of all immobile factors. From a given site price comes a given location distance from the market. That site price, when compared to costs, indicates a certain output quantity which may lead to an economic rent that is, in this case, the site rent from production at that location.

Speed–flow and speed–cost relationships: see congestion costs.

Subsidy: an amount of money provided to a demander or supplier of a good or service in order to encourage a greater usage of it. The subsidy may be lump-sum meaning that it is a general allotment of funds, or it may be an amount per quantity used. A yearly subsidy to a transit authority is lump-sum while a discount to bulk purchases of transit tickets represents a per unit subsidy.

Taper effect: occurs as a direct result of the economies of distance transported. A transport firm facing fixed costs will find that these costs are easier to carry when freight is transported over longer distances. The fall in the average total cost of transport services with respect to distance is the result of this effect.

Terms of trade: the ratio of the value of export prices to import prices faced by a region or country. This ratio defines the value of what it intends to export in terms of what it intends to import in return.

Third degree price discrimination: occurs when the firm charges different prices based on different price elasticities of demand from among the buyers. Profits increase when the firm charges high (low) prices to price-inelastic (-elastic) buyers. Because business travelers have more price-inelastic demands than casual travelers, the former usually pay more for car rentals (because they are apt to be rented for only single days) and for airline tickets (because they are less apt to stay at their destinations over weekends). Knowing these traits about business travelers, firms can price their products such that the higher price falls on the business traveler and not the casual traveler. See price discrimination.

Time utility: the value added to products by changing their time of availability to users. In the supply chain this is usually provided by warehousing and inventory holding. This is also referred to as temporal utility.

Tit-for-tat strategy: the optimal strategy for any player to employ when under the conditions of a repeated Prisoners' Dilemma game. What is required is: (1) all players make their moves simultaneously; and (2) the number of games has no end. Whatever one player's move is in the previous game period, the player in question will match it in the present game. Of course, if a player "defects" in the previous game, the player in question will "defect" in the present game so as to punish the other player. However, the player in question will then "cooperate" in the next game. This strategy will allow the "defecting" player to come to the conclusion that only the "always cooperate" strategy will ensure the highest set of payoffs for him when facing another player using the tit-for-tat strategy. This then becomes the dominant strategy. See self-regulation and also see the Prisoners' Dilemma.

Total social welfare: the net of producer and consumer benefits over and above the cost of production. It is measured by: total revenue plus consumer surplus minus total social cost.

Traceability problem: occurs when it is not possible to breakdown (or trace) the total costs of production into all of its sub-components. Joint, common and constant costs existing in a firm can lead to this problem. Transportation firms find this problem in terms of, for example: (1) setting fronthaul and backhaul freight rates; and (2) allocating an amount of track maintenance costs, for a common railway, to passenger trains and freight trains.

Tragedy of the commons: is the idea that common property is doomed to overuse or misuse because each user, though a small contributor to the total negative effect, does not consider this total damage caused by all people thinking along the same lines. Each person's small, marginal, effect will lead to a large total effect because this is the sum of all of the marginal effects. For example, a person taking a fast curve on a highway causes a small amount of curve damage, thus justifying his action; but all others thinking in this way lead, in total, to significant highway damage.

Tramp shipping: port-to-port ocean vessel transport at rates negotiated between the shipper and vessel owner in contrast to scheduled ocean liner shipping.

Trans-shipping: the movement of freight over one or more transfer points. The goods are switched from one vehicle to another as in the case of transferring containers from ocean vessels onto flatbed railcars.

Two-part pricing: a compromise between average cost pricing and marginal cost pricing. In this way, the economic loss that marginal cost pricing causes to monopolies operating with economies of scale will be overcome by charging a higher price to another segment of the consumers. The charging of the marginal cost price and a monopoly price to two segments of the consumer class is a form of price discrimination.

Two-part tariff: a tax or user charge designed to handle two problems at once. Specifically, a toll charge can simultaneously handle peak-load and congestion problems. The toll may be two-tiered in order to account for peak loads but it may also be distance-related so that a vehicle's contribution to congestion can be accounted for.

Value of the marginal product (VMP): the value to the firm of the marginal product of a factor of production. This value comes from the sale price of the output this factor is producing. In this way, the VMP measures one's willingness to pay for use of a factor and is thus the determinant of the derived demand for that factor.

Value-added: the value of output less the contributions to all intermediaries, which leaves the payment to the primary factors of production. Can also be considered at the firm level as the firm output less all goods and services purchased from other firms. In this case, value-added refers to the sum of profits and wages paid by the firm.

Walras' Law: shows how all markets in the world are related in terms of excess supply and excess demand. If there were only two markets, when one is in equilibrium so must be the other. If one is experiencing excess demand the other must be experiencing excess supply. In this way, the world as a whole cannot experience excess supply or excess demand in the aggregate taken across all markets.

Weighted demand curve: a demand curve developed for peak load pricing when the peak and off-peak demands do not have the same time durations. The willingnesses to pay by peak and off-peak users for a given quantity is summed with the appropriate time weights attached.

Yield Management: this is a combination of price discrimination and inventory management that employs historical patterns of sales to determine the quantity and prices available to buyers where sales are made through a reservation system.

Glossary and Index Items

Printed in the United States
By Bookmasters